THE FIGURE OF THE POET
IN RENAISSANCE EPIC

THE FIGURE OF THE POET

IN RENAISSANCE EPIC

By

ROBERT M. DURLING

HARVARD UNIVERSITY PRESS

Cambridge, Massachusetts

1965

Distributed in Great Britain by Oxford University Press, London

Publication of this volume has been aided by a grant from the
Ford Foundation

Library of Congress Catalog Card Number: 65-22060

Printed in the United States of America

TO MY STUDENTS AT CORNELL UNIVERSITY

1957-1965

Acknowledgments

Many persons have helped and encouraged me in the writing of this book, and it is a pleasant duty to express my gratitude to them. My deepest obligation is to my teachers at Harvard College and the Harvard Graduate School, especially to Douglas Bush and Charles S. Singleton, who first aroused my interest in the literature of the Renaissance and who have helped and encouraged me at every step of the way. At Cornell University, James Hutton has answered my many queries with unfailing learning and kindness. Meyer H. Abrams, Gian-Paolo Biasin, Harry Caplan, Eugenio Donato, John Freccero, and David Novarr have read portions of the manuscript and made valuable suggestions. Robert M. Adams, Joseph A. Mazzeo, and Rachel Jacoff read and commented on an earlier version. Certain chapters received the benefit of criticism so detailed and incisive as to enable me to rethink and rewrite them: that on Ariosto from Donald Carne-Ross, that on Chaucer from Robert E. Kaske, that on Petrarch from Ephim G. Fogel and Piero Pucci, and the introduction from Joyce Lebowitz of Harvard University Press, whose editorial assistance has in general been invaluable. I owe an especially important debt to Paul de Man, who has repeatedly awakened me to the critical and philosophical implications of this subject and who has deeply influenced the evolution of my views. I owe more than I can say to the support and stimulation of countless talks with Max Bluestone and Norman C. Rabkin, who have also repeatedly read and criticized parts of the manuscript. Finally, since this book has grown directly out of my teaching, the obligation expressed in the dedication is—along with that to my own teachers—perhaps the most pervasive and important of all.

The writing of this book has been supported by the Grant-in-Aid Fund of the Department of English, Cornell University, whose grants in 1958 enabled me to travel and in 1960 and 1961 relieved me of part of my teaching load.

A section of Chapter I appeared in different form as "Ovid as Praeceptor Amoris," *The Classical Journal*, 53:157-167 (January 1958); part of Chapter V, now thoroughly revised, appeared as "The Divine Analogy in Ariosto," *Modern Language Notes* (published by the Johns Hopkins Press), 78:1-14 (January 1963); and parts of Chapter VI, also greatly revised, appeared as "Tasso's Epic Rhetoric," *The Romanic Review*, 50:81-94 (April 1959), copyright 1959 by Columbia University Press. I should like to thank the original publishers for permission to use this material here.

All translations not otherwise identified are my own.

April 1965   R. M. D.

CONTENTS

CONTENTS

THE FIGURE OF THE POET
IN RENAISSANCE EPIC

Introduction

M<small>Y</small> <small>SUBJECT</small> is the figure of the narrating poet in four Renaissance epics. The importance of the narrator in any fiction was perhaps first pointed out by Aristotle, in his discussion of the three ways of distinguishing among imitations of human action (according to the means, the objects, and the modes of imitation). The principal modes of literary mimesis, he said, are drama and narrative: in drama "the imitators . . . represent the whole story . . . as though they were actually doing the things described";[1] in narrative, however, the events themselves are not before us, and we learn of them through the telling of a narrator. This means that strictly speaking no event of a narrative is given immediately, not even dialogue; everything comes to us with the emphasis and structure given to it by an intervening consciousness.[2]

Since there is nothing in a narrative except the words—except what a narrator says or implies—it could be maintained that all statements about any narrative are in fact statements about its narrator. But every reader of fiction recognizes the possibility of certain distinctions, fluid though they may be, such as that between the imagined events and the narrator's telling of them. I should like to explore here some of the most important distinctions concerning the figure of the narrator and to make clear the scope of this book.

The first and perhaps most fundamental of these distinctions is that between the actual author, who exists outside the work, and the figure of the narrator, which exists within the work. Both for us and for the author, the figure of the narrator is a mental construction. We know very well that the words on the page have been manipulated—selected, revised, rearranged, and so forth. The succession of words we read does not necessarily, as we know, correspond to any particular actual utterance of the author

1

and does not necessarily reflect any actual temporal order, except that of our own reading. Nevertheless, as we read we *receive* the printed words as if they were a continuous utterance; we imaginatively construct a source for them, such as they might have in a dramatic reading. From the point of view of the author, the figure of the narrator is a role in which the author casts himself; it is a dramatic projection of some kind. The failure to maintain the distinction between the figure of the narrator—or the speaker of any poem—and the author has led, at worst, to such abuses of biographical criticism as taking for literal fact the statements about "themselves" made by highly conventionalized narrators like Ariosto. In such cases the mistake is double: the critic has mistaken the nature of biographical evidence, and he has misunderstood the nature of poetic or narrative rhetoric.[3] To be sure, the figure of the narrator must in some way be consistent with the subjective awareness of the author: the author must be able to assume the role. By the same token, the role will reveal a great deal about the author—but usually not facts.

Though the figure of the narrator must at some level be consistent with the subjectivity of the author, the exact level of congruence may be rather difficult to determine. A narrative expresses, with more or less completeness and explicitness, its author's vision of experience. The particular individuality of that vision permeates the work to its most apparently trivial details. The work reveals the author even in ways of which he is unaware, for it dramatizes or projects the structure of his consciousness through his most sensitive tool, his linguistic activity.[4] But that we can distinguish, in a narrative, between the imagined events and the telling of them is most important. Stated in general terms, it means that we distinguish the synthesis of the whole from its projection in the sentence-by-sentence, page-by-page activity of narration. The progressive unfolding of the whole takes place in time and is always partial and provisional; it is by definition in tension with the totality.

The figure of the narrator, then, is the focus, the fixed point, of this act of linguistic projection. The author has a whole story to tell; he wishes to achieve the synthesis of a whole fictional world. He moves from the silence before the beginning to the great variety of means, ranging from the imposition, at the level of syntax and on up, of chronological and other logical structures that do not correspond to the free play of the reflector's consciousness, through indirect discourse, to direct quotation. Understanding what is happening in a James novel depends to a large extent upon grasping this complex interplay:

After the young woman in the glass cage had held up to him across her counter the pale-pink leaflet bearing his friend's name, which she neatly pronounced, he turned away to find himself, in the hall, facing a lady who met his eyes as with an intention suddenly determined, and whose features —not freshly young, not markedly fine, but on happy terms with each other—came back to him as from a recent vision. For a moment they stood confronted; then the moment placed her: he had noticed her the day before, noticed her at his previous inn, where—again in the hall—she had been briefly engaged with some people of his own ship's company.[7]

What is going on in this passage is not that the author's narration is being mediated through a fictional Narrator, but that the character's (Strether's) consciousness is being mediated through the Author's narration.

Participation. Is the Narrator an actor in the story or not? This distinction is of course much the same as the traditional one between first- and third-person narration. But, although most Authors are not participants and many fictional Narrators are, it is not the same as the distinction according to identity. Like the Renaissance epic Poets I shall examine, Henry James speaks as Author but not as participant. Huck Finn is a participant, but he is not the author. Marlow is neither the author nor, except in a peripheral way, a participant. Yet Dante, in the *Vita nuova* and the *Divina Commedia*, is both Author and participant. Note that the distinction has nothing to do with that between factuality and fictitiousness; there is, I take it, no doubt that the *Commedia* is a fiction.

Usually the identity and the participation or nonparticipation of the Narrator reinforce each other. But it is still possible to distinguish critical problems deriving from differences in participation as opposed to differences in identity. The Narrator who also participates has, both as Narrator and as participant, a *past* that must be thought of as continuous with the narrative present in which he speaks, a present that is thus anchored in temporality; the synthesis he attempts or claims to attempt (not necessarily the same as the one the author intends or achieves) will always be retrospective from a particular point in time, and a looking back on an inner trajectory. The nonparticipating Author, as Author of this story and not some other one, has no past except as he chooses to refer to one; his narrative present transcends specific temporality. In other words, nonparticipating Authors are always omniscient, while the participant's knowledge is by definition limited. I am not referring to the so-called omniscient-author style; by definition, the Author of any story knows—even though he may not choose to reveal his knowledge—everything there is to know about the story. As soon as the participating Narrator violates the restrictions on his knowledge, we understand that it is the Author speaking to us, the Author who could theoretically tell us about anything at all within the fictional world. When the difference is crucial, then, it is basically one of authority: we expect the participant to be interested, the Author to be disinterested. But no matter how lacking in authority—how unreliable—a participant is, we must be able to cooperate with him in the imagining of the world of the story.

One of the most interesting cases is of course that of Dante, who claims both the vantage and the past of a participant and the authority of the Author. As Singleton has shown, the allegory of the *Divina Commedia* is intended to be analogous to that of the Bible as interpreted by the Middle Ages. While the allegory of the poets conveys its meaning through a literal sense that is fictitious, the allegory of the Bible—of theologians—presents a literal sense that is historically true; the allegorical senses of the Biblical narrative are meanings possessed by the *events* themselves. So in the *Commedia*: as Singleton puts it, "The fiction of the *Divine Comedy* is that it is not a fiction."[8] This strange effect is achieved precisely by the coincidence in the Narrator of participant and Author.

Character or nature. I group under this heading differences among Narrators that spring not from the modalities of the narration itself—the questions of identity and participation—but from the personal character of the Narrator. The difference between "objective" and "intrusive" narration is often thought of as a difference in modality,[9] but it is rather a difference in the characters of the Narrators. In both Thackeray and James, for example, the Narrator is usually the Author; the difference between their Narrators is not one of identity. When the Author narrates, in Trollope or James, he is not a participant. But there is a great difference in manner, and it springs from a difference in these Authors' characters, or ethos, as Narrators. The objective Author ostensibly limits himself to discourse about the narrative moment; the intrusive Author apparently regards himself as free to talk about other matters as well, including himself. I say "ostensibly" and "apparently" because both aim at controlling local response and, through it, total response. In other words, the intrusive Author is just as dialectically immersed in the moment as the objective, and the objective Author is just as interested in relating the moment to the underlying norms and structure of the totality as the intrusive Author is.[10] Furthermore, the Jamesian Author is just as omniscient about his story—about each of the characters, say—as Thackeray or Trollope, and he had better be. The difference is, first, that his knowledge of them has a different content from Thackeray's and Trollope's knowledge of their characters and, second, that he chooses to reveal the content of his omniscience in a different way. This amounts to saying that the categories "objective" and "intrusive," "omniscient" and "dramatic," are not logical or absolute, but historical. Omniscience in the abstract is unobjectionable. What Lubbock was objecting to was the particular things the Victorian novelists chose to know in their omniscience. He thought he was objecting to a technique; in fact he was objecting to a whole style of humanity, a whole projected ethos.

For a narrative style is, metaphorically, a style of life. It is the style of life the author chooses to adopt insofar as and while he is a Narrator, and the greater the intensity of life he can pour into his writing, the closer to being literally a style of life his narrative style will be. Changes in narrative styles thus reflect changes in men's attitudes toward themselves and toward the world. To understand the ultimate significance of the cult of "objective" narration in Flaubert and James—and its later vogue among literary critics—it is necessary to develop a historical view of the varieties of Narrators' characters. As a matter of fact, the differences in manner between the Victorians and James have been greatly

exaggerated, and at our point in time it is becoming easier to
see the essential similarities between them. Placed in a larger
historical perspective, the difference between the one's intrusive-
ness and the other's objectivity seems relatively unimportant
compared with those aspects of character they share.

A Narrator's self-projection reflects an entire conception of
man: the Narrator is projected in terms of fundamental philosophical and religious categories; he acts out fundamental attitudes; and he shows implicitly just what claims to human perfection his readers will allow him to make. Homer, for example,
speaks as one who seriously believes the Muses speak through
him; we know enough about oral-formulaic improvisation to have
some understanding of the psychological plausibility, especially
in an age that still hypostasized some psychological processes,[11]
of his attributing to the Muse his memory of the "past" and his
capacity to bring it forth. What Homer attributes to the Muse we
attribute to his humanity, to the humanity that his culture made
it possible for him to attain. He shows us not only what his
opinions were about the gods (though not very ingenuously), but
also the way in which he attempted to *be* godlike, and thus the
degree to which it was in fact possible for a human being to
attain—in a special way, to be sure—what was thought of as
resemblance with the gods. And that the Greeks thought him godlike is beyond dispute.

The dominant convention of traditional epic from Homer on
was that its Narrator, the Poet, was inspired. In the *Aeneid*, such
conventions of Homeric epic as the invocations of the Muse are
partly literary mannerism, but the Stoic doctrine of the presence
of the divine spark in every man and the Stoic leaning toward an
allegorical habit of mind—both very strong in Virgil—account
rationally for the mythological veiling of a passionate sense of
inspiration. Because of the element of learned imitation, however,
the inspiration of the Poet is endangered and thematically crucial
in Virgil; it is parallel to the dilemma of Aeneas, who must mediate between an intolerable past and a distant future by means of
whatever elusive capacity for transcendent vision he possesses.
In later ages, particularly in the Renaissance, when neoclassical
ambitiousness in literature collides with the decline of medieval

faith, the conventions of traditional epic become the focus of a deeply significant transition.[12]

For if the dominant convention of epic is that its Narrator is a supernaturally inspired man who *transmits* a story received from outside himself, the dominant convention of the novel is that its Narrator (whether Author or character) is a natural man, limited to natural powers, who has (when Author) created the story out of his own experience and observation.[13] In the perspective of this fundamental change, the vogue of "objective" Narrators, which goes hand in hand with the increasing tendency to exploit epistemological relativism among the characters (the more objective the Narrator, the more subjective the character[14]), is clearly part of the cultural movement away from a religious or supernatural conception of man. What studying Narrators can help us to see is that this movement is not merely a reshuffling of opinions, a chapter in the history of unit-ideas, but that it is a change taking place in the very texture of the human attitudes, the projects, to use Sartre's term, enacted by writers.

Just as the novel has from the eighteenth to the twentieth century moved toward the central theme of the epistemology of nontranscendant subjectivity, a process that reveals the inner logic of its basic conventions, so the traditional epic, when it was revived in the Renaissance, increasingly revealed the centrality of its fundamental convention, the inspired Narrator. It became less and less feasible to assume the pose of an inspired Poet unless your subject was religious. The last great traditional epic, *Paradise Lost*, was possible only because of Milton's sublime faith that his prayers to the Spirit were in fact being answered. Less self-confident poets, poets who were uncertain that any supernatural entity would deign to speak through them—Tasso is a good example—often turned to religious subject matter for epic because they believed that a mediated supernatural inspiration was available in ecclesiastical tradition.

The Renaissance fascination with the ancient epic and its general inability to produce epics of its own are of course danger signals, and the official culture of the Renaissance ultimately broke down when its inability to express men's changed sense of what was most significant in their experience became in-

tolerable. The poems I shall examine share—except for Tasso's—
a typical Renaissance characteristic: the tendency to combine
conventions of ancient epic (which involved an abstract, trans-
cendant, or superpersonal "I" as Narrator) with a strong assertion
of a more discursively established, concrete identity for the Poet.
This chatty, discursive strain—which derives both from such
ancient genres as formal satire and didactic parody, especially
Horace and Ovid, and from medieval romance—is the ancestor of
the elaborate development of the discursive Narrator in the
eighteenth- and nineteenth-century novel. This development of
the novel[15] is a continuation of the earlier development and, like
it, reflects a continuing crisis in the way authors and readers
viewed themselves as human beings. The Romantic critics were
well aware of the debt the novel owed to Renaissance literature.[16]
But modern students of narrative have so far devoted too little
attention to the continuity of the tradition. Except for a growing
interest in this aspect of classical and medieval literature, the
early tradition has received little attention.[17]

    The central theme of this book is the significance of the Narra-
tor's changeability or instability. In Part Two, I discuss four Renaissance epics which, although they belong to the same tradition—
and although the writer of each of them was influenced by all of
the previous ones—reflect significantly different approaches to
the variability and potential inconsistency of the self. In Part
One, I discuss the most important writers of the older tradition of
self-contradiction and deprecation: Horace, Ovid, and Petrarch.
I include a chapter on Chaucer's *Troilus and Criseyde* in Part
One both because it is a major example in European literature
of the humorous, discursive style and because its medieval treatment of the theme of human instability provides a useful point of
reference. Chaucer's treatment of the theme is in fact much more
conservative than Petrarch's, in spite of Petrarch's being the older
man; I therefore violate chronology by discussing *Troilus and
Criseyde* before the *Canzoniere*. My approach and emphasis vary
somewhat from chapter to chapter, but I use throughout the critical method—a dangerous one, as I have already suggested—of
singling out passages where the Poet–Narrator refers to "himself."

Part One

ANCIENT AND MEDIEVAL
INFLUENCES

I

Two Roman Poets

IT OUGHT not to be supposed that writers before the eighteenth century were unaware of the importance of the projected Narrator. The persuasive power of the character (ethos) of the speaker is a commonplace of classical rhetoric. Aristotle classifies it as one of the three modes of persuasion proper to the art of rhetoric: "Of the modes of persuasion furnished by the spoken word there are three kinds. The first depends on the personal character of the speaker; the second on putting the audience into a certain frame of mind; the third on proof, or apparent proof, provided by the words of the speech itself."[1] Many pages of Aristotle's *Rhetoric* are devoted to the principles of ethical persuasion; and Cicero,[2] the *Auctor ad Herennium*,[3] and Quintilian,[4] to mention only the rhetoricians most popular in the Renaissance, all give attention to it. Aristotle's opening exposition is a convenient summary of the doctrine.[5]

Persuasion is achieved by the speaker's personal character when the speech is so spoken as to make us think him credible. We believe good men more fully and more readily than others; this is true generally whatever the question is, and absolutely true where exact certainty is impossible and opinions are divided. This kind of persuasion, like the others, should be achieved by what the speaker says, not by what people think of his character before he begins to speak. It is not true, as some writers assume in their treatises on rhetoric, that the personal goodness revealed by the speaker contributes nothing to his power of persuasion; on the contrary, his character may almost be called the most effective means of persuasion he possesses.

The persuasiveness of a work of literature, of course, is of a different kind from that of "practical" oratory. Like the orator, however, the author of narrative must somehow—perhaps by very indirect means—make his audience "attentive, docile, and benevolent"; he must control their attitudes toward the fictional world and their conception of its structure and ontology; he must make them accept, first as interesting and ultimately as valid, his vision of experience. In ages that thought of imaginative literature as closer to rhetoric than we ourselves do, the traditional doctrine of ethical persuasion served to call the attention of writers to this central problem of narrative, if they were not led to consider it by their own reflections on their art or by the examples of other writers.

It is well known that Roman writers, especially under the Empire, were deeply influenced by rhetorical doctrine, and in this chapter I shall discuss works that are overtly intended to persuade and that make self-conscious use of the possibilities of ethical persuasion. Horace's *Satires* were called by their author *Sermones* (talks) in allusion to the tradition of the Stoic diatribe; they are, then, short, informal orations. Ovid's *Art of Love* is a didactic poem—a series of lectures, as it were.

1

In formal satire, the rhetorical importance of the character of the speaker is especially plain. The satirist must somehow establish his own relation to the norms by which he measures others. Juvenal found the problem so important that he devoted an entire introductory poem to his reasons for writing—"It is difficult not to write satire," and "If talent won't do it, indignation will compose the verse." Horace's urbane self-portraits are of course justly famous. No one would seriously question their truthfulness; in this case clearly, the style is the man. Yet Horace is by no means artless. He is a conspicuous example of success in the rhetorical task of establishing "faith" with the audience. He never loses sight of the necessity of establishing himself as a representative of the social norm, and he manages to do so without ever seeming fatuous or pompous. His methods are various. Several autobiographical passages are devoted to explicit self-defense. At other times, as in *Satires* I.1, he relies exclusively upon lively, witty, familiar tone and vivid incident. In the dramatic satires, his method is even more indirect.

The sixth satire of the first book is a good example of fairly explicit and straightforward ethical persuasion. The autobiographical passage (lines 45-131) is a defense against the charge that Horace is a favorseeker, that he gained Maecenas' friendship by pushing, and that he is ambitious. In a first brief section, Horace combats the charge by outright denial and by describing how the friendship actually developed. In this account (lines 52-62) he naturally represents himself as the opposite of the pushing or self-interested man and Maecenas as the opposite of the hasty or gullible man.

The rest of the satire falls into two parts; the first is a proud assertion of his virtue and his gratitude to his father, in which he gives the well-known account of his education: the second is a disclaimer of ambition as inconvenient, with an amusing and amiable account of his contented, free life of moderate self-indulgence. There is no need to examine this passage in detail. It begins with the frequently repeated assertion that, while Horace has small faults, his nature is fundamentally sound:

> Atqui si vitiis mediocribus ac mea paucis
> Mendosa est natura, alioqui recta, velut si
> Egregio inspersos reprendas corpore naevos,
> Si neque avaritiam neque sordes nec mala lustra
> Obiciet vere quisquam mihi, purus et insons,
> Ut me collaudem, si et vivo carus amicis,
> Causa fuit pater his.*   (65-71)

Here the assertion is direct and serious in tone; elsewhere Horace expertly turns his supposed faults to comic effect, as we shall see.[6] In several respects the satire demands that we accept Horace himself as a norm. First, in preferring his wise and virtuous father to one escorted by lictors and possessing the insignia of public office and the consular class (line 97), he represents a norm both of filial piety and of rational preference of true virtue to hollow titles. Second, his rejection of the discomfort and bother of a life of affairs—his preference of ease to the strenuous activity of the "distinguished senator" and the thousand others (110-111) —is presented as the principal alternative to depraved ambition

---

* Anyway, if my nature is marred by a few minor faults but is otherwise flawless—as if you should note a few moles or freckles scattered over a beautiful body —if no one ever rightly accused me of avarice or miserliness or low living, if I live blameless and innocent (allow me to praise myself) and dear to my friends, the cause of all this was my father.

(128-129). This passage joins an earlier one (23-44) on the subjection of the ambitious to envy and slander in identifying the good life with political quietism. What happens to the figure of Maecenas, then? "Born of ancient kings" (*Odes* I.1), Maecenas is above the dazzling attractions of ambition, and he knows how to discern what is truly virtuous. Of course, as we know and as Horace's public knew, he does not lead the life of *otium*, because of his self-sacrificing public spirit. He is one of the few born to rule, and others should not concern themselves with politics. Readers who are won over by the charm of Horace's self-portrait in this satire should not overlook the fact that it is an ethical persuasion to a quietistic acceptance of the current Roman regime.

Elsewhere the ethical persuasion is much less straightforward, for instance in *Satires* I.4, Horace's most elaborate defense of the genre of satire. Most of the satire is taken up with the answer to the question "whether this kind of writing deserves your distrust" (64-65). The chief objections to which he replies are that the satirist is merely a compulsive scribbler with no discrimination (34-38), that the satirist is to be feared (70), and that Horace himself writes out of ill nature and a desire to wound (77-78). The second and third of these charges are dealt with directly, the first indirectly.

The reply to the second is the direct assertion that only the vicious need fear the satirist (65-70) and need not detain us. The third charge, that of ill nature, is more important, and some sixty-five lines are devoted to it (78-143), almost half of the satire. It falls into two parts. The first is an angry rejection of the accusation of back-biting and an extended attack on that vice. It depends on the distinction between slander and speaking freely and jocosely—"liberius . . . forte iocosius" (91-93, 103-105). The second part attributes Horace's criticism of others not to spleen but to the habit of learning from others' misfortunes instilled in him by his father—a habit he still follows for his own benefit ("neque . . . desum mihi," 134). Horace's freedom of speech is, then, a privilege the reader should grant him (104-105), and his incessant writing *compressis . . . labris*, with a frown, is merely a minor vice (139-140) to be indulgently allowed ("concedis," 140) unless the reader wishes to risk offending the whole tribe of poets (140-143).

Here is a characteristic Horatian obliquity. The charge of ill nature is dealt with directly enough—and in a most urbane and amiable way—though we should notice the use of the tone of filial piety to dispel the charge of depravity (*pravitas*). Actually, whether we like Horace or not may have a great deal to do with our reaction to his poetry, but it is not entirely relevant to the question "meritone tibi sit suspectum genus hoc scribendi" (64-65); it is instead a most skillful example of ethical persuasion. To phrase the question in such terms is to see at once that this self-defense involves an implicit theory of satire—that satire is socially valuable as a means of moral instruction for the reader. But the theory is not made fully explicit, for the reader is told that his office is to pardon Horace, not to learn a lesson; rather it is implied, first by the assertion of the efficacy in Horace's own case of his father's instruction (129-131) and, second, by the analogy between Horace's reflections, which are written down, and his father's, which were delivered orally. There is, to be sure, a slight shift in the categories here—Horace's warnings to himself (133-137) are not the same as the poems addressed to the reader; between the two moments there must occur the conscious intent to instruct the reader. That Horace avoids making explicit his own function as teacher is a good instance of his skill and tact.

The last of the three accusations—that the satirist is a mere scribbler who will not spare even his friends if he can raise a laugh (34-38)—is essentially a charge of lack of discrimination. The earlier passage on Lucilius' prolixity and Horace's refusal to race with Crispinus (9-21) has already suggested that the Speaker is quite discriminating; it has, in fact, undermined the criticism before it has been stated. The very first section of Horace's defense is devoted to a nice distinction between the poet and the writer of *sermoni propiora*, things close to speech. The poet has "ingenium . . . mens divinior atque os magna sonaturum" (genius . . . more divine mind and a more resounding mouth—43-44). The distinction seems to place satire along with comedy in a class that differs from prose (*sermo*) only in having meter (47-48).

Although Horace has begun with a disclaimer to the title of poet (39-40), a properly modest gesture, he is careful not to say that what he and Lucilius have written are not poems. Lines 43 and 44 do not mean that writers of the grand style are the only poets. Horace does not say that he doubts that comedies are poems but that *quidam*—certain people—do. The sense of lines 56-62 depends upon the force given to the *ut* clause. Is it restrictive or nonrestrictive? *Eripias si tempora certa modosque,* if you take away the metrical structure, would Horace's satires be *etiam disiecti membra poetae?* The consensus of readers would, I have no doubt, answer yes, and most would regard them as better poetry than the rather ridiculous example from Ennius. *Quod prius ordine verbum est posterius facias* (make the first word the last in order): Horace is so skillful a manipulator of the resources of tone and emphasis of the Latin language—which, more than in most languages, depend on word-order and pauses—that it is hard to imagine him seriously derogating from their value in poetry. Horace is indulging in a quibble; while agreeing for the moment that the term *poema* might be restricted to works in the grand style, he contrives to make the grand style seem a bit inflated in comparison with his own supple and subtle style.

> "At pater ardens
> Saevit, quod meretrice nepos insanit amica,
> Filius uxorem grandi cum dote recuset,
> Ebrius et, magnum quod dedecus, ambulet ante
> Noctem cum facibus." numquid Pomponius istis
> Audiret leviora, pater si viveret? ergo
> Non satis est puris versum perscribere verbis,
> Quem si dissolvas, quivis stomachetur eodem
> Quo personatus pacto pater.*   (48-56)

Here Horace seems to be suggesting that the exemplary character which is a specific virtue of comedy—that *decorum personae* of which he makes so much in the *Ars poetica*—works against its being truly poetic. For comedy presents characters that follow a pattern of probability (see Aristotle, *Poetics,* 1454a) —they are ordinary, or at least representative. To be a poet, then, one must not write as just anyone (*quivis*) would speak, with the

---

* "But the father rages that his spendthrift son, mad with love for a hetaira, refuses this wife with her large dowry, and—what is really terrible—walks around drunk having torches borne with him before nightfall." Well, would Pomponius hear less serious reproaches if his father were alive? Therefore it is not enough to write out in flawless verses something which, if you took it apart, is what any father would thunder forth, just like the one in the play.

mere superaddition of meter. Here again we have another quibble. The antithesis *quivis-poeta* can be understood as referring
simply to the hierarchy of styles—*genus tenue* as against *genus
grande*—or to the nature of the speaker. The selection of words,
the diction, of Horace's satires comes perhaps from *sermo quoti-
dianus*, everyday speech, but the thought does not. Indeed,
Horace is at great pains, from the beginning of *Satires* I.1, to
separate himself and Maecenas from the mass of mankind;
Horace represents the norm, not the average. In this passage, the
emphasis on the representativeness of characters in comedy—
along with the sly implication that the plots of most comedies
are trite—invites the reader to consider whether or not the words
he is reading are such as an ordinary man would use in his rage
(*quivis stomachetur pater*); his answer, of course, must be no.

It is interesting to remember in this connection that in comedy
the *senex*—usually a father—should, according to the famous
lines, be

> Dilator, spe longus, iners, avidusque futuri
> Difficilis, querulus, laudator temporis acti
> Se puero, castigator censorque minorum.*
> (*Ep.* II.3.171-174)

Some of these details apply to Lucilius as Horace paints him. Of
course, the chief cause of the tiresomeness of *senes* in comedy
is their loquacity (173-174). *Satires* I.4 begins with an attack on
Lucilius' prolixity, his uncritical garrulity in verse. As applied to
a versifier such as Lucilius or Crispinus, the criticism is a literary
one; if Horace is exempt from the fault, as he claims to be, it is
an aesthetic virtue.

In the end, Horace explicitly leaves the whole question open—
iustum sit necne poema. The implication is that he hopes ultimately to persuade the reader that it is a poem. At the end of the
satire there is an implied resolution of the question—a piece of
subliminal advertising, as it were; for in the humorous conclusion
he identifies himself as one of the band of poets. The term *poeta*
is here used in the broadest sense, including pretenders as well

---

* A delayer, but long on hope; lazy but eager for the future, fastidious,
querulous; a praiser of the times when he was a boy, the corrector and censor
of the young.

as true heirs (*nam multo plures sumus*). It is a humorous assertion of what is so modestly denied in lines 39-40:

> Cui si concedere nolis,
> Multa poetarum veniet manus, auxilio quae
> Sit mihi—nam multo plures sumus—ac veluti te
> Iudaei cogemus in hanc concedere turbam.*
>
> (140-143)

The question is finally and unambiguously resolved in *Satires* I.10, where Horace gives a much more straightforward account of the poetic virtues he has aimed for.

Horace thus has a considerable repertory of devices of ethical persuasion. He is perhaps most persuasive when we are least aware of his rhetorical purpose. The method becomes even more indirect in the so-called dramatic satires. One of the most charming of these is I.9, in which Horace represents himself as incapable of getting rid of an obnoxious coxcomb who hopes to obtain an introduction to Maecenas. After much preliminary talk, the man comes to the point in a way designed to put him in the worst possible light. First (45-48) he offers to become Horace's ally in an effort to exploit Maecenas. Horace answers with an explicit defence of Maecenas' circle: "Non isto vivimus illic, / Quo tu rere, modo; domus hac nec purior ulla est / . . . est locus uni / Cuique suus" (we don't live there in the way you suppose; there is no more virtuous house . . . each has his place—49-52). The boor finds this difficult to believe and goes on to brag that he will bribe the servants in order to gain entry and will pester Maecenas until he is received into the circle; Horace does not answer his boasts, and at this point the conversation is interrupted by the arrival of Horace's friend, Aristius Fuscus. The poet offers no comment on the conversation about Maecenas beyond what he represents himself as having said on the occasion. He preserves the natural, apparently haphazard flow of actual events, and the defense of Maecenas' circle, though clearly the purpose of the entire poem, is not insisted upon. It is the boor, not Horace, who does most of the talking.

The conversation about Maecenas occupies roughly the third

---

* If you won't allow me that, a whole crowd of poets will come to my help— for we outnumber you by a lot—and, like Jews, we will make you join the crowd.

quarter of the poem and is thus arrived at gradually. Before and after it, attention centers on Horace's inability to rid himself of the fellow. The man is oblivious to Horace's obvious reluctance to talk with him and impervious to Horace's only weapon, irony. Horace represents himself as simply incapable of handling him:

> Misere discedere quaerens
> Ire modo ocius, interdum consistere, in aurem
> Dicere nescio quid puero, cum sudor ad imos
> Manaret talos.* (8-11)

At first the man had followed Horace (6). Soon Horace recognizes he is beaten and now follows his tormentor (42-43). When Fuscus arrives, Horace frantically tries to enlist his aid in getting rid of the boor, but Fuscus is so amused by Horace's desperation that he deliberately ignores his appeals and leaves him "under the knife." Only the arrival of the unnamed boor's angry and vociferous adversary at law releases him from the long torture: "sic me servavit Apollo" (so Apollo saved me, 79)—divine intervention is necessary, so futile are Horace's own efforts.

The rhetorical purpose, of course, underlies the entire poem. The intention of discrediting the view of Maecenas' circle as a power-hungry and corrupt clique by attributing the view to a comically obtuse and distasteful (as well as venal) braggart is clear enough. It is a concealed argument *ad hominem*; it implies that those who so view Maecenas and his circle do so because they themselves are venal and obtuse. The foolishness of the boor is therefore firmly established before he gets around to his real purpose in singling out Horace. Equally important is the contrast between the boor and Horace. The fact that Horace makes no explicit defense of himself (although the boor's offer to become his ally implies that the boor sees him as one of the corrupt) is characteristic of the oblique method of the satire. If Horace is so comically incapable of handling this crass tormentor, he can hardly have achieved his position in Maecenas' circle through intrigue and pushing. The angry adversary can handle this man, not Horace. The humorous self-representation in the poem is, then, an ethical proof of the defense of Maecenas and his circle.

---

* Wretchedly trying to get away, I now walked fast, now stood still, now whispered some nonsense into the ear of my slave, as the sweat dripped down to my very heels.

Just as comic, but concerned with much more general issues, is the third satire of the second book. This is the longest of the *Satires* (326 lines) and is cast entirely in dialogue form. Here Horace is the prey of an even more garrulous person than the boor. Damasippus is a bankrupt spendthrift who was on the brink of suicide and has been converted to Stoicism. He treats Horace to a verbatim account of the formal diatribe with which the Stoic Stertinius dissuaded him from drowning himself. The diatribe itself, dedicated to the familiar Stoic paradox, "None but the wise man is sane," is Horace at his best: lively and witty, filled with telling exempla, incisively phrased, it is a demonstration of the insanity of mankind in general, with special emphasis on the avaricious, the ambitious, the libidinous, and the superstitious. Horace's favorite theme in the *Satires* and *Epistles*, of course, is not the extreme viciousness that Juvenal excoriates, but rather those deviations from a right standard that deserve the name of folly rather than of guilt. Much of the purport of Stertinius' diatribe is entirely consistent with Horace's direct statements in other poems (see II.3.82-157, on avarice, and I.1). What reservations Horace has will appear in a moment.

The diatribe, however much truth it may contain, is put in the mouth of Damasippus, himself a comic example of a further kind of madness—that of the convert. Just as Damasippus was once a fanatical, improvident collector of bronzes, so now he has become a fanatical Stoic (20-30). He has seized on the external marks of the philosopher, growing a beard and learning by rote the precepts of his master. But his philosophy is only hair-deep, so to speak. His chief pleasure, as he himself says, now that he has no business of his own, is minding other people's—"aliena negotia curo / Excussus propriis" (19-20). The poem in fact opens with Damasippus' fifteen-line exhortation of Horace to forsake his laziness. Horace congratulates Damasippus on having lost his craze for statues, and the implied rebuke is what sets Damasippus off. Horace has no right to criticize him, he says, since, like everyone else, Horace is himself insane; then, like a true convert, Damasippus repeats word for word what his master has taught him. Damasippus' reasons for relating the diatribe are thus a comic indication of his lack of the dispassionate harmony expected of the sage. Indeed, at the end of the diatribe Damasip-

pus shows that he regards Stertinius' instructions not as a guide
for his own conduct, but as a weapon against others:

> Haec mihi Stertinius, sapientum octavus, amico
> Arma dedit, posthac ne compellarer inultus.
> Dixerit insanum qui me totidem audiet atque
> Respicere ignoto discet pendentia tergo.*
>   (296-299)

There is much satire of the Stoics in the picture of both
Damasippus and Stertinius (whose very name is comic—
"Snorer"). The first, and basic, appeal Stertinius makes to
Damasippus is to his pride:

> Nam male re gesta cum vellem mittere operto
> Me capite in flumen, dexter stetit et "Cave faxis
> Te quicquam indignum . . ." inquit.†
>   (37-39)

The dogmatism and narrowness of Stoicism are frequent objects
of attack in Horace (as in *Serm.* I.3), who prides himself on never
swearing by any master's words (*Ep.* I.1.16). Damasippus is a
meddling bigot who shows himself to be more insane than the
man he sets out to convict of insanity. Although the problem is
never stated explicitly, an important purpose of the dialogue is
to display the dangers and reveal the discreditable foundations
of unself-critical dogmatism. Being a fanatical Stoic is just as
bad as being a fanatical art collector.

It is thus no accident that in the figure of Horace qualities
are emphasized that contrast strongly with Damasippus' bigotry.
He is the representative of a norm of balance and common sense.
The effect is paradoxically achieved by his agreeing that he is
in fact insane. At the outset he accepts Damasippus' abusive
counsel against his own idleness:

> Di te, Damasippe, deaeque
>   Verum ob consilium donent tonsore. Sed unde
>   Tam bene me nosti?‡   (16-18)

---

* These arms Stertinius, the eighth wise man, gave to me his friend, lest people
call me names with impunity. Whoever calls me insane will get just the same in
return, and will learn to see the bag hanging behind his own unwitting back.

† For when with veiled head I was about to jump into the river, he stood
suddenly on my right and said, "Look out—don't do anything unworthy of
yourself."

‡ For this true counsel, Damasippus, the gods and goddesses give you to the
barber. But how do you know me so well?

Horace's willingness to listen to criticism of himself (though in part ironic) is contrasted sharply with Damasippus' resentment and abusiveness, and makes it possible to show up his exaggerated cant:

> "Stoice, post damnum sic vendas omnia pluris,
> Qua me stultitia, quoniam non est genus unum,
> Insanire putas? Ego nam videor mihi sanus."
> "Quid? caput abscissum manibus cum portat Agave
> Gnati infelicis, sibi tunc furiosa videtur?"
> "Stultum me fateor—liceat concedere veris—
> Atque etiam insanum; tantum hoc edissere, quo me
> Aegrotare putes animi vitio?"*   (300-307)

Part of the point here is an attack on the Stoic oversimplification of ethical problems in regarding all departures from reason as equally insane or criminal (see *Serm.* I.3.76-112). Damasippus is shown to be ridiculous in speaking about Horace as if his insanity were comparable to Agave's. He is so firmly in the grip of his bigotry that the only way to get some sense from him is to agree to whatever he says. Horace therefore speaks in the passage before us with clear ironic overtones. Part of his motivation is that of drawing Damasippus out; when Damasippus answers his claim of sanity with the senseless example of Agave, he quickly changes his position in an effort to get the Stoic to talk sense. In his willingness to listen to Damasippus and to entertain criticism of himself, there is a generous dash of ironic detachment—Damasippus is not to be taken seriously. Thus although Horace calls Damasippus' remarks on his idleness "verum consilium," he shows his amusement by suggesting that Damasippus go to the barber.

Ultimately, of course, Horace's detachment is broken down. The trace of irritation visible in "Sed unde/ tam bene me nosti?" becomes greater when, toward the end of the poem, Damasippus begins to list Horace's faults. He attacks Horace for living beyond his means, for trying to keep up with rich men like Maecenas, for writing poetry (no sane man writes poems!), for his temper—

---

* "Stoic, so may you after all your losses sell everything at a profit, with what form of insanity, for there is not just one kind, do you think me ablaze? For I seem perfectly sane to myself."—"What? when Agave is carrying her unfortunate offspring's head cut off with her own hands, does she then seem crazy to herself?"—"Well, I confess I am foolish—one ought to admit the truth—and even crazy; but tell me just this, what vice of the mind is making me ill, do you think?"

and at this point, appropriately, Horace loses his temper: "Iam
desine!" (323)—equivalent to "all right now, that's enough!"
But Damasippus goes on to accuse him of "the thousands of
girls, thousands of boys you're infatuated with." Horace silences
him with "O maior tandem parcas, insane, minori" (pick on a
madman your own size, 326).

Now there are two points to be considered about the effect
and purpose of Horace's impatience: its relation to the norm
and its role in suggesting the author behind the dramatic character. The character's loss of patience is made to seem natural
by the exaggerations of Damasippus' attitude; its function is
precisely to emphasize the difference between the pretensions of
the would-be superhuman sage and the more natural Horace.
Ne quid nimis is the key to the figure of Horace—he listens to
much with patience, including sharp and direct criticism of
himself, but he is not such a wise man as never to resent im-
pertinence. The last line, in which he reverts to irony, states
directly the point that the contrast between Horace and Damasippus has sought to establish: Horace has his failings, but he recognizes them and, after all, they are comparatively mild. He is
sane enough to view with ironic skepticism not only Damasippus'
pretensions but his own as well. Horace is not merely patting
himself on the back; he is making a serious comment on fanati-
cism and dogmatism, and he not only presents a fanatic in a
comic light but contrasts him with a figure whose qualities make
him incapable of immoderation.

It is on this level that the figure of the Speaker Horace and
that of the author are consistent. We know that the author is
not losing patience as he makes the character Horace lose
patience. By portraying himself humorously and by implying
that criticisms of himself are valid, the author demonstrates his
balance and sanity. The effect is greatly strengthened by the
author's having Damasippus adopt some of his own devices in
criticizing him; in lines 314-320, for example, Damasippus drives
his point home with a beast fable, a favorite device of the Stoic
diatribe and characteristic of Horace. Horace also puts into
Damasippus' mouth mockery of his own small stature when he
has Damasippus discuss his style of living in terms of a metaphor
of physical size:

Accipe: primum
Aedificas, hoc est longos imitaris, ab imo
Ad summum totus moduli bipedalis, et idem
Corpore maiorem rides Turbonis in armis
Spiritum et incessum: qui ridiculus minus illo?*
(308-311)

The qualities in himself that the poet chooses to emphasize in *Satires* II.3 are thus not quite the same as in *Satires* I.9, but the method is fundamentally similar: representation of a norm and indirect comment through humorous self-portrayal. (*Satires* II.7, to mention one other example, follows a pattern almost identical with that of II.3.) It is one of the triumphs of Horace's art that the illusion of naturalness is so well maintained. The rhetorical purpose never becomes obtrusive; nor does the poet represent himself as such a paragon of virtue that the reader is alienated.

2

When the poet Horace constructs a Speaker Horace, he wishes the reader to identify the two. Paradoxically, the more elaborate his methods become, the less likely the reader is to make the identification; his pleasure depends upon his awareness of the skill and subtlety of the self-dramatization. Such refinement of poetic ethical persuasion as Horace practices perhaps inevitably calls forth a further refinement: transparent pretense, the specialty of Ovid in his love poetry.

It had been the intent of earlier elegists to achieve an effect of sincerity,[7] but Ovid deliberately plays with convention in such a way as to emphasize the pretenses involved. Book I of the *Amores*, for instance, opens with an elaborate prologue in which the Poet first decides that he will write love poetry rather than epic (I.1); second, formally submits to the power of Cupid (I.2); third—and only third—mentions meeting the girl (I.3).[8] This deliberately artificial opening, with all of its explicit discussion of the distinctions between the genres, is in marked contrast to the opening of Propertius' first book: "Cynthia prima suis miserum me cepit ocellis/Contactum nullis ante cupidinibus"

---

* Here goes: first, you are building, that is, you're imitating the big fellows, though you're only two feet tall from top to bottom, and at the same time you make fun of the spirit and strutting in arms of Turbo, which are so much bigger than his body—how are you any less ridiculous that he?

(Cynthia first captured me with her eyes, miserable me untouched before by any passion).

The *Amores* plays all manner of games with the traditional themes of elegy, such as twisting the Propertian injunction of simplicity of dress (I.2) into the parodic "I told you so" of *Amores* I.14, in which the woman is represented as having lost her hair because of dyeing it. In the *Amores* Ovid may be said to have introduced the trick of juxtaposition of opposites that he turned to such effect in the *Ars amatoria,* as we shall see, and that had so much influence on later writers. Perhaps the clearest instance is the pair of poems, II.7 and 8. In the first, supposedly addressed to Corinna, his mistress, the poet indignantly refutes the accusation that he has slept with her maid. The whole is a study in the *topics* of self-defense, ending with a solemn oath by Venus and Cupid. In the next poem, II.8, he turns to the maid and asks her, "How the deuce did Corinna find out about you and me? Did someone see us?" and so on through a number of mythological examples to persuade the maid, now intimidated by her mistress' anger, to continue the deception.

The *Amores,* however, is not my chief concern. It was in the *Ars amatoria* and the *Remedia amoris* that Ovid's particular technical gifts found the material most suited to them. The originality of the *Ars amatoria* is generally said to be the casting of erotic instruction in the form of the didactic poem.[9] As has long been recognized, the precepts Ovid offers are largely derived both from other elegists and from the whole tradition of erotic literature. A. L. Wheeler pointed out some time ago that even the role of *praeceptor amoris* is assumed by Propertius and Tibullus and introduced his discussion by saying: "The role of *praeceptor amoris* is seen in its fullest development in Ovid's *Ars amatoria*. But the *Ars amatoria,* like so much else in the work of that facile poet, was only the expansion and development to more definite form of an element already present in Roman elegy."[10] As Wheeler pointed out in his conclusion, however, the "profession of experience" of the *praeceptor* "connects the eroto-didactic element with the personal, rendering it part and parcel of the subjective-erotic note, which is the chief characteristic of Roman elegy."[11] Indeed, the instruction Propertius and Tibullus give is motivated by the supposed intensity of their personal experiences, and so there is a fundamentally serious note in their assumption of the role. Ovid's presentation of the role, however, is profoundly different because it is primarily facetious, and it is here, it seems to me, that his greatest originality lies.

As I have said, much of the amusement of the poem derives from its parody of the serious didactic poem.[12] The irony of the parody is intensified by the fact that the traditionally ungovernable passion which the Poet claims to have reduced to a system is no longer a serious matter involving the entire existence, the status in society, and the very sanity of the poet, but instead the sophisticated pursuit of pleasure—as Emile Ripert aptly put it, "the art of loving without love."[13] It is part of the game for the fashionable rake as Ovid envisages him to ape the truly passion-stricken lover. (This may be the real reason why Ovid "killed" Roman elegy—after him, the conventions could not be used without the taint of pretense.) The heroic and mythological comparisons, which are usually serious in Propertius and which, because of the intensity of emotion he conveys, are not out of keeping with the subject, become in the *Ars* and *Remedia* a principal source of humor precisely because the discrepancy is so great and is given such emphasis.

The vehicle of all this irony and parody is the figure of the Poet. Let us examine a few passages.[14]

> Siquis in hoc artem populo non novit amandi,
>   Hoc legat et lecto carmine doctus amet:
> Arte citae veloque rates remoque reguntur,
>   Arte leves currus: arte regendus Amor.
> Curribus Automedon lentisque erat aptus habenis,
>   Tiphys in Haemonia puppe magister erat:
> Me Venus artificem tenero praefecit Amori;
>   Tiphys et Automedon dicar Amoris ego.*
>
> (I.108)

The very first lines of the poem begin a complex play of irony. The subject of the poem is slyly announced in the first line as

* If there is anyone among these people who does not know the art of loving, let him read this poem and then love learnedly! It is by skill that the rapid ships are moved with their sails and oars, by skill the light chariots: Love is to be ruled by skill. Automedon was skilled with the chariot and the supple reins; Tiphys was the pilot aboard the Haemonian bark. Venus has made me the master craftsman in charge of tender Love; I shall be called the Tiphys and Automedon of Love.

something most people know about already, although Ovid takes care to signalize again and again the novelty of his poem. The second line suggests that all one needs to do in order to become a learned and up-to-date lover is to read through the poem once —*lecto carmine*. After drawing the parallel between the arts of sailing and chariot driving and this new art of love, the Poet makes an elaborate boast. He says that Venus herself has appointed him tutor to Cupid, that he will be known as the Automedon and Tiphys of Love. We know, of course, that he is speaking figuratively: he does not mean that he has actually tutored the god or that he has mastered his own passions, but that he has been clever enough to systematize an approach. We also know at once that it cannot be the insane furor of true love that is so governable, for his method is applicable only where the passions are but shallowly stirred. This is the first appearance of the pretense that the pursuit of pleasure is violent and involved passion. Indeed, the boast of controlling Cupid is, in its ironic exaggeration, a way of suggesting the author's technical control of the poem, since it focuses our attention on the verbal wit.

This last point becomes even clearer in the next few lines:

> Phillyrides puerum citharae perfecit Achillem
>   Atque animos placida contudit arte feros:
> Qui totiens socios, totiens exterruit hostes,
>   Creditur annosum pertimuisse senem;
> Quas Hector sensurus erat, poscente magistro
>   Verberibus iussas praebuit ille manus.
> Aeacidae Chiron, ego sum praeceptor Amoris:
>   Saevus uterque puer, natus uterque dea.*
> (I.11-18)

Here the discrepancy between the witty amorous Poet and the heroic centaur Chiron is given such emphasis, and is so comic, that the serious idea of the rational control of passion—if it was ever present—evaporates; and the parallel itself suggests the

* Chiron instructed the young Achilles in the lyre and soothed his fierce spirit with placid skill; he who was to terrify so many times both his friends and his enemies is believed to have been afraid of the year-laden old man; and those hands that Hector was to feel he held out for punishment at the command of his master. Chiron was the teacher of the son of Aeacis, I of Love: both boys are wild, both born of goddesses.

taming of love will be as impermanent as was Chiron's of Achilles. We laughingly submit to the outrageous impudence. What these lines prepare us for is a brilliant display of virtuosity, and we might note at this point that the metaphors of sailing and chariot driving, used here to illustrate the idea of the art of love, are the regular topoi in terms of which the divisions of the poem are referred to. Another metaphor identifies the course of the poem with that of a love affair—the reader's.[15] This raises a point of fundamental importance. The art of love is applicable only in an imaginary world, a world in which human beings have no profound needs or passions; as soon as the question of genuine passion arises, the problem of responsibility presents itself, and the cynical manipulation of others can no longer be treated lightly. This is a world of "as if," and the identification of the poem with the reader's love affair calls our attention to that fact. In effect, it shifts the problem of the application of the art from the practical sphere to the poetic, where we are led to admire Ovid's technical brilliance.

The Poet claims that his instruction has a firm basis in actual experience. The claim is made, however, in such a mock-serious tone that we are immediately alert for the irony, for the technique. In lines 22-30 the Poet's personal experience is impudently made to seem a far better guide than anything Hesiod learned from birds or Muses:

> Non ego, Phoebe, datas a te mihi mentiar artes,
>   Nec nos aeriae voce monemur avis,
> Nec mihi sunt visae Clio Cliusque sorores
>   Servanti pecudes vallibus, Ascra, tuis;
> Usus opus movet hoc: vati parete perito!
> Vera canam: coeptis, mater Amoris ades!*
>   (I.25-30)

He has not been staying in an isolated valley tending sheep. The claim of personal experience is thus an integral part of the elaborate bravura of this pose, and we have Ovid's word (*Tristia*

---

* Phoebus, I am not going to lie and say you have taught me my art, nor am I instructed by the voices of airy birds, nor did I see Clio and Clius and the sisters while I was keeping sheep in your valleys, Ascra. Experience impels this poem: make way for a bard who's an expert! I shall sing the truth: mother of Love, favor my undertaking!

2) that the personal experiences the Poet mentions to support his instructions are fictitious.

In Book II, the same vaunts of authority—and of success in teaching the techniques—are made, and the boasts are even more exaggerated. Here again we find the identification of the poem, the instructions, with the successful application of the technique: "Arte mea capta est, arte tenenda mea est" (she has been captured by my art; she must be kept by my art—II.12). The teacher's success is so great that the lover will bestow on him the palm taken away from Homer and Hesiod:

> Dicite "io Paean!" et "io" bis dicite "Paean!"
> Decidit in casses praeda petita meos;
> Laetus amans donat viridi mea carmina palma
> Praeferor Ascraeo Maeonioque seni.*
> (II.1-4)

The second book will be concerned with an even harder task:

> Magna paro, quas possit Amor remanere per artes,
> Dicere, tam vasto pervagus orbe puer.
> Et levis est et habet geminas, quibus avolet alas:
> Difficile est illis inposuisse modum.†
> (II.17-20)

The difficulty of holding Cupid back leads into one of the frequent decorative tales, that of Daedalus and Icarus. Typical in its wit of the virtuosity with which Ovid connects his digressions with the main movement of the poem, the tale demonstrates again the verbal resolution of the control of love: "Non potuit Minos hominis conpescere pinnas: /Ipse deum volucrem detinuisse paro" (Minos could not hold down a mortal's wings: but I am about to restrain a god from his flight—II.97-98).

At the end of Book II, the Poet returns to the language of the boasts of the opening of Book I. He claims to have fulfilled the promises made there and extends even further the humorous amplification in literal statement of what began as metaphor:

---

* Cry "Io Paean," and call out "Io Paean" twice! The prey has fallen into my snares; the happy lover gives green palms to my poem, and he prefers me to the Ascraean or Maeonian bards.

† I am preparing great things—to say through what arts can Love be made to stay, that boy who so wanders through the vast world. He is light, and he has two wings with which to fly away: it is hard to impose a stay on him.

Quantus apud Danaos Podalirius arte medendi,
Aeacides dextra, pectore Nestor erat,
Quantus erat Calchas extis, Telamonius armis,
Automedon curru, tantus amator ego.
Me vatem celebrate, viri, mihi dicite laudes,
Cantetur toto nomen in orbe meum!*
(II.735-740)

Here the successful teaching of the art (actually, the completion
of a unit of the poem) is identified with its successful application;
previously the steps in the instruction were metaphorically seen
as steps in the pupil's love affair, but now the (metaphorical)
success of the pupil is seen as the teacher's own amatory prowess.
The placing of the successful lover (*praeceptor*) among the
heroes[16] is a further inflation of the initial idea that the *magister
amoris* is the rival of such great heroic *magistri* as Chiron. In
finally demanding recognition as *poet*, Ovid explicitly identifies
his amatory prowess with his poetic virtuosity.

The comic juxtaposition we find in these vaunts of the Poet
is one of the basic comic devices of the poem. The citation of
heroic and mythological precedents for each of the precepts is
a delightful parody of pedantry, and involves reducing heroes
and gods to the level of the Roman demimonde, just as the boasts
of the Poet place him among the heroes. Most frequent and important are the ironic references to the Homeric stories. For example, Menelaus is to blame for his own troubles: an expert
cannot blame Helen; she could not bear to sleep alone, and Paris
—like a true gentleman—merely helped her out (II.359ff). The
lover is urged to learn from Agamemnon the advisability of
hiding his infidelities from his mistress, since it was Agamemnon's
unfaithfulness that caused Clytemnestra to take a lover—and we
all know how that ended (II.399ff).

The legends of Rome's noble past do not escape unscathed.
In a parody of the aetiological poem, the Poet explains that the
theater is a good hunting ground for the young rake because it
was at a theatrical festival that the Romans carried off the Sabine

---

* However great Podalirius was among the Greeks for the art of healing,
Achilles for his right hand, Nestor for his great courage, however great Calchas
was with the omens, Ajax with arms, Automedon with the chariot, that's how
great a lover I am. Celebrate me the bard, men, sing praises to me, let my name
be sung around the world!

women (I.101-134). The decorative tale is told with great skill, and the application is brilliantly sardonic: "Romule, militibus scisti dare commoda solus!/Haec mihi si dederis commoda, miles ero!" (Romulus, you're the only one who knew how to treat soldiers right! If you will give me these comforts, I'll be a soldier, too!—I.131-132).

Many fine passages depend upon this kind of impudent manipulation and juxtaposition. In Book I, for example, Ovid presents a long digression on the prospective victories of Gaius Caesar over the Parthians (I.177-228). The praises of Gaius are sung with ostensible patriotic fervor, with all the pomp of heroic diction, invocation of the gods, and righteous indignation. The victorious battle is imagined, and the whole ends with Gaius' triumph: "Ergo erit illa dies, qua tu, pulcherrime rerum, / Quattuor in niveis aureus ibis equis" (so the day will come when you, wonder of the world, will ride golden behind four white steeds —I.213-214). Then the Poet shows the triumph to be an occasion for seduction. Not only that, but the young stay-at-home rake is urged to lie about the triumph in order to seem well informed:

> Omnia responde: nec tantum siqua rogabit;
>   Et quae nescieris, ut bene nota refer!
> Hic est Euphrates, praecinctus harundine frontem;
>   Cui coma dependet caerula, Tigris erit.
> Hos facito Armenios, haec est Danaeia Persis;
>   Urbs in Achaemeniis vallibus ista fuit;
> Ille vel ille duces; et erunt quae nomina dicas
>   Si poteris, vere, si minus, apta tamen.*
>
> (I.221-228)

Until he comes to the end of it, the reader expects the parenthesis to Gaius to be a conventional compliment to an important personage. At first the interest lies principally in the vivacity with which Ovid is able to inform the convention in his description of the triumph. When we come to the application, however, the tables are turned, and Gaius is shown to exist for the commodity of the fashionable rakes of Rome.[17]

---

* Answer everything, and not only when she asks; and what you're ignorant of, speak as if you knew it well! This is the Euphrates, his brow circled with reeds; that one with blue hair shall be the Tigris. Make these the Armenians, let this be Danaeian Persis; that over there was a town in the Achaemenian valley; let this fellow or that be the leaders. And let the names that you give them all be true, if you can; if not, at least well chosen.

In much the same way, philosophy and cosmology are wrenched to the purposes of the *magister amoris*. The witty sensualist reminds his pupils that beauty is fleeting and urges them to cultivate the things of the spirit—in order to continue to attract girls (II.113-122). And just as concord succeeded chaos in the formation of the world, so one should silence the reproaches of his furiously (and justifiably) jealous mistress by administering the strong medicine of love (II.467-492). Just after this passage, Apollo appears to the Poet and offers additional advice. The effect here is complex. We admire the cleverness with which the usual method of direct precept is varied by the pretense of divine help. More important, the advice Apollo gives is highly comic—he shows how the Delphic oracle's most famous words—*nosce teipsum*—are applicable to philandering: know your strong points and how to capitalize on them (II.494-510). Our awareness of the manipulating hand is intensified by the Poet's mock-serious appeal to the authority of the god: "Sic monuit Phoebus: Phoebo parete monenti!" (so Phoebus advised: obey the god and his precepts—II.509).

The structure of the four books of the *Ars* and *Remedia* depends as much on the increasing complexity of this ironic manipulation as it does on an ordering of the subject matter. In the third book, the teacher displays his virtuosity by arming the other side in the war between the sexes. He has plenty of weapons left over, and Venus has in fact ordered him to arm the women, since he has given the men an unfair advantage. That the girls need help is clear. The most famous heroines were unhappy in love, and the whole list of them (Medea, Ariadne, Dido, and the rest) lost their lovers simply because they were ignorant of the *Ars*. Ovid will take pity on them (III.33-44). The effect of the third book thus depends to a large extent upon the cleverness with which parallels to the preceding books are exploited. Similar advice is given about dress (I.505; III.129), cleanliness (I.513; III.193), the habitat of the prey (I.67; III.387), the relative virtues of youth and maturity (II.665; III.555), the use of letters (I.437; III.350; III.469), and so forth. More important, the girls are given weapons to counteract those given to the men. Thus in Book I the teacher urges the men not to worry about perjuring themselves when making promises:

Nec timide promitte: trahunt promissa puellas;
  Pollicitis testes quoslibet adde deos!
Iuppiter ex alto periuria ridet amantum.*
                    (I.631-633)

And in Book III he warns the girls against believing men when they swear and advises them to play the same game:

Parcite, Cecropides, iuranti credere Theseo:
  Quos faciet testis, fecit et ante, deos . . .
Si bene promittent, totidem promittite verbis,
  Si dederint, et vos gaudia pacta date.†
                    (III.457-462)

And both sides of the battle are instructed in the essential techniques of arousing and allaying jealousy as need arises (II. 425; III.555).

The *Remedia amoris* carries these methods yet a step further: not only can Ovid arm both sides of the struggle, but he can arm anyone who wants to get out of it. The figure of the teacher is presented much as it was in the other books, but the comedy is pushed a step further. In Book III he claims that the heroines could have kept their lovers if only they had had his treatise. Here he says that his book would have saved the lives of Phyllis and Dido; it would have prevented the crimes of Tereus, Pasiphae, Medea, Phaedra, Paris, Scylla (*Rem.* 161-168), since all these suicides and criminals only needed the benefit of his expert advice in order to overcome their unfortunate passions. As usual, the fun depends on our keeping clearly in mind the distinction between genuine human passion and its metamorphosis into shallow pleasure-seeking. If we mistake the Poet's Phaedra for a real Phaedra, or this pretended world for the real world, we lose the effect of the wit, which again has the effect of drawing our attention to the poet's technical control of the entire fabric.

The *Remedia* opens with the Poet's seeking—and receiving—

* And do not make timid promises: promises conquer the girls; so promise and call on whatever gods you please as witnesses! Jupiter on high laughs at the perjuries of lovers.
† Beware, daughters of Cecrops, of believing Theseus when he swears: he has sworn by those same gods before . . . If they promise well, give promises back with just as many words; if they fulfill them, then you too give the joys you have promised.

Cupid's approval of his writing a cure for love on the ground that, in preventing suicides and crimes, it will keep Cupid from getting a bad name (1-40). Not only that, but Cupid himself is to contribute effective ways of overcoming love (555ff). The whole point of the *Remedia*, indeed, is announced in the lines presenting the teacher's ultimate boasts:

> Discite sanari per quem didicistis amare:
> Una manus vobis vulnus opemque feret.*
> (43-44)
> Naso legendus erat tum cum didicistis amare:
> Idem nunc vobis Naso legendus erit.†
> (73-74)

This completion of Ovid's brilliant demonstration of his command of his medium naturally includes the most impudent of Ovid's many references to his own works. Just as in Book III he referred the girls to his treatise on make-up, so in this book on the cure of love he works in a footnote to the *Ars*: follow the example of Agamemnon, he says, who rid himself of his passion for Chryseis by taking on Briseis:

> Ergo adsume novas auctore Agamemnone flammas,
> Ut tuus in bivio distineatur amor!
> Quaeris, ubi invenies: artes, i, perlege nostras:
> Plena puellarum iam tibi navis erit.‡   (485-488)

The defense of his poems against detractors, which forms one of the lengthier digressions of the *Remedia*, is just as bold. It begins with the proclamation that he does not care what his critics say in the first place—why should he? Everyone is reading his poems (363-364). The complaint he sets out to dispose of is that his Muse (his style) is *proterva*—shameless—as if, indeed, that were a fault. He does not deny the charge, but claims rather that he is not to be blamed, since the decorum of elegy requires such a manner. Surely he is not to write like an epic poet! This

---

* Learn how to get well from him who taught you to love: one and the same hand gives you the wound and its cure.

† You had to read Ovid when you were learning to love: the same Ovid must be read now.

‡ Therefore learn from the example of Agamemnon to take a new flame, so that your love, divided, may be weakened! You ask where to find one? Go, read my *Art of Love:* your ship will be speedily filled with girls.

is of course the most transparent begging of the question: as Zoilus might well point out, why choose a *materia proterva?* And it conveys a further suggestion: that the poet is just as capable of epic or tragedy as he is of elegy, his *protervitas* being simply a literary manner adopted for the moment. The whole passage ends with a triumphant taunt, in which Ovid says he has just begun to write. His detractors have begun too soon, since they will be even more shocked by his next poems (391-392). Indeed, he will not stop until he knows writers of elegy will confess they owe as much to him as the epic does to Virgil (393-394).

So far we have been examining passages in which the Poet explicitly proclaims his mastery of both the subject matter and the literary medium, and in which his virtuosity is displayed by ironic manipulation and juxtaposition. There are some interesting passages, both in the *Ars* and in the *Remedia*, in which he suggests some kind of lack of control. The passage in the *Remedia* in which Cupid appears to him is a good example (549-578). Like the appearance of Apollo in Book II of the *Ars*, it serves several purposes: variation, elaboration of the figure of the Poet, fun at the expense of Cupid. Its effect depends on our awareness of the artificiality and pretense behind it. The Poet even calls our attention to the pretense by expressing doubt as to whether it really was Cupid or a dream that appeared to him. Then he decides that it was not the real Cupid (555-556, 576). After relating the advice Apollo gave in *Ars* II, we remember, the Poet made an appeal to the authority of the god. Here the equally facetious decision that it was only a dream diminishes the divine authority of the advice—it is a kind of bravura of control. So too is the note on which the passage ends—he pretends to be at a loss about how to go on, since Cupid, his Palinurus, has deserted him in unknown waters (577-578).

The effect of such pretenses of doubt and lack of control is obviously a function of the general pose of absolute control. If here he pretends to doubt or to be ignorant of the material, elsewhere he pretends to be forgetful: "Quam paene admonui, ne trux caper iret in alas!" (how close I came to warning you not to let the rank goat go around in your armpits—*Ars* III.193), or unwilling: "Eloquar invitus: teneros ne tange poetas" (unwillingly I say it: stay away from the tender poets), and then immediately reminds us of the virtuosity with which he has put himself in such a position: "Summoveo dotes ipsius ipse meas" (I myself banish my own talents—*Rem.* 757-758). Sometimes he pretends to be ashamed: "Et pudet et dicam" (I am ashamed but I shall tell—*Rem.* 407), which is merely a signal that something surpassingly impudent is to follow.

One of the most amusing examples of this pretended lack of control occurs in *Ars* III.663-672, where Ovid warns the women to beware of good-looking friends and servants. He pretends to be so carried away by the pedagogical instinct that he gives himself away:

> Haec quoque, quae praebet lectum studiosa locumque,
>   Crede mihi, mecum non semel illa fuit.
> Nec nimium vobis formosa ancilla ministret:
>   Saepe vicem dominae praebuit illa mihi.
> Quo feror insanus? quid aperto pectore in hostem
>   Mittor et indicio prodor ab ipse meo?
> Non avis aucupibus monstrat, qua parte petatur;
>   Non docet infestos currere cerva canes.
> Viderit utilitas! ego coepta fideliter edam
>   Lemniadum et gladios in mea fata dabo.*

This supposedly autobiographical reference appears in the poem for the sake of demonstrating the poet's control. No one is fooled, and of course no one is expected to be. The pretense of unwitting self-betrayal is a further emphasis on the absolute artistic will, just as the claim that *usus opus movet hoc* of Book I is part of the parody of the serious didactic poem. Most of the little incidents Ovid presents as taken from his own experience in fact involve some kind of mistake, gaucherie, or lack of control:

> Me memini iratum dominae turbasse capillos:
>   Hei mihi quam multos abstulit ira dies!
> Nec puto nec sensi tunicam laniasse, sed ipsa
>   Dixerat: et pretio est illa redempta meo;

---

* And that friend who seems so eager to lend you her place and bed, believe me, she has been with me more than once. Nor should you have too pretty a maid: she has often taken her mistress' place with me. Where am I going, fool that I am? Do I walk to my enemies with unarmed breast and am I betrayed by my own testimony? The bird does not show the fowler where to hunt him; the deer gives no lessons in running to the hounds. To hell with advantage! I will follow through with what I've begun, though it guide the sword to my heart.

At vos, si sapitis, vestri peccata magistri
Effugite et culpae damna timete meae!*
(*Ars.* II.169-174)
Haeserat in quadam nuper mea cura puella:
Conveniens animo non erat illa meo;
Curabar propriis aeger Podalirius herbis,
Et, fateor, medicus turpiter aeger eram.†
(*Rem.* 311-314)

The mistakes of the Poet as lover, of course, make it possible for him to be all the more effective as teacher, and all the more amusing.[18] This posture of lack of control—whether over the process of writing or over the course of a love affair—is thus one of the important subsidiary devices by which the absolute technical control of the poem is suggested.

The advice Cupid gives when he appears to the Poet in the *Remedia* is typical of all the advice in these poems in that it envisages the means of dealing with categories of personal experience. We should note the ways in which ends and means are related:

Filius hunc miles, te filia nubilis angat!
Et quis non causas mille doloris habet?
Ut possis odisse tuam, Pari, funera fratrum
Debueras oculis substituisse tuis.‡
(571-574)

The imagined pupil wants to rid himself of an attachment that for some reason has become irksome. To remind oneself of one's duties is only a means toward this other end—as if sons who are soldiers, marriageable daughters, or dying brothers exist simply as distractions for the man who wants to get over a love affair and have no claim upon him in themselves. This is the same kind of irony that introduced Gaius' victories into the

---

* I remember that once I tore at my mistress' hair: ah, how many days did her anger deprive me of! I did not feel her tunic tearing, nor do I think it did, but she said it did: and so my money replaced it; but you, if you are wise, avoid the mistakes of your teacher and beware of the punishment my faults received!

† Recently I was stuck on a girl but she was not at all my type, really; another sick Podalirius, I had to treat myself with my own herbs, and, I confess it, Doctor Ovid was most wretchedly ill.

‡ This man can worry about his son in the army, you can worry about your marriageable daughter. Who does not have a thousand causes for pain? Paris, to be able to hate your girl, you should have kept in mind the funerals of all your brothers.

poem by pointing out how they could serve the purposes of the seducer. It is no accident, therefore, that Gaius and the claims of patriotism reappear in the *Remedia,* now serving the purposes of the renouncer of love (149-158).

This marshaling of *loci communes* in the *Remedia* leads us again to the question of the relation of the *Ars* and *Remedia* to rhetoric. It has often been pointed out how deeply Ovid was affected by the rhetoric of his day.[19] What I wish to emphasize is something quite fundamental, something in Ovid akin to what Socrates attacked in Gorgias. The attitude of absolute control of the subject matter and of the audience that we have been examining in Ovid's Poet is precisely the attitude of the sophist. The ability to arm both sides in a struggle—or to do away with the struggle itself—all with equal effectiveness (*modo das, modo demis*) is the ability that the sophist claimed and that the central tradition of ancient rhetoric sought to develop in the student. Since rhetoric and sophistic in themselves afford no critique of ends, they lead ultimately to the glorification of the orator as superior to all possible subjects of discourse. In the *Ars* and *Remedia* we have a display of pure technique, which is disinterested in the sense that it remains above and uncommitted to any of the possible subjects or to the moral positions one can take toward them. What Ovid does, perhaps not deliberately, by applying the techniques of rhetoric to an unconventional problem, the didactics of love, is to unveil the fundamental impudence of sophistic rhetoric itself. Such an unveiling can in fact be best achieved by showing how the categories and topics and *loci communes* are applicable to what is obviously outrageous and immoral.

The unveiling of rhetorical technique is well illustrated by those passages in the *Ars* where Ovid deliberately contradicts himself. The principal instances of this kind of bravura are the passages in which he first indicts and then defends the morals of the female sex.

> Prima tuae menti veniat fiducia, cunctas
>   Posse capi: capies, tu modo tende plagas.
> Vere prius volucres taceant, aestate cicadae,
>   Maenalius lepori det sua terga canis,
> Femina quam iuveni blande temptata repugnet:

Haec quoque, quam poteris credere nolle, volet.
Utque viro furtiva Venus, sic grata puellae:
    Vir male dissimulat, tectius illa cupit;
Conveniat maribus, ne quam nos ante rogemus,
    Femina iam partes victa rogantis agat.
Mollibus in pratis admugit femina tauro,
    Femina cornipedi semper adhinnit equo;
Parcior in nobis nec tam tam furiosa libido:
    Legitimum finem flamma virilis habet.
Byblida quid referam, vetito quae fratris amore
    Arsit et est laqueo fortiter ulta nefas?
Myrrha patrem, sed non qua filia debet, amavit:
    Et nunc obducto cortice pressa latet.*
                            (I.269-286)

I omit the long tale of Pasiphae that follows here, as well as the other examples of female lust (Aerope, Scylla, Clytemnestra, Medea, Clytia, Phaedra), and skip to the application:

Omnia feminea sunt ista libidine mota:
    Acrior est nostra plusque furoris habet.
Ergo age, ne dubita cunctas sperare puellas!
    Vix erit e multis, quae neget, una tibi.†
                            (I.341-344)

With this should be compared such passages as

Penelopen ipsam, perstes modo, tempore vinces;
    Capta vides sero Pergama, capta tamen.‡
                            (I.477-478)

and

---

* First make up your mind that they can all be caught. You will catch them, just set your snares. The birds will be silent in the springtime, the cicadas in the summer, the Maenalian hound will flee the hare, before a woman sweetly tempted by a young man will refuse: even the one you thought had no desire, she wishes it. Stolen love delights the girls just as much as the men: men dissemble ill, the girls burn more secretly. If we men should agree not to ask them first, the women, already overcome, would woo us. The cow moans to the bull in the flowering meadows, and it is the mare who always whinnies to the hoof-shod stallion; in the male passion is more moderate and less furious: male passion seeks a lawful goal. Why should I bring up Byblis, who burned for her brother with forbidden flame and bravely avenged her guilt with a noose? Myrrha loved her father, but not as a daughter ought; and now she is hiding within the bark that covers her.

† All of these crimes were caused by the lust of women: women's lust is sharper than men's and has more madness in it. Go on, then, don't doubt you can win any girl! Hardly a one out of thousands will refuse you.

‡ Just persist, and you will win Penelope herself. As you can see, it took a long time to capture Troy, but it was finally captured.

> Reddite depositum, pietas sua foedera servet;
> Fraus absit, vacuas caedis habete manus:
> Ludite, si sapitis, solas inpune puellas.
> Hac magis est una fraude pudenda fides.
> Fallite fallentes: ex magna parte profanum
> Sunt genus; in laqueos quos posuere cadant!*
>
> (I.641-646)

But in Book III, when he announces his intention of arming the weaker sex, Ovid imagines one of his audience as objecting:

> Dixerit e multis aliquis "cur virus in angues
> Adicis et rabidae tradis ovile lupae?†

He answers:

> Parcite paucarum diffundere crimen in omnes;
> Spectetur meritis quaeque puella suis;
> Si minor Atrides Helenen, Helenesque sororem
> Quo premat Atrides crimine maior habet,
> Si scelere Oeclides Talaioniae Eriphylae
> Vivus et in vivis ad Styga venit equis,
> Est pia Penelope lustris errante duobus
> Et totidem lustris bella gerente viro.
> Respice Phylaciden et quae comes isse marito
> Fertur et ante annos occubuisse suos;
> Fata Pheretiadae coniunx Pagasaea redemit
> Proque viro est uxor funere lata viri.
> "Accipe me, Capaneu! cineres miscebimur" inquit
> Iphias in medios desiluitque rogos.
> Ipsa quoque et cultu est et nomine femina Virtus:
> Non mirum, populo si placet illa suo.
> Nec tamen hae mentes nostra poscuntur ab arte:
> Conveniunt cumbae vela minora meae.
> Nil nisi lascivi per me discuntur amores:
> Femina praecipiam quo sit amanda modo.
> Femina nec flammas nec saevos discutit arcus;
> Parcius haec video tela nocere viris.
> Saepe viri fallunt, tenerae non saepe puellae
> Paucaque, si quaeras, crimina fraudis habent.‡
>
> (III.9-32)

---

* Return what has been entrusted to you, and let your piety keep true faith; let fraud be far from you, and keep your hands free of blood: if you are wise, deceive only the girls, which you can do with impunity! All other faith shines brighter in such fraud! Deceive those deceivers: they are a sex mostly beyond the law; let them be caught in their own snares!

† One of my many readers will say, "Why do you give the serpent more poison? Why do you turn the lamb over to the raging she-wolf?"

‡ Don't impute the crimes of a few to all; let every girl be judged on her

Now this is quite deliberate. I will resist the temptation to discuss the subsidiary ironies of the individual passages (such as the mention of *Virtus* and the quick rejoinder that he is, after all, teaching women vice), and will comment upon the broad contradiction. We are not asked by Ovid to adjudicate the case; we are asked to admire the ease with which arguments and examples are found for both sides and the bravura of the juxtaposition. Each passage embodies that adaptation to the audience which is the basic principle of rhetoric; the beginning of Book III is in fact a transparent *captatio benevolentiae*.[20]

The rhetoric is unmasked; the audience to which this transparent *captatio* is directed is not the actual readers of the poem, but a fictitious audience, the appliers of the art of love, who exist in the amoral world of "as if." The actual audience, in the real world, observes and appreciates the sophist's manipulations. The *Ars* and the *Remedia* are primarily an elaborate literary game, and it is for precisely this reason that the figure of the Poet—in its protean role—is so central to them. To arouse the reader's awareness of the artificiality of conventions, the contrivance, the pretense, and his admiration of the virtuosity of bold manipulation is the primary intention of these poems.

---

own merits. If Menelaus had good reason to do Helen in, and Agamemnon to do Clytemnestra in, if Amphiauraus came living and drawn by living horses to the Styx through the fault of Eriphyle, still Penelope was faithful to her husband while he waged war for ten years and then wandered for ten more. Look at Protesilaus and his wife who is supposed to have gone to Hades with her husband before her time; and the wife of Pagasaean Admetus redeemed him from fate and was carried to the pyre instead of her husband. "Receive me, Capaneus, let our ashes be mixed," said the daughter of Iphis and cast herself onto the pyre. Virtue herself is in dress and name a woman: small wonder if she pleases her people. But such exalted minds are not required by my art—my little bark takes smaller sails! Here you will learn nothing but wanton loves; I shall teach a woman how to be loved. Women do not brandish fire nor the cruel bow; they harm others with these weapons less often than men. Men are often deceivers, tender girls not often, and they have seldom been convicted of fraud.

II

Chaucer

In the first chapter I tried to show some of the ways in which Horace's and Ovid's careful definition of their roles as Poets is central to their poetry in both conception and effect. We turn now to Chaucer, and, while the chronological leap is a great one, the connection is not arbitrary. Along with Virgil, Horace and Ovid were during the Middle Ages the most widely studied and influential of the classical poets, and we should expect that an age so conscious of the rhetorical aspects of poetry and so dominated by the Horatian *iuvare-delectare* would understand and prize those technical aspects that I have been pointing out. We can also expect first-rate poets to have had a much broader conception of poetic rhetoric than the formalistic bias of the handbooks of the period might lead us to suppose, particularly since these Roman poets were directly available to them.

There is great need for a historical survey of both the techniques and the rhetorical function of self-conscious discursive narration in the Middle Ages. Self-conscious Narrators appear in most kinds of medieval imaginative narrative, especially from the twelfth century on (courtly romance, love-vision allegory, beast epic, theological allegory, to name only a few), and the influence of their example extends well into the Renaissance. Chaucer's[1] and Chrétien de Troyes'[2] Narrators have attracted considerable attention, but E. R. Curtius' monumental *European Literature and the Latin Middle Ages* is perhaps the first to attempt to cover such matters as invocation of the muses for the Middle Ages as a whole. The study of self-conscious Narrators has the tendency to lapse into mere listing of topoi and counting of authorial interventions; both Lüdecke and Curtius demonstrate

the danger. What is needed for medieval literature in general
—and it has begun to appear in Chaucer studies—is analysis of
the thematic and rhetorical function of the figure of the Poet in
individual works.

In this chapter I present an analysis of the function of the
Poet of *Troilus and Criseyde* that differs in some respects from
those suggested so far.[3] The Poet's "intrusions" have already been
catalogued and classified,[4] the formal arrangements deriving
from rhetorical doctrine have been pointed out,[5] and I shall not
go over that ground again in the case of Chaucer. What I wish
to focus on is the rhetorical function of the apparent self-contra-
dictions of the Poet and of his self-deprecation.

1

This is not the place to argue the pros and cons of various
interpretations of *Troilus and Criseyde,* but of course any view
of the function of its Poet necessarily implies an interpretation.
Paying close attention to the figure of the Poet should help us
to avoid two extremes of interpretation—one that the epilogue
is merely tacked on or that the poem has a "double morality";[6]
the other that a rigid and scornful theological puritanism informs
the poem from the outset.[7] Neither of these views is reconcilable
with the manner and tone adopted by the Poet. It is better to see
the poem as governed by a dialectical movement: at the beginning the assumption is that the audience has not yet learned the
particularly hard lesson that the conclusion will make explicit.
The action of the poem—and the commentary of the Poet—leads
us through sympathetic participation in Troilus' joy and woe to
an intellectual and emotional grasp of the point made in the
epilogue. We are intended to participate as fully as possible in
the intensity of Troilus' joy in order to share as fully as possible
in his disappointment and in the wisdom that can be derived
from it.

The strategy of the poem thus requires the Poet to adopt a
perspective which at the beginning is not very much wider than
that of the characters themselves and which is sometimes inconsistent with the conclusion. For we are not meant to react
like rigid theologians contemptuously clucking our tongues.
Even if we have already learned the lesson the poem will teach,

to read the poem effectively we must adopt the stance of one who has not.[8] In Book III the poem grants the love of Troilus and Criseyde all the poignancy of bliss that might be claimed for it by the lovers themselves. Then the action shows how abruptly it is destroyed. Book IV brings a radical shift in the Poet's attitude: while losing none of its compassion, it becomes increasingly hard-headed and more critical of the characters. Finally, when the action has demonstrated the incapacity of all three major characters to find any satisfactory principle for coping with the disaster and has made us share their agony and sense of futility, the vision of Troilus after death and the epilogue make explicit the Christian solution of the impasse. Let us examine this process in more detail.

The opening of the poem sets up the terms by which we are to receive the narrative. It gives some idea of the kind of story it will be, characterizes both Poet and audience, and provisionally indicates the kind of response the story will demand. The first two stanzas tell us the essential outline of the story:

> The double sorwe of Troilus to tellen,
> That was the kyng Priamus sone of Troye,
> In lovynge how his aventures fellen
> Fro wo to wele, and after out of joie,
> My purpos is, or that I parte fro ye.
> Thesiphone, thow help me for tendite
> Thise woful vers, that wepen as I write.
>
> To the clepe I, thow goddesse of torment,
> Thow cruel furie sorwynge evere yn peyne,
> Help me that am the sorwful instrument
> That helpeth loveres, as I kan, to pleyne;
> For wel sit it, the sothe for to seyne,
> A woful wight to han a drery feere,
> And to a sorwful tale a sory chere.[9]
>
> (1-2)

It is noteworthy that both in these stanzas and in stanza 8 the Poet asserts his knowledge of the entire story but withholds the interpretation of the story, the *sentence* with which the poem will end. It would not do, of course, to pretend that he did not know the outcome; he must therefore strike a delicate balance between his knowledge and the sympathetic participation he wishes to evoke.

Next the Poet characterizes himself and his motives for writing.
He represents himself as one who helps lovers to lament, who
serves the servants of love but who is not one of them. Here
again a careful balance is struck. There were three possible
stances the Poet could have taken here. He could have spoken
as one who had never loved, as one who was at the moment in
love, either happily or unhappily, or as one who had passed
through the experience of love to some position beyond. He
speaks instead as one who does not "dar to love, for myn un-
liklynesse, Preyen for speed," but who nevertheless sympathizes
with lovers. He thus establishes a certain essential detachment
without suggesting that he is in any way *superior* to lovers. (The
second possibility, of course, is that chosen by Boccaccio in the
Filostrato, where it accompanies a much narrower conception of
the moral problems; the third, as we shall see, is chosen by
Petrarch for the introduction to the *Canzoniere*. For Chaucer's
purposes, the second method lacks detachment, and the third
implies too great a detachment and superiority of wisdom.)

The next four stanzas reinforce the partial identification of
the Poet with lovers, who are now identified as the audience to
whom the poem is addressed, and they outline a wide spectrum
of possible fortunes in love, calling upon fortunate lovers to
have compassion for those less fortunate and also for each other.
Such compassion is equated with what the Poet feels, and the
experience of the *hevynesse* of love is identified as making possible the correct—the compassionate—understanding of the
story.

> But ye loveres, that bathen in gladnesse,
> If any drope of pyte in yow be,
> Remembreth yow on passed hevynesse
> That ye han felt, and on the adversite
> Of other folk, and thynketh how that ye
> Han felt that love dorste yow displese,
> Or ye han wonne hym with to grete an ese.
>
> And preieth for hem that ben in the cas
> Of Troilus, as ye may after here,
> That love hem brynge in hevene to solas;
> And ek for me preieth to god so dere,
> That I have myght to shewe in som manere

Swich peyne and wo as loves folk endure,
In Troilus unsely aventure.

And biddeth ek for hem that be despeired
In love, that nevere nyl recovered be,
And ek for hem that falsly ben apeired
Thorugh wikked tonges, be it he or she;
Thus biddeth god, for his benignite,
So graunte hem soone out of this world to pace,
That ben despeired out of loves grace.

And biddeth ek for hem that ben at ese,
That god hem graunte ay good perseveraunce,
And sende hem mygth hire ladies so to plese,
That it to love be worship and plesaunce;
For so hope I my soule best avaunce,
To preye for hem that loves servauntes be,
And write hire wo, and lyve in charite.

(4-7)

These stanzas implicitly adopt the evaluation of love as the greatest of earthly goods; there is no hint of religious condemnation. Although the greater context of human life is referred to repeatedly—"god so dere," "hevene," "out of this world"—the references are presented as consistent with the attitudes of lovers. They are similar to the references we shall later find Troilus making. Now the reader of the poem is meant to identify himself hypothetically with this attitude, and part of the function of mentioning these diverse fortunes in love is to include as many persons as possible in the supposed audience and at the same time to exclude others. Like any poem, this one sets up a world of discourse into which we can enter only by accepting its postulates, only by theoretically putting ourselves in the position from which it starts. That position is defined carefully here in order to exclude the position we reach at the end of the poem. This is why the poem is addressed to lovers, not to theologians. When we do reach the end and look back, we may see that this proem does in fact make veiled reference to the poem's hortatory purpose. Living in charity with lovers, we shall see, means bringing them to wisdom. But that perception is carefully kept in abeyance at the outset.

The Poet, of course, represents himself as possessing a con-

siderable degree of worldly wisdom. He is not the naive dreamer
of Chaucer's love visions. He constantly calls upon his audience
to share his ironic perception of the limited vision of his characters, especially Troilus:

> O blynde world, O blynde entencioun!
> How often falleth al the effect contraire
> Of surquidrie, and foule presumpcioun;
> For kaught is proud, and kaught is debonaire.
> This Troilus is clomben on the staire,
> And litel weneth that he moot descenden;
> Bul al day faileth thing that fooles wenden.

> As proude Bayard gynneth for to skippe
> Out of the wey, so pryketh hym his corn,
> Til he a lassh have of the longe whippe,
> Than thynketh he, "though I praunce al byforn,
> First in the trays, ful fat, and newe shorn,
> Yit am I but an hors, and horses lawe
> I moot endure, and with my feres drawe."

> So ferde it by this fierse and proude knyght;
> Though he a worthy kynges sone were,
> And wende no thing hadde had swich myght,
> Ayeyns his wil, that sholde his herte stere,
> Yit with a look his herte wax a-fere,
> That he, that now was moost in pride above,
> Wax sodeynly moost subgit unto love.
>   (31-33)

Now one of the marks of the dialectical participation I am speaking of is that Chaucer takes pains to avoid imposing on the story
at this point any theological judgments about the blindness of
lovers. He does so by taking the opposite tack, by having the
Poet preach subjection to love in terms worthy of the most
faithful devotee:

> Now sith it may nat goodly ben withstonde,
> And is a thing so vertuous in kynde,
> Refuseth nat to love for to be bonde;
> Syn as hym selven list he may yow bynde.
> The yerde is bet that bowen wole and wynde
> Than that that brest; and therefor I yow rede
> To folwen love that yow so wel kan lede.
>   (37)

And we shall find in the course of the first three books that love has precisely the ennobling effect on Troilus that the Poet claims for it here (III.257-258).[10]

This passage early in the poem and the many others like it that poke fun at the characters have several important functions. They keep the story from seeming stiff or ridiculous. They suggest an experience of the world and of love which, though it may be vicarious in the case of the Poet, is more inclusive than that of the characters; still it is essentially on the same plane as theirs, and so insulates the characters at least temporarily against theological incursions. Finally, the gently mocking view of the characters sets them up as objects of irony—if we allow ourselves to share the irony, we grant the "reality" of the character, and our sense of the vividness of the story is enhanced; by the same token, our compassion for the characters is deepened insofar as our perception of their limitations takes the form of affectionate humor based on recognition of a common humanity.[11]

The Poet's skillfully balanced mixture of worldly wisdom and inexperience in love is important in the proem to Book II, which begins by a particularly striking assertion of his immersion in the local moment:

> Owt of thise blake wawes for to saylle,
> O wynde, O wynde, the weder gynneth clere;
> For in this see the boot hath swych travaylle,
> Of my konnyng that unneth I it steere.
> This see clepe I the tempestous matere
> Of desespoir that Troilus was inne;
> But now of hope the kalendes bygynne.
>
> O lady myn, that called art Cleo,
> Thow be my speed fro this forth, and my Muse,
> To ryme wel this book, til I have do;
> Me nedeth here noon othere art to use.
> Forwhi to every lovere I me excuse,
> That of no sentement I this endite,
> But out of Latyn in my tonge it write.
>
> Wherfore I nyl have neither thank ne blame
> Of al this werk, but prey yow mekely,
> Disblameth me, if any word be lame;
> For as myn auctour seyde, so sey I.
> Ek though I speeke of love unfelyngly,

No wonder is, for it no thyng of newe is;
A blynd man kan nat juggen wel in hewis.

                            (1-3)

Here we have a protestation of ignorance similar to that with
which the poem opened. The function of this proem is slightly
different, however. The focus is on strengthening our sense that
the events of the poem have a sanction independent of the
author's personal views and limitations. The Poet is but trans-
lating "myn auctour"; the story is received and not invented.
Furthermore, the Poet says he speaks of love "unfelyngly." It is
to "every lover" that this excuse is directed, and the appeal to
figures outside the poem is meant to enhance the impression that
the feelings of Troilus and Criseyde are ideally intense and that
love is a human reality which is independent of the poem as well
as of the Poet's powers of expression.

    The next stanzas again identify lovers as the primary audience
and answer a possible objection to the poem:

> Ye knowe ek, that in forme of speche is chaunge
> Withinne a thousand yeer, and wordes tho
> That hadden pris, now wonder nyce and straunge
> Us thinketh hem, and yit thei spake hem so,
> And spedde as wel in love as men now do;
> Ek for to wynnen love in sondry ages,
> In sondry londes, sondry ben usages.
>
> And forthi, if it happe in any wyse,
> That here be any lovere in this place
> That herkneth, as the story wol devise,
> How Troilus com to his lady grace,
> And thenketh, "so nolde I nat love purchace,"
> Or wondreth on his speche, or his doynge,
> I noot, but it is me no wonderynge.
>
> For every wight which that to Rome went,
> Halt not o path, nor alwey o manere;
> Ek in som lond were al the game shent,
> If that men ferde in love as men don here,
> As thus, in opyn doyng, or in chere,
> In visityng, in forme, or seyde hire sawes;
> Forthi men seyn, ech contree hath his lawes.
>
> Ek scarsly ben ther in this place thre,

That have in love seid lik, and don in al;
For to thi purpos this may liken the,
And the right nought, yit al is seid, or shal;
Ek som men grave in tree, som in ston wal,
As it bitit; but syn I have bigonne,
Myn auctour shal I folwen, if I konne.

(4-7)

The point of this passage is not, it seems to me, to establish "historical distance" between us and the characters, but just the opposite. It asserts that, beneath the superficial diversity of human customs, the reality of the heart is essentially the same. The differences between Troilus' *purchacing* of love and the approach of the listener imagined in stanza 5 are first introduced in connection with differences in "forme of speche" (*verba* as opposed to *res*, in the traditional distinction); then the disparity due to "thousand yeer" changes is shown to be the same in kind with differences between *contemporary* cultures and, in stanza 7, with differences between individuals within the same society. The distance is progressively diminished; it is only superficial, in any case, for all are going to Rome—love (the word appears five times) is constant for all. The passage thus claims for the love of Troilus and Criseyde an importance it could not have in any relativistic view.[12] It becomes representative of human love in general; it becomes a test case. We are invited to forget our differences from Troilus and Criseyde and to accept the two as essentially like ourselves.

The passage has a second important function, which has to do with the specific terms of the contrast between the customs of Troy and those of the audience. The latter's *opyn doyng, chere, visitying,* and *forme* are in obvious contrast to the secrecy with which Troilus and Criseyde pursue the same "game." Futhermore, the objections attributed to lovers in the audience, imagined as coming from men, are clear references to Troilus' lachrymose dependence on Pandarus. The Poet has all along been inviting us to view Troilus with a wordly-wise, affectionate humor that springs from our shared notion of a more masculine and assertive norm of behavior in the lover. The decision to cast Troilus in an exaggeratedly passive role, emphasizing his subjection to love and his failure to see beyond it, results from a special strategic necessity: when in this proem to Book II the Narrator insists that any *purchacing*—hunting, pursuing—is really the same as Troilus': he is preparing us for the perception that assertiveness in love may be fully as much a subjection to love.[13]

The climax of the Poet's dialectical participation in the vision and emotions of his characters is in Book III. Although he reminds us several times of the dependence of the lovers' happiness on Fortune (III.89, 245) and maintains in the early part his affectionate humor at their expense (III.64, 139, 166), he adopts an attitude of full sympathy and approval of their bliss. He hopes that Troilus will come to bliss (III.152); he urges women to act with Criseyde's loving "gentilesse" (III.175); he wishes he himself had known such bliss (III.189); he thanks God the lovers' sadness was turned to joy (III.198) and wishes us no worse hap (III.178). We are intended to admire the gentilesse with which the lovers give themselves to each other and to judge their joy as the highest kind of earthly love. The Poet repeatedly emphasizes the nobility of their love:

> Lord, trowe ye a coveytous, or a wrecche,
> That blameth love and halt of it despit,
> That, of tho pens that he kan mokre and crecche,
> Was evere yit yyeven hym swich delit,
> As is in love, in o poynt, in som plit?
> Nay, douteles; for, also god me save,
> So parfit joie may no nygard have.
>
> They wol seyn "yis"; but, lord, so that they lye,
> Tho besy wrecches, ful of wo and drede!
> They clepen love a woodnesse or folie;
> But it shal falle hem as I shal yow rede:
> They shal forgon the white and ek the rede,
> And lyve in wo, ther god yeve hem mischaunce,
> And every lovere in his trouthe avaunce!
>   (195-196)

The same note is struck in the description of the second night of love, with the addition that their joy is now forgetful of self and therefore inexpressibly poignant:

> Nat nedeth it to yow, syn they ben met,
> To axe at me if that they blithe were;
> For if it erst was wel, tho was it bet
> A thousand fold, this nedeth nat enquere.

> Agon was every sorwe and every feere;
> And bothe, ywys, they hadde, and so they wende,
> As muche joie as herte may comprende.
>
> This is no litel thyng of for to seye;
> This passeth every wit for to devyse;
> For eche of hem gan otheres lust obeye;
> Felicite, which that thise clerkes wise
> Comenden so, ne may nat here suffise.
> This joie may nat writen be with inke;
> This passeth al that herte may bythynke.
>   (241-242)

The Poet's tone here is that of an authority on love, and he is implicitly challenging the lovers in the audience to measure their own experience of love against this exemplar. Earlier he had spoken "under correction," in his more customary pose as inexperienced in love:

> But how although I kan nat tellen al,
> As kan myn auctour of his excellence,
> Yit have I seyd, and god toforn, and shal,
> In every thing the gret of his sentence;
> And if that I at loves reverence,
> Have any thing in eched for the beste,
> Doth therwithal right as youre selven leste.
>
> For myne wordes, heere and every part,
> I speke hem alle under correccioun
> Of yow that felyng han in loves art,
> And putte hem hool in youre discrecioun,
> Tencresce or maken diminucioun
> Of my langage, and that I yow biseche;
> But now to purpos of my rather speche.
>   (201-202)

The effort to enlist the participation of the audience, to ensure that we will accept the love night as exemplary, is central to both passages.[14] The effectiveness of the poem—its power and persuasiveness—depends upon our acceptance of its descriptions of love as authoritative and upon our emotional participation. The Poet's participation is, finally, signalized also by the proem of Book III, which anticipates the terminology and the mood of Troilus' praise of love (III.250-253), and by the conclusion of the book, which rounds it out by recalling the proem and thanking Venus for having given the requested aid.

2

By the end of Book III, then, the lovers have reached a "hevene" of earthly happiness on which they rely without any thought of its impermanence. The last two books narrate the two changes that destroy this happiness: the change in external circumstances and the change in Criseyde. Events ironically frustrate the characters' expectations, and the narration proceeds by a series of abrupt juxtapositions of expectation and outcome. Each of the three principal instances of this discontinuity, is announced by emphatic pronouncements.

The proem to Book IV, with its mention of the disastrous outcome, is in sharp contrast to the picture of undisturbed happiness with which Book III ends. This is the most emphatic juxtaposition of the poem, and the effect of abrupt discontinuity with Book III is a major structural fulcrum which has been prepared with the utmost care. The Poet speaks now from the fullness of his knowledge of how the world goes. He does not yet invoke the religious synthesis of the epilogue, for we must fully contemplate the evil before we entertain its remedy. But he begins with a generalization whose inclusiveness and severity are equal to what the epilogue will have to say about worldly hopes; "swich joie"—all purely earthly happiness—is asserted to last "al to litel," and all those who rely upon it are branded fools.

> But al to litel, weylawey the whyle,
> Lasteth swich joie, ythonked be Fortune,
> That semeth trewest whan she wol bygyle,
> And kan to fooles so hire song entune,
> That she hem hent and blent, traitour comune;
> And whan a wight is from hire whiel ythrowe,
> Than laugheth she, and maketh hym a mowe.
>
> From Troilus she gan hire brighte face
> Awey to wrythe, and took of hym non heede,
> But caste hym clene oute of his lady grace,
> And on hire whiel she sette up Diomede;
> For which right now myn herte gynneth blede,

And now my penne, allas, with which I write,
Quaketh for drede of that I moste endite.
(1-2)

This is a radical shift from the attitude the Poet has taken in
Book III, or indeed in all the preceding books.[15] The closest
approach to it is in I.31-37, whose deliberate avoidance of moral
implications we have noticed. It is significant that IV.2 omits
mention of the circumstances that separate the lovers and that
will be the focus of Book IV. It leaps to the very end, to Criseyde's ultimate betrayal, and the effect is to emphasize a violent
discontinuity with the picture of Criseyde as wholeheartedly
devoted to Troilus. It is in fact the first explicit reference to her
coming unfaithfulness since the beginning of the poem. Stanzas 3
and 4 relate the structure of the poem to the action:

For how Criseyde Troilus forsook,
Or at the leeste how that she was unkynde,
Moot hennesforth ben matere of my book,
As writen folk thorugh which it is in mynde.
Allas! that they sholde evere cause fynde
To speke hire harm! and if they on hire lye,
Iwis, hem self sholde han the vilanye.

O ye Herynes, Nyghtes doughtren thre,
That endeles compleynen evere in pyne,
Megera, Alete, and ek Thesiphone,
Thow cruel Mars ek, fader to Quyryne,
This ilke ferthe book me helpeth fyne,
So that the losse of lyf and love yfeere
Of Troilus be fully shewed here.
(3-4)

Again we find the Poet claiming extrapersonal sanction for his
story in the appeal to his sources and, at the same time, adopting
the sorrowful, compassionate attitude toward Criseyde that will
dominate his comments about her in the last book. The suggestion that the sources may be lying about Criseyde has the function both of suggesting that she existed independently of the
Poet and of strengthening the conviction that she did in fact
forsake Troilus. The fourth stanza further qualifies the compassion by adding the important fact, not yet referred to, that
Troilus lost "lyf and love *yfeere*."

The Poet's commentary in Book IV is principally devoted to emphasizing the intensity of his characters' woe. After the proem there is no direct reference to Criseyde's approaching infidelity. On the contrary, there are two explicit claims that her devotion to him is still unimpaired (IV.97 and 203-205). We are meant, of course, to remember that her mind will change, but we should accept these assertions of her devotion at face value. The most important single digression in Book IV is not concerned with the lovers at all, but with the ironic outcome of the Trojan eagerness to ransom Antenor. It occurs near the beginning of the book and is meant to be thought of in connection with the proem:

> O Juvenal, lord! soth is thy sentence,
> That litel wyten folk what is to yerne,
> That they ne fynde in hire desir offence;
> For cloude of errour lat hem nat discerne
> What best is; and, lo, here ensaumple as yerne.
> This folk desiren now deliveraunce
> Of Antenor, that broughte hem to mechaunce.
>
> For he was after traitour to the town
> Of Troye; allas, they quytte hym out to rathe!
> O nyce world, lo thy discrecioun!
> Criseyde, which that nevere dide hem scathe,
> Shal now no lenger in hire blisse bathe;
> But Antenor, he shal come hom to town,
> And she shal out; thus seyde here and howne.
>
> (29-30)

This exclamation has several functions. First, it broadens the context of the story of the lovers to include the fate of Troy, an instance of the brittleness of worldly fortune whose magnitude far transcends their fate. Second, it shows that a major historical event, the fall of a great empire, stems at least in part from exactly the same cause as the private disaster of a lover; that is, it provides us with another instance of human betrayal—Criseyde, who will betray Troilus, is to be exchanged for Antenor, who will betray Troy. That the lines mention Antenor's future betrayal and Criseyde's past loyalty, but omit mention of Antenor's past loyalty and Criseyde's future betrayal, has the effect of bringing the reader up sharp and making him complete the pattern for himself; the irony is thereby considerably sharpened. Finally, the Trojans themselves are shown to be examples of the same kind of blindness Troilus has been guilty of, with the added suggestion, which the Poet has not as yet applied to Troilus, that not merely reliance on Fortune but, more important, the Trojans' own willful choice of a wrong object is to blame for their downfall. All of this serves to suggest how Troilus' loss is representative of human experience in general, on both the public and the private level. We are moving closer, especially in the final suggestion, to the inclusive religious perspective of the epilogue.

The third major juxtaposition of expectation and outcome is, of course, that in Book V of Troilus' trust and Criseyde's unfaithfulness. Criseyde's unfaithfulness is gradual in the length of time—repeatedly emphasized—it takes her to come round to it; but it is abrupt absolutely, in relation to her devotion to Troilus. The abruptness is emphasized both by a violation of chronology, the sudden mention of the fait accompli, and by the comments of the Poet. Book V is divided into four parts. In the first (1-28), Criseyde leaves Troy and arrives at the Greek camp; the action itself ironically passes Criseyde from Troilus' hand to Diomede's and contrasts the earlier part of the episode, where the woebegone Troilus is unable to act or speak, with the later part, where Diomede so vigorously lays siege to Criseyde. The second part (29-98) shifts to Troy, where Troilus waits out nine of the ten days after which Criseyde had promised to return. The third part (99-157) takes place in the Greek camp and carries us forward over an unspecified time to Criseyde's final betrayal of Troilus; and the fourth part (158-end) returns to Troilus on the evening of the ninth day and continues with him to his death and vision. After the third part of the book, Criseyde is never again on stage.

The disruption of chronology at the beginning of the fourth part of the book, the return to the ninth day, is an important ironic juxtaposition. The third part itself, however, has begun with an equally important anticipation. After relating Criseyde's sincere and unqualified suffering and her resolve to return to Troy, the Poet adds,

> But, god it wot, or fully monthes two,
> She was ful fer fro that entencioun;
> For bothe Troilus and Troie town

Shal knotteles thorughout hire herte slide;
For she wol take a purpos for tabyde.
(110)

And the touching picture of Criseyde's longing for Troilus is immediately qualified further by the appearance of the future seducer, Diomede. After recounting Diomede's resolve to win Criseyde, the Poet pauses to describe Diomede, Criseyde, and Troilus (115-120). The three descriptions are themselves in sharp contrast, and the series begins and ends with Diomede, for after giving the last portrait, that of Troilus, the Poet effectively follows it with his renewal of the narrative: "But for to tellen forth of Diomede" (121). These stanzas serve, as it has often been noted, to objectify and distance the figures of the protagonists. They also present them in attitudes of poised fixity just before the account of the radical change in Criseyde's actions, and help to intensify our sense of the abruptness of her passage from fidelity—fixity in love—to fickleness.

The reader's view of Criseyde's unfaithfulness is naturally crucial to his view of the story as a whole, and the Poet takes elaborate pains to control it. It is essential that Troilus' misery not seem merely the result of choosing the wrong woman.[16] Before her betrayal of Troilus, what we are shown of Criseyde in Book V is her state of uncertainty. In her soliloquies (99-101, 105-110) and in her speech to Diomede (137-144), there is a complex interplay of her yearnings for Troilus, her assessment of the practical situation (her father's unwillingness to let her depart, the certain doom of Troy), her regard for the *convenances*, her desire to take advantage of whatever can protect her in the Greek camp, her now disastrous capacity for hypocrisy, and even the beginnings of the idea of Diomede as a lover. She begins the evening by soliloquizing that she will follow her lover in spite of what other people say (109); she ends it by rationalizing her continuance in the Greek camp as determined by her need of other people (147). This initial stage of self-aware uncertainty, which culminates in the pathetic, demoralized "I mene wel, by god that sit above" (144), is not the act of betrayal itself or the act of will that will precede it. The betrayal itself comes some undertermined time later, and the Poet hides from us the moment of decision; he disclaims knowledge of what her motives were at that moment—"men seyn, I not, that she yaf hym hire herte" (150). He shows us rather her state *after* she has taken the practical step, "whan that she falsed Troilus" (151ff).

It is striking that a similar, though unmarked, reticence governs the narrative of Books II and III. In them we see Criseyde moving through the gradual, shifting process of falling in love with Troilus and ultimately accepting him as her lover; she does not fall in love lightly, and in a mood of urbane comedy we watch the interplay of sometimes only half-acknowledged desires and half-naive hypocrisies. Although Chaucer pays close attention to the process by which Criseyde falls in love, he contrives his account of events between the interview at Deiphobus' house and the love night so as to avoid the necessity of commenting on her internal dialogue with herself; we see her only externally. He hides from us, although we may not realize it at the time, the moment in which Criseyde decides that she will sleep with Troilus; he makes it clear, however, that there was such a moment and that the decision has been consciously taken when Criseyde says to Troilus, "Ne hadde I or now, my swete herte deere, Be yolde, iwys, I were now nat here" (III.73).

The difference in the results of the two processes is immense and crucial: in the earlier books Criseyde moves through uncertainty to the fixity of her acceptance of Troilus; in the later books she moves from that fixity through uncertainty to permanent inner conflict. At the beginning of her last soliloquy, she recognizes with bitter clarity and equally bitter regret the nature of her betrayal of Troilus; by the end of it, she is taking refuge in an elaborate series of hypocrisies (she will at least be true to Diomede, she will love Troilus like a brother) and finally in the nihilism of "al shal passe."

One of the things Criseyde's clarity enables her to see is that for future ages she will be the exemplar of unfaithfulness in love (152). It is of course only in relation to the perfection of the adjustment between the lovers in Book III that the charge makes any sense. In Book III Criseyde has been presented as exemplary in the opposite sense—not only in her beauty and womanliness, but also in her capacity to rise to the level of Troilus' love and to give herself wholly and consciously. It is through no mere pecu-

liarity of character that she is able to do so—it is through her
womanly humanity as such. By the same token, her betrayal does
not spring from some accident of her character; rather, it is the
result of the existential problem of being human, and the danger
Criseyde succumbs to is one to which anyone, no matter what
his particular traits, may succumb.[17]

The easiest way of stating what is at stake here is to say that
Criseyde has placed her faith in an earthly happiness which
depends upon the caprice of Fortune and that, when Fortune
turns against her, she is entirely defenseless. This statement is
found in Boethius and Boccaccio, and Chaucer made ample use
of it. For Boethius, Fortune is the personification of the radical
instability, mutability, of created things, and the danger to
human beings lies as much within them as without. This is why
it makes perfect sense, on one level, for Troilus to blame Fortune
for Criseyde's betrayal. Criseyde's fixity-in-love, which we are
made to feel so strongly at the end of Book III, is the centering
of her being on a single object of love. It is a full, genuine integration because the object is single—hence the reader's sense that
Criseyde has transcended her earlier uncertainties and hypocrisies. But her relationship with Troilus is itself subject to Fortune,
and when Fortune disrupts it she is no longer able to focus her
actions on that one center. In other words, she lacks a principle
that will enable her to transcend change; unable to rise above the
flux of the world, she is caught in it and exemplifies it within
herself.[18]

The conflict within Criseyde, then, is the result not of her
"character," but of the lack of a transcendental principle of fixity.
It is most significant that the same pattern governs the presentation of Troilus. Like Criseyde, Troilus reverts in Books IV and V
to an earlier pattern of behavior—somnambulant passivity—
which he had transcended at the end of Book III. But the later
passivity and dependence on circumstance are not comic. Before
he is uncertain of Criseyde's unfaithfulness, Troilus lives in an
unceasing welter of hope and fear, which shows him to be not
only subject to Fortune but also in a state of psychological flux.
The account of his inner state stops as soon as he becomes certain
of her infidelity: Troilus is not permitted to reach any point of
fixity until after death, for the frantic fighting into which he

throws himself expresses his futile lust for vengeance and recon-
nects his history with the greater disaster of Troy. Troilus and
Criseyde can be seen to represent the alternatives inevitably
faced by those whose love is directed outward to earthly goals—
either frustration of love for one object or fickle enjoyment of a
succession of objects.

The Poet's own view of both Troilus and Criseyde is a mixture
of mercilessly uncompromising clarity, which often takes the
form of irony at the expense of their self-deceptions, and compassion. His sympathy for Troilus remains largely implicit, but he
chooses to express his feeling for Criseyde, most emphatically as
he takes leave of her in stanza 157:

> Ne me ne list this sely womman chyde,
> Forther than the storye wol devyse.
> Hire name, allas, is punysshed so wide,
> That for hire gilt it oughte ynough suffise.
> And if I myghte excuse hire any wise,
> For she so sorry was for hire untrouthe,
> Iwis, I wolde excuse hire yit for routhe.

The Narrator's forgiveness of Criseyde is important to the
strategy of the poem, and central to his representation of her. He
has shown with remarkable brilliance the rationalizations she
takes refuge in (and he will go on doing so in her letters later
in the book), but he wishes to establish regret and compassion as
the norm of response. He so views Criseyde because she is representative of human unfaithfulness. Her fall is that of a genuinely
superior being. To view her with scorn here would be to deny her
representativeness and to adopt a worldly perspective that would
be no more inclusive than Pandarus'. The Poet's pity and forgiveness thus exemplify, without naming it, the Christian charity of
the conclusion.

The last two books of the poem, then, demonstrate the inability of the characters to deal with the abrupt discontinuities of
worldly change. They have placed their faith in earthly happiness, which depends upon the caprice of Fortune, and when
Fortune turns against them they are vulnerable. They lack a
principle that will enable them to transcend change. Therefore, in
different ways, they themselves, caught in earthly flux, exemplify
it in their own psychological states. Everything leads to the

announcement in the epilogue of the only principle by which one may become invulnerable against the inevitable flux of worldly fortune and the danger of flux within the soul itself. It is for Chaucer the only possible resolution of the agonizing futility of the last two books.

The epilogue gives the last word on the action, the audience, and the Poet himself:

O yonge fresshe folkes, he or she,
In which that love up groweth with youre age,
Repeyreth hom fro worldly vanyte,
And of youre herte up casteth the visage
To thilke god that after his ymage
Yow made, and thynketh al nys but a faire
This world, that passeth soone as floures faire.

And loveth hym which that right for love
Upon a cros, oure soules for to beye,
First starf, and roos, and sit in hevene above;
For he nyl falsen no wight, dar I seye,
That wol his herte al holly on hym leye.
And syn he best to love is, and most meke,
What nedeth feyned loves for to seke?

(V.263-264)

The "yonge fresshe folkes" are the lovers who have all along been envisaged as the audience of the poem. The Poet now expects them to accept him as superior in wisdom, which would have alienated them at the beginning of the poem, and he reminds them of their age and inexperience, exhorting them to profit from the vicarious experience the poem has furnished for them. The advice he gives follows the Augustinian sequence— they should return home (*intra*) from worldly vanity (*extra*) in order to look above themselves (*supra*) to God. They are reminded of both kinds of instability that the poem has shown, external and internal; the first is directly referred to ("this world, that passeth soone as floures faire"), the second—human betrayal —by implication in the substitution, for earthly "feyned loves," of the love of him who "nyl falsen no wight." Stanza 262 sets against this transcendental possibility of wholeness the discontinuity of Troilus' initial and ultimate fortunes; stanza 265 emphasizes the blindness of both Troilus and the Trojans.

After his eloquent appeal to his audience, which makes definitively clear the implications of the story and his own reasons for writing, the Poet further qualifies his own attitude. In a stanza that balances the proem to Book I, he dedicates the poem to "moral Gower" and "Philosophical Strode"; he thus identifies himself at the last not with poets of love or with lovers, but with moral and philosophical poets, the spokesmen of wisdom. Finally, as the poem opened with a prayer for lovers and showed us the Poet not daring to pray to the god of earthly love, the poem ends with a prayer in which he unites himself with all men in worshipful recognition of God's transcendence ("uncircumscript, and al maist circumscrive") and of his own and their dependence upon God's grace.

I do not mean to suggest that the epilogue presents no awkwardness or difficulties, or that my view accounts for everything. A revision, for instance, accounts for the awkwardness of transition in stanzas 258-262.[19] Originally stanza 262 directly followed stanza 258, in a natural transition from Troilus' death to the vanity of the gifts of fortune, which death destroys:

> But, weilawey, save only goddes wille!
> Ful pitously hym slough the fierse Achille.
>
> Swich fyn hath, lo, this Troilus for love!
> Swich fyn hath al his grete worthynesse!
> Swich fyn hath his estat real above!
> Swich fyn his lust! swich fyn hath his noblesse!
> Swich fyn hath false worldes brotelenesse!
> And thus began his lovyng of Criseyde,
> As I have told, and in this wise he deyde.

The point is not that, if Troilus had not loved Criseyde he would not have died at this time or in this way, but that his death reveals the ultimate vanity of all worldly fortune. In the conjunction of love, valor, and royal estate, Chaucer is identifying a particular prevalent attitude toward worldly goods, the courtly one. The passage suggests that there is not much point in renouncing love if you do not also renounce the other gifts of fortune. In any case, the insertion of stanzas 259-261, which adapt Boccaccio's account of Arcite's translation, disrupts the smooth transition by making the "swich fyn" series, which dwells on the negative reasons (death, the most radical change of fortune) for turning away from the world, follow a passage that mentions some positive reasons for doing so, thus producing a sense of strain and anticlimax. To attribute the anticlimax and the revision to a supposed intent on Chaucer's part to undercut the Narrator here seems to me to miss the point of the poem; probably the attribution springs from a modern unwillingness to suppose that Chaucer could have meant anything so puritanical to be taken straight. The whole poem, however rich its understanding and compassion for earthly lovers, is a demonstration of the negative reasons for turning away from the world. Although Chaucer does not wish us to be scornful of human beings caught in the delusions of earthly love, he does wish to instill a *contemptus mundi*.[20] For a contemporary of Chaucer's, more used than we are to that view of earthly life, the transition at stanza 262 may well have seemed acceptably smooth.

From the vantage point of the epilogue, then, we look back upon the role of the Poet. We see that our contemplation of the action after Book III has involved a continual and gradual qualification of our view of what occurred in the first three books. The Poet dramatizes the inadequacy of the position of Book III by a series of abrupt juxtapositions. We may see more clearly into the rhetorical function of his adoption of the perspective of the lovers in Book III and earlier. We see also that much of what he had said, although we may not have understood it at the time, is consistent with the epilogue: for example, the characterization of his motive as that of charity in the proem to Book I. We realize also that, although the proem to Book III sounds the praises of Venus in terms similar to Troilus' praise of love, it does so with a significant difference—it identifies the "pleasaunce of love" as instrumental and makes more modest claims for it. It does not make the mistake Troilus does, that of confusing a natural principle with the transcendent principle of love. The remarks that are consistent with the epilogue are a guarantee of the Poet's singleness of purpose; those that are inconsistent with it, we can see as having a rhetorical and thematic function in the general strategy of the poem.

Thus there is a gradual unveiling of the full thematic implications of the poem through the increasing inclusiveness of the Poet's commentary as well as through the action itself. The fullest understanding of the statement of the poem is possible only in retrospect. In this respect there is an important kinship between *Troilus and Criseyde* and the other chief poetic monument of the fourteenth century, the *Divina Commedia*. The Narrator of the *Commedia*—Dante looking back over the journey as a whole—cannot in his commentary at the beginning of the poem convey the full measure of his understanding. By definition, that understanding can only come through the experience itself. The beginning of the *Commedia* requires the reader to adopt the perspective of the inexperienced voyager. Of course the reader lacks the experience of the world beyond; allegorically, however, the world beyond is this world, and the reader is being maneuvered into hypothetical acceptance of inexperience of this world as well. The *Commedia*, like *Troilus and Criseyde*, leads the reader through sympathetic participation in the protagonist's experience to a perspective that transforms and transcends the nature of each step along the way. Both as a whole and in its parts, the *Commedia* proceeds by a process of retrospective illumination.[21]

The rhetorical strategies of the *Divina Commedia* and *Troilus and Criseyde* both depend upon a hierarchy of vision that makes possible the ordering of the various perspectives adopted by the Narrator. *Troilus and Criseyde* limits itself to portraying the consequences of misdirected love in this life and does not rise to the beatific vision as such; but the epilogue reminds us of that goal, whose existence and possibility is every bit as fundamental here as in the *Commedia*. Like the *Commedia*, then, *Troilus and Criseyde*, in its very essence as poetry, rests upon the Christian conception of the ascent in truth through experience. (The description applies equally well, of course, to such other fourteenth-century works as *Piers Plowman* and *The Pearl*.) Among the many lessons Chaucer learned from Horace and Ovid, we may no doubt include a sense of the concrete poetic possibilities of self-deprecation and apparent self-contradiction; his use of the devices is, however, radically different and deeply medieval.

III

Petrarch

In the sixteenth century, the hierarchy of perspectives that had enabled Dante and Chaucer to unify potentially contradictory modes of vision was in crisis, and a principal subject of my later chapters will be the approach to the fragmentation of experience taken by Ariosto, Tasso, and Spenser. Before turning to them we must look at Petrarch's *Canzoniere*, both because it presents one of the earliest Renaissance studies in spiritual multiplicity and because it directly influenced all the major Italian writers of the sixteenth century. The *Canzoniere* consists of three hundred and sixty-six sonnets, canzoni, sestine, madrigals, and ballate; it is intended as a unified work and is thematically and structurally extremely complex. It is not a narrative. It presents us with a series of lyrical poems supposedly arranged in the order of composition.[1] At times the poems purport to be immediate reactions to specific incidents, but even when they refer to no incidents the basic presupposition is that they are occasional, in the sense of expressing the mood of the Poet at the time of writing. The passage of time is continually referred to—is in fact a major theme of the sequence—and our sense of it is strengthened by the effect of the succession of separate units as well as by the appearance of anniversary poems. The *Canzoniere* presents itself as a kind of diary, and thus in an important sense its form is dramatic, except that the protagonist is supposed to be the actual author. The fact that the poems are poems, deliberately shaped by the Poet-Lover, is an integral part of their dramatic significance, especially when they are arranged to suggest a chronological sequence of changes in attitude. That the writing of poetry may be a mode of self-examination threatening to replace

the more traditional religious modes of self-examination indeed
becomes one of the thematic issues.

1

I shall describe the themes and structure of the *Canzoniere* by
discussing the relation, in each of its two parts, between several
of the canzoni and the shorter poems.[2] In Part I canzone 126,
"Chiare fresche e dolci acque," is of special interest (and is
perhaps Petrarch's greatest single poem). Its theme is the perma-
nence in his memory of a particular sight of Laura:

Chiare fresche e dolci acque
ove le belle membra
pose colei che sola a me par donna,
gentil ramo ove piacque
(con sospir mi rimembra)
a lei di fare al bel fianco colonna,
erba e fior che la gonna
leggiadra ricoverse
co l'angelico seno,
aere sacro sereno
ove Amor co' begli occhi il cor m'aperse:
date udienza insieme
a le dolenti mie parole estreme.

S'egli è pur mio destino,
e 'l cielo in ciò s'adopra,
ch' Amor quest' occhi lagrimando chiuda,
qualche grazia il meschino
corpo fra voi ricopra
e torni l'alma al proprio albergo ignuda;
la morte fia men cruda
se questa spene porto
a quel dubbioso passo,
che lo spirito lasso
non poria mai in più riposato porto
né in più tranquilla fossa
fuggir la carne travagliata e l'ossa.*

* Clear, fresh, and sweet waters, where she who alone seems Lady to me rested
her lovely body; gentle branch, where it pleased her (with sighing I remember) to
make a column for her lovely side; grass and flowers that her rich garment covered,
along with her angelic breast; sacred bright air, where Love opened my heart
with her lovely eyes: Listen all together to my sorrowful dying words. If it is
indeed my destiny and Heaven exerts itself that Love may close these eyes
while they are still weeping, let some grace bury my poor body among you and let

The existence of this physical site, the place where he saw Laura, has brought the past event into the present, preserved it; and so the first stanzas, which address the place and identify the dramatic present, already define the present in terms of the past intensity of the sight of the lady, though that sight is only fragmentedly and allusively referred to (by being connected with the separated items in the scene—waters, branches, grass, flowers). The present is a time in which essentially nothing is happening: the lover is deprived of the sight of his lady. He envisages the probability of eternal frustration and foresees his death; he identifies his words as his last words. The first important change of focus comes in the third stanza, when he looks forward into the future:

> Tempo verrà ancor forse
> ch' a l'usato soggiorno
> torni la fera bella e mansueta
> e la 'v' ella mi scorse
> nel benedetto giorno
> volga la vista disiosa e lieta
> cercandomi, ed, o pieta,
> già terra infra le pietre
> vedendo, Amor l'ispiri
> in guisa che sospiri
> sì dolcemente che mercé m'impetre
> e faccia forza al cielo,
> asciugandosi gli occhi col bel velo.*

This looking forward to a time when Laura shall seek him only to find that he is dust is, of course, quite self-indulgent and lachrymose, and designedly so. It is also concrete, calling up a vividly imagined scene. This intensity of imagined wish fufillment in the future, projected precariously in the fantasy, triggers a breathtaking shift back to the past:

---

my soul return naked to its own dwelling; death will be less harsh if I bear this hope to the fearful pass, for my weary spirit could never in a more restful port or a more tranquil grave abandon my laboring flesh and my bones.

* There will come a time perhaps when to her accustomed haunts the lovely, gentle prey will return, and, seeking me, will turn her desirous and happy eyes toward where she saw me on that blessed day; and oh the pity! seeing me already dust amid the stones, Love will inspire her to sigh so sweetly that she will win mercy for me and force Heaven, drying her eyes with her lovely veil.

Da' be' rami scendea,
dolce ne la memoria,
una pioggia di fior sovra 'l suo grembo,
ed ella si sedea
umile in tanta gloria,
coverta già de l'amoroso nembo;
qual fior cadea sul lembo,
qual su le treccie bionde
ch'oro forbito e perle
eran quel dì a verderle,
qual si posava in terra e qual su l'onde,
qual con un vago errore
girando parea dir, "Qui regna Amore."

Quante volte diss' io
allor pien di spavento,
"Costei per fermo nacque in paradiso."
Così carco d'oblio
il divin portamento
e 'l volto e le parole e 'l dolce riso
m'aveano, e sì diviso
da l'imagine vera,
ch' i' dicea sospirando,
"Qui come venn' io o quando?"
credendo esser in ciel, non là dov' era.
Da indi in qua mi piace
quest' erba sì ch' altrove non ò pace.*

These two stanzas evoke the poignancy of the lover's immobile contemplation of Laura in the rain of flowers, which by their motion help to express both the fixity of his gaze and her immobility in the eternity of the memory and the moment. It is never quite clear at what point the transfiguration of the event by the activity of obsessive memory takes over from the accurate factual account of the original vision.

* From the lovely branches was descending, sweet in memory, a rain of flowers over her bosom, and she was sitting humble in such glory, already covered by the loving cloud; this flower was falling on her skirt, this one on her blonde tresses, which were burnished gold and pearls to see that day; this one was coming to rest on the ground, this one on the water, this one, with a lovely wandering, turning about seemed to say, "Here reigns Love." How many times did I say to myself then, full of awe, "She was surely born in Paradise!" Her divine bearing, and her face, and her words, and her sweet smile had so laden me with forgetfulness and so divided me from the real image, that I was sighing, "How did I come here, and when?" thinking I was in Heaven, not there where I was. From then to here this grass pleases me so, that elsewhere I have no peace.

Although this poem is the fullest development in the *Canzoniere* of the theme of his memory of that first day, it is by no means the only one. The theme of the lover's obsession with this vision has been the subject of dozens of poems in the sequence *before* this one, and they have been very carefully placed to lead up to it. They describe his dwelling on the memory; they give provisional descriptions of it; they describe his attitude toward the place; they refer to other moments of that first day and perhaps of other days—but they tend to do only one of these things at a time. They do not unite all aspects of the theme into one complete whole, as does canzone 126, and do not describe the vision directly. The most important poems in this anticipatory process are 90, 108, 109, 112, 116, and 125. I shall quote only the first two of these in order to suggest the kind of expectant tension their repetitions bring about until we reach the fulfillment in 126:

> Erano i capei d'oro a l'aura sparsi
> che 'n mille dolci nodi gli avolgea,
> e 'l vago lume oltra misura ardea
> di quei begli occhi ch'or ne son sì scarsi,
>
> e 'l viso di pietosi color farsi—
> non so se vero o falso—mi parea;
> i' che l' esca amorosa al petto avea,
> qual meraviglia se di subito arsi?
>
> Non era l'andar suo cosa mortale,
> ma d'angelica forma, e le parole
> sonavan altro che pur voce umana;
>
> uno spirto celeste, un vivo sole
> fu quel ch' i' vidi, e se non fosse or tale,
> piaga per allentar d'arco non sana.*
>
> (90)
>
> Aventuroso più d'altro terreno,
> ov' Amor vidi già fermar le piante
> ver me volgendo quelle luci sante
> che fanno intorno a sé l'aere sereno,

---

* Her golden hair was loosed to the breeze, which turned it in a thousand sweet knots, and the lovely light burned without measure in her beautiful eyes, which are now so chary of it; and it seemed to me her face took on the color of pity, I know not whether truly or falsely; I, who had the tinder of love in my breast, what wonder if I suddenly caught fire? Her walk was not that of a mortal thing but of some angelic form, and her voice sounded differently from any human voice; a celestial spirit, a living sun was what I saw, and if she were not such now, a wound is not healed by the loosening of the bow.

prima poria per tempo venir meno
un' imagine salda di diamante
che l'atto dolce non mi stia davante
del qual ò la memoria e 'l cor sì pieno;

né tante volte ti vedrò già mai
ch' i' non m'inchini a ricercar de l'orme
che 'l bel piè fece in quel cortese giro.

Ma se 'n cor valoroso Amor non dorme,
prega Sennuccio mio, quando 'l vedrai,
di qualche lagrimetta o d' un sospiro.*

(108)

If 126 represents a structural node, which fully develops
themes scattered through many poems preceding and following it,
23 anticipates the appearance of many separate themes. Canzone
23, the first canzone and the longest, describes the six metamorphoses the lover undergoes in his love: he is turned into a
laurel; after his hope has been struck down like Phaeton (he has
evidently declared himself), he grieves for it like Cycnus and
becomes a swan—a lamenting poet. In a second cycle, after she
steals his heart, he breaks her commandment not to speak of his
love, and like Battus he is turned into a stone, reduced to crying
out to her with pen and ink since he cannot speak. But his
humility merely inflames her pride, and so like Byblis he turns
into a fountain of tears; then, like Echo, into bones and a dis-
embodied voice; then, like Actaeon, into a stag pursued by his
own dogs. The whole is a brilliant, surrealistic-allegorical adaptation of six Ovidian accounts of metamorphosis, using much of the
traditional allegoresis of them. Now this poem is a pillar of the
structure of the *Canzoniere* in several ways. First of all, the
theme of metamorphosis is ubiquitous. The transformation into
the laurel, the myth of Apollo and Daphne, so permeates the
sequence that it has called forth several studies.[3] Other individual
metamorphoses are often referred to—the myth of Actaeon in 52,
of Echo and Narcissus in 45. There may well be a connection,

---

* Luckier than any other ground, where I once saw Love stop her footsteps,
turning toward me those holy lights that make the air clear all around her; a
statue of solid diamond could wear away before I could forget her sweet bearing,
of which my memory and my heart are so full; and however many times I shall
see you yet, I shall still bend over to look for the print made by her lovely foot
in that noble place. But if Love is not asleep in worthy heart, beg Sennuccio,
when you see him, for some little tear or for a sigh.

incidentally, between the Actaeon myth (Diana in the fountain) and the scene described in "Chiare fresche e dolci acque."[4] Next to the transformation into the laurel, the most frequently recurring change is that into stone, about which I shall have more to say later.

The theme of metamorphosis serves to express the mutability of the lover. He is changed instantaneously by the power of his love. His state varies abruptly from the extreme of hopelessness to manic joy. One of the basic structural principles in the *Canzoniere* is the juxtaposition of such conflicting—and chronologically sequential—states. Let me comment briefly on one such sequence of poems.

In sonnet 60, the Poet vents a passionate anger against his lady: her cruelty has turned all this thoughts to grief, and so some other lover who had high hopes of his poetry might now curse the laurel tree that prevents their fulfillment. In the next poem, a famous and much-imitated tour de force, all shadow of anger is gone:

> Benedetto sia 'l giorno e 'l mese e l'anno
> e la stagione e 'l tempo e l'ora e 'l punto
> e 'l bel paese e 'l loco ov' io fui giunto
> da' duo begli occhi che legato m'hanno;
>
> e benedetto il primo dolce affanno
> ch' i' ebbi ad esser con Amor congiunto,
> e l'arco e le saette ond' i' fui punto,
> e le piaghe che 'nfin al cor mi vanno.
>
> Benedette le voci tante ch' io
> chiamando il nome de mia Donna ò sparte,
> e i sospiri e le lagrime e 'l desio;
>
> e benedette sian tutte le carte
> ov' io fama l'acquisto, e 'l pensier mio
> ch' è sol di lei sì ch' altra non v'à parte.*
>
> (61)

---

* Blessed be the day and the month and the year and the season and the time and the hour and the instant and the beautiful city and the place where I was struck by the two lovely eyes that have bound me; and blessed be the first sweet trouble I felt on being made one with Love, and the bow and the arrows that pierced me, and the wounds that reach my heart. Blessed be the many words that I have scattered calling the name of my Lady, and the sighs and the tears and the desire; and blessed be all the pages on which I gain fame for her, and my thoughts, which are only of her, so that no other has part in them.

Something has happened since the previous poem—if only that the lover's state has changed radically, to produce almost the most exalted outpouring of joy in the whole *Canzoniere.* Perhaps there has been no external incident at all. It is the peculiar quality of this work that there is no narrative mediation between such extreme states. We do not know how he moved from the one to the other; they are juxtaposed in all their ir- reconcilability. In particular, the sestet blesses *all* the lover's cries, sighs, tears, desire, poetry, and thoughts: it is not merely that blessing his poetry in praise of Laura rescinds the anger of the last poem; the last poem is itself one of his "pages" and is thus included in the blessing.

So far we have seen a self-regarding (because based on am- bition, even though poetic ambition) denunciation of Laura's cruelty and then a joyous declaration of thankfulness for his love. The motif of blessing the day on which he fell in love has occurred earlier, in sonnet 13, which is explicitly echoed here and which makes it clear that the reason for the Poet's thankful- ness is that his love is leading him toward heaven: "da lei vien l'animosa leggiadria / ch' al ciel ti scorge per destro sentero / sì ch' i' vo già de la speranza altero" (from her comes the buoyant hopefulness that leads you to heaven along a straight path, so that already I go high with hope). The explicitness of the allusion implies a similarity of reason between the two, although the question is not raised within 61.

There is another abrupt shift in the next sonnet, which raises some interesting questions about the benedictions:

> Padre del ciel, dopo i perduti giorni,
> dopo le notti vaneggiando spese
> con quel fero desio ch' al cor s'accese
> mirando gli atti per mio mal sì adorni,
>
> piacciati omai, col tuo lume, ch' io torni
> ad altra vita et a più belle imprese,
> sì ch' avendo le reti indarno tese
> il mio duro avversario se ne scorni.
>
> Or volge, Signor mio, l'undecimo anno
> ch' i' fui sommesso al dispietato giogo
> che sopra i più soggetti è più feroce;
>
> miserere del mio non degno affanno;

reduci i pensier vaghi a miglior luogo;
ramenta lor come oggi fusti in croce.*

(62)

This is an even more sudden change than the last one. Here
the theological condemnation of his vain love is imposed with
particular severity, and from this vantage point the benedictory
spasms of the previous poem have to be seen as, precisely, ravings
(once a liturgical context of some kind has been invoked, it is
tempting also to see a relation between the anaphora and poly-
syndeton of sonnet 61 and the style of the great psalms of praise
that were the staple of the office of Lauds[5]). As it happens, sonnet
62 is a particularly important poem; its implications about preceding—and following—poems extend far beyond the points I
am considering. For example, it is the second poem purporting
to present the lover's meditations on the anniversary of his
falling in love. The first one was 30, supposed to have been
written on the seventh anniversary. As we were told in the third
poem of the *Canzoniere*, the poet fell in love on the day of
Christ's crucifixion. But 30 makes no mention of the fact, ignor-
ing the crucifixion in its fixation on Laura's beauty: "Gold and
topaz in the sun above the snow are vanquished by the golden
locks next to those eyes that lead my years so quickly to shore."
Sonnet 62 thus raises an important question about 30 and about
all the other anniversary poems that disregard the religious
significance of the day.

The very next poem, 63, which has several explicit echoes of
the language of 62, reasserts the poet's love, and it does so in
terms which, in the context of the religious condemnation of 62,
are most emphatic: by greeting him, Laura has kept him alive;
he recognizes that his being comes from her; she has both keys
to his heart in her hand; anything from her is a sweet honor, and
he is ready to set sail with any wind. The image of a ship in
storm and in danger of not reaching port becomes an important

---

* Father of Heaven, after the lost days, after the nights spent raving with that
fierce desire which was lit in my heart when I looked on those gestures, so lovely
for my hurt, let it please You at last that with Your light I return to a different
life, and to more beautiful undertakings, so that, having spread his nets in vain,
my harsh adversary may be disarmed. Now turns, my Lord, the eleventh year
that I have been subject to the pitiless yoke, which is always more fierce to the
most submissive; have mercy on my unworthy pain; lead my thoughts back to a
better place; remind them that today You were on the cross.

metaphor for the disruption of the lover's soul; this is one of the first appearances of the metaphor of sailing, which is to receive independent treatment in 80, as the storm does in 66 and as the ship does again in innumerable poems, such as the famous one translated by Wyatt as "My galley charged with forgetfulness."

But the important point here is that the abrupt changes, the metamorphoses, are utterly irreconcilable with each other, incoherent, discontinuous, juxtaposed in such a way as to sharpen, rather than mediate, the differences. Unreasoning anger, unreasoning joy, half-sincere repentance, brazen back-sliding (I am calling these states by their theological names)—these juxtapositions are related to the traditional antitheses of the lover's state: I hope and fear, I burn and freeze, and so forth.

At this point we may look at 62 again. It is not saying, after all, "I do repent, I will conquer my love," but "Help me to repent, lead my thoughts back to You." By its phraseology it imposes the religious condemnation of the Poet's love so strongly that we may fail to see the implication that his heart and his thoughts are *even now* straying off to Laura. Hence also we feel the peculiar pathos of those eleven years: although he recognizes and is able to express with matchless eloquence the vanity of his love, although he wishes he could free himself, he cannot. The schema of this representation of moral conflict is, of course, Pauline: "The good that I would do, that do I not; the evil I would not, that do I" (Rom. 7:19). It is also the schema according to which Augustine describes the agony of his division against himself just before the instant of conversion. It is the moment at which grace must intervene, to heal the split in man's will. But grace does not intervene, in spite of the intensity of the Poet-Lover's desire for it. Instead, the opposite movement takes place —defection, in which the lower tendency of the will wins out and even perverts the rational categories, attributing to the lady a causality that belongs to God alone.[6]

In sonnets 60-63, then, we witness a series of inconsistent and even contradictory attitudes deriving from conflicts of the will. The theme of metamorphosis is developed also in canzone 129, the last in the group that includes "Chiare fresche e dolci acque." The abrupt variations of the lover's state are described at the beginning.[7]

... ivi s'acqueta l'alma sbigottita,
e come Amor l' envita
or ride or piange or teme or s'assecura;
e 'l volto che lei segue ov' ella mena
si turba e rasserena
et in un esser picciol tempo dura;
onde a la vista uom di tal vita esperto
diria, "Questo arde e di suo stato è incerto."*

But a chief theme of the poem is the metamorphosis of external reality in the lover's projection of the image of Laura (also the theme of 127):

I' l' ò più volte (or chi fia che m' il creda?)
ne l' acqua chiara e sopra l'erba verde
veduto viva, e nel troncon d'un faggio
e 'n bianca nube.†

Of equal importance is the lover's own metamorphosis—he is changed by the fixity of his own thought into stone:

Poi quando il vero sgombra
quel dolce error, pur lì medesmo assido
me freddo, pietra morta in pietra viva.‡

We can see, then, that the organization of Part I of the *Canzoniere* is, within the fundamentally narrative chronology, extremely complex: it defines by the alternation of states from poem to poem the fluctuations of the lover's will, and, at the same time, by a careful placement of longer poems in linked groups which I have called thematic nodes, it suggests increasingly rich thematic interconnections. Recurrent motifs thus acquire new resonances and significances in context, and the meaning of individual poems is sometimes sharply modified by the contrast with their neighbors.[8]

This kind of structure is a variation of the kind we have seen

* . . . there my frightened soul is quieted; and, as Love leads it on, now it laughs, now weeps, now fears, now is confident: and my face, which follows wherever it leads, is clouded and made clear again and remains but a short time in any one state; whence anyone who had experienced such a life would say, "This man is burning with love, and his state is unstable."

† I have many times (now who will believe me?) seen her alive in the clear water and on the green grass, and in the trunk of a beech tree, and in a white cloud.

‡ Then, when the truth drives away that sweet deception, right there in the same place I sit, cold, a dead stone on the living rock.

in *Troilus and Criseyde*, one based on retrospective illumination. Experiences are not fully understood when we are having them; later they reveal significances undreamed of at the time. What differentiates Petrarch from Chaucer and most fourteenth-century poets is that, although doctrine and experience keep challenging his immediate sense of the significance of his love, it is not clear that he is convinced by them or that his self-examination enables him to progress at all.

2

The most important contextual modification of the immediate significance of the lover's experience is the death of the lady, the most poignant instance of the mutability of the created world and a metamorphosis unaccounted for in Part I. Part II of the *Canzoniere* is thus the essential complement of Part I.

Even at first glance, the formal outlines of Part II suggest some complexity. There are ten longer poems: nine canzoni and one sestina (the sestina is a double one, so that the total number of sestine in both parts is nine or, counting the double one as two, ten). The longer poems occur in three groups at the very beginning, somewhat past the middle, and at the very end. On either side of the central group (323, 325, 331, 332) are two fairly long groups of sonnets and other short forms—one contains 51 poems; the other, 25 poems. These two groups are analogous in structure; they lead, through a similar alternation of themes, to the canzoni that begin the second and third groups of long poems. I shall discuss two canzoni from Part II in relation to the shorter poems of Part II and to the *Canzoniere* as a whole.

Canzone 359 begins the final group of long poems (359, 360, 366). It narrates in 71 lines a dialogue between the lover and Laura, whose soul he imagines to have come down from Heaven to visit him:

> Quando il soave mio fido conforto,
> per dar riposo a la mia vita stanca,
> ponsi del letto in su la sponda manca
> con quel suo dolce ragionare accorto,
> tutto di pietà e di paura smorto
> dico, "Onde vien tu ora, o felice alma?"
> Un ramoscel di palma

ed un di lauro trae del suo bel seno
e dice, "Dal sereno
ciel empireo e di quelle sante parti
mi mossi, e vengo sol per consolarti."*

The lover asks how she knows his state; she replies that his incessant weeping has disturbed her and that if he loved her he
should rejoice that she has gone to a better life. He replies
that he weeps not for her but for himself. Yet, he says, without
her he is nothing. She now urges him to lift himself up from
earth by plucking one of the two branches—palm and laurel—
and by begging for God's help:

"Or tu, s' altri ti sforza
a lui ti svolgi, a lui chiedi soccorso,
sì che siam seco al fine del tuo corso."†

At this moment comes a characteristic shift, an emphatic one in
view of what Laura has just been saying:

"Son questi i capei biondi e l'aureo nodo,"
dich' io, "ch' ancor mi stringe, e quei belli occhi
che fur mio sol?"‡

It is as if Laura's mention of his relying on God's grace precip-
itated the assertion of his fixation on her body. We recall that
the two branches came from "her lovely bosom." She rebukes
him:

"Non errar con li sciocchi
né parlar," dice, "o creder a lor modo;
spirito ignudo sono, e 'n ciel mi godo.
Quel che tu cerchi è terra già molt' anni . . ."

I' piango, ed ella il volto
co le sue man m'asciuga.§

* When my gentle, faithful comforter, to give repose to my weary life, sits
on the left side of my bed with that sweet skillful talk of hers, all pale with
anguish and fear I say, "Where do you come from now, o happy soul?" A little
palm branch and a laurel branch she draws from her lovely bosom and says,
"From the bright Empyrean Heaven and from those holy places I have come,
and I come only to console you."
† "Now you, if another is overpowering you, turn to Him, ask Him for
help, so that we shall be with Him at the end of your course."
‡ "Is this the blond hair and the golden knot," I say, "which still binds me,
and those beautiful eyes which were my sun?"
§ "Do not err with the foolish," she says, "nor speak nor believe in their

Now this poem, in all its intellectual and emotional complexity, is structured to pass through a number of topics we have seen before: Laura's virtue, the Poet's grief, her disciplining of him. Because of the imagined visit, the poem itself is recognizable as a literary indulgence in fantasy—its literary elaboration does not permit us to take it literally. At one point Laura says to the lover that he should weigh his chatter (*ciance*), meaning his poems, in a just scale. Complexly situated in the fictional nature of the poem is the ultimate psychological basis: the indulgence in imagining the beatified Laura. As a piece of self-analysis, the poem functions to identify the apparently sacrosanct figure of Laura as a sexual fantasy. The lover's interest is still—primarily or ultimately or also—in her body. It was significant that she sat on the *left* side of his bed rather than on the right side.[9]

Now the fantasy of Laura's visits to her lover in Part II is analogous to the fantasy of memory that was the subject of "Chiare fresche e dolci acque." I shall not explore the relation between the two fantasies themselves beyond saying that now, after death, Laura moves and speaks, whereas in canzone 126 she was immobile and silent in that fixed gaze. Like 126, 359 is prepared by a long series of poems, of which there are two principal groups in Part II, one in each of the two groups of sonnets that surround the central group of longer poems. In the first group, the fantasy of her presence is evoked by the places the lover associates with her. One instance:

> Quante fiate al mio dolce ricetto,
> fuggendo altrui e—s' esser po—me stesso,
> vo con gli occhi bagnando l'erba e 'l petto,
> rompendo co' sospir l'aere da presso.
>
> Quante fiate sol, pien di sospetto,
> per luoghi ombrosi e foschi mi son messo,
> cercando col penser l'alto diletto
> che Morte à tolto, ond' io la chiamo spesso.
>
> Or in forma di ninfa o d'altra diva
> che del più chiaro fondo di Sorga esca
> e pongasi a sedere in su la riva,

---

fashion; I am a naked spirit and I rejoice in Heaven. What you seek has been in the earth for many years now . . ." I weep, and she dries my face with her hands.

or l'ò veduto su per l'erba fresca
calcare i fior com' una donna viva,
mostrando in vista che di me le 'ncresca.*

(281)

Except for the fact that Laura is dead, these glimpses of her are
almost indistinguishable from the two forms of the old fantasy
(Laura sitting and Laura walking). It is close to the projections
of 129 and can hardly be distinguished from an intense memory.
The next step is actual dreams, and the very next poem (282)
introduces them: "Alma felice che sovente torni / a consolar le
mie notti dolenti" (happy soul who often comes back to console
my sorrowing nights).

Later, in the second long section of sonnets, following the
central group of long poems in Part II (323, 325, 331, 332), the
return of this theme is explicitly announced by 340, which complains that Laura has not recently visited him in dreams. Sonnet
341 promptly relates a visit:

Deh qual pietà, qual angel fu sì presto
a portar sopra 'l cielo il mio cordoglio?
ch' anchor sento tornar pur come soglio
Madonna in quel suo atto dolce onesto.†

In this poem she explains her former cruelty: "Fedel mio caro,
assai di te mi dole / ma pur per nostro ben dura ti fui" (my dear
faithful one, I am much grieved for you; but still I was cruel to
you for our own good).

The most significant sonnet in this series is 345, which denounces such fantasies as dangerous nonsense:

Spinse amor e dolor ove ir non debbe
la mal lingua, aviata a lamentarsi,

* How many times, fleeing others and—if it is possible—myself, to my sweet
hiding place I go, bathing with my tears the grass and my breast, disturbing with
my sighs its air! How many times alone, full of fear, have I gone into shadowy
dark places, seeking in my thought the high delight that death has taken away,
because of which I often cry out for death! Now in the form of a nymph or other
goddess who comes forth from the deepest floor of Sorgue and sits on the bank,
now I have seen her on the fresh grass treading the flowers like a living woman,
showing by her face that she is sorry for me.
† Ah, what pity, what angel was so swift to carry above to Heaven my heart-
felt sorrow? for again I sense my Lady returning as she is wont, with that
virtuous sweet bearing of hers.

a dir di lei per ch'io cantai et arsi
quel che se fosse ver torto sarebbe;

ch'assai 'l mio stato rio quetar devrebbe
quella beata e 'l cor racconsolarsi,
vedendo tanto lei domesticarsi
con colui che vivendo in cor sempre ebbe.

E ben m'acqueto e me stesso consolo,
né vorrei rivederla in questo inferno,
anzi voglio morire e vivere solo;

che più bella che mai con l'occhio interno
con li angeli la veggio alzata a volo
a piè del suo e mio Signore eterno.*

Now this is very clear and very harsh. The fantasy is wrong: it is the fruit of self-pity and an obstacle to true repentance. But the Poet-Lover is caught in that golden knot—this clear recognition fades; the fantasy recurs and is developed fully in 359, "Quando il soave mio fido conforto." That canzone does not of course resolve the ambiguity—except insofar as its literary presuppositions remove all the doubt as to the cause of the fantasy (inherent in its identification with dreams)—but it presents the ambiguity with matchless eloquence.

The importance in Part II of this fantasy is suggested by the key position of "Quando il soave mio fido conforto": it is the last poem before the final summing up of the lover's inability to resolve his dilemmas, canzone 360, the second longest poem in the collection. Here the lover arraigns Love before the bar of Reason, and the two debate at great length. At the end Reason smiles and declares that she cannot decide so great a question in "so little time." But it has been thirty years, according to the *Canzoniere's* fictional chronology, since the beginning! About the placement of 360 I shall only mention that this detailed summing up of the conflict, at the very end of Part II, balances the first poem in Part II, 264. That one had been placed just

---

* Love and sorrow incited my ill tongue—accustomed to lament—to where it should not go, to say of her for whom I sang and burned that which, if it were true, would be wrong: that she is in heaven ought to quiet my torment and console my heart, seeing that she is now so close to Him whom in her life she carried always in her heart. And I do grow calm again, and console myself, nor would I wish to see her here in this hell; rather I wish to live and die alone. For more beautiful than ever do I see her with my internal eye, risen in flight to the feet of her and my eternal Lord.

before Laura's death, as if to summarize the conflict prior to her death, when the lover was of course equally unable to resolve it.

A system of elaborate symmetries begins to emerge from Part II.[10] The other canzone I wish to discuss is the one that occurs closest to the midpoint of Part II—323, "Stando un giorno solo a la finestra," the first poem in the second group of long poems. This poem develops further the theme of metamorphosis, this time death as metamorphosis. You will remember the six metamorphoses undergone by the lover in canzone 23. These six metamorphoses actually fall into three cycles, whose rhythm is as follows: the lover loves, declares his love and is repulsed, and mourns in poetry. Except for the fact that we would have to add the fact of the lady's death, this repeated cycle bears a strict resemblance to the movement of the entire *Canzoniere*: a lover loves the mutable, is repulsed by it (loses it), and mourns. The metamorphoses of Laura, presented in 323, are also six; and they echo the events of 23 and also canzone 135, which describes the lover and lady as six marvels of the world. The six emblematic visions of Laura's death are as follows: a *fera*— no doubt a deer—killed by two dogs; a ship sunk by a tempest; a young laurel tree struck—contrary to usual practice—by lightning; a fountain (echoing 135) carried away by an earthquake; a phoenix (also 135, picked up again in 185) killing itself; a lady in a meadow bitten in the heel by a snake (the allusion is to Eurydice). Within Part II, coming as it does after the first long group of sonnets, 323 serves emblematically to renew the shock of Laura's death and to emphasize its abruptness and thus the mutability of the created world. Within the *Canzoniere* as a whole, it balances 23, the canzone of the lover's mutability, and casts ironic light back on it and on 135.

It is no accident that the theme of metamorphosis recurs in the ending of the *Canzoniere*. After the lover's inability to resolve his conflicts has been definitively set forth in 360, there follow sonnets of regret and renunciation, but not of final liberation or conversion, and the great prayer to the Virgin Mary (366), also a prayer for help in overcoming his attachment to the flesh and to the world, not the celebration of the accomplishment. This last canzone is the most sustained and penitentially

inclusive prayer for grace in the *Canzoniere*. As Father Kenelm
Foster has pointed out, it attempts to substitute the figure of
the Virgin Mary—a *vera beatrice*—for that of Laura, who is now
judged to have been a Medusa.[11] But one must be quite clear
about the difference between this religious ending and, say,
that of the *Divina Commedia*. If we describe it in the terms of
Dante's poem, Petrarch is still where Dante was at the beginning
of the *Commedia*—turning his back on the darkness, struggling
out of the water with laboring breath, yearning to climb the
mountain, but unable to make it on his own. And so far the
Virgin has not intervened.

As the most rigid theological view must define her, Laura was
a Medusa for Petrarch. When he fixed his gaze on her, his heart
turned to stone. He also turned her into stone in the immobility
of that ecstasy: he made her into an idol. Here we may recall
that the description of that contemplation given in "Chiare
fresche e dolci acque" relates it to the vision of God in terms
suggesting that it is idolatrous:

> Quante volte diss' io
> allor pien di spavento,
> "Costei per fermo nacque in paradiso."
> Così carco d'oblio
> il divin portamento
> e'l volto e le parole e 'l dolce riso
> m'aveano, e sì diviso
> da l'imagine vera,
> ch' i' dicea sospirando,
> "Qui come venn' io o quando?"
> credendo esser in ciel, non là dov' era.*

Laura is seen in *glory*, fixedly, ecstatically, in a mode of vision
that forgets her real being. The essence of idolatry is that the
idolater perverts the categories of the love and vision of God,
applying them to lesser things. I cannot here pursue the rich
and varied theme of idolatry in Petrarch.[12] I shall limit myself to
an aspect that leads us back to the nature of the formal structure
of the *Canzoniere*. The idolater wishes time to stand still:

---

* How many times did I say to myself then, full of awe, "She was surely
born in Paradise!" Her divine bearing, and her face, and her words, and her
sweet smile had so laden me with forgetfulness and so divided me from the
real image, that I was sighing, "How did I come here, and when?" thinking I
was in Heaven, not there where I was.

Prima ch' i' torni a voi, lucenti stelle,
o torni giù ne l'amorosa selva,
lassando il corpo che fia trita terra,
vedess' io in lei pietà, che 'n un sol giorno
può ristorar molt' anni e 'nanzi l'alba
puommi arricchir dal tramontar del sole.

Con lei foss' io da che si parte il sole,
e non ci vedess' altri che le stelle,
sol una notte e mai non fosse l'alba!
E non se transformasse in verde selva
per uscirmi di braccia, come il giorno
ch' Apollo la seguia qua giù per terra!

Ma io sarò sotterra in secca selva,
e 'l giorno andrà pien di minute stelle,
prima ch' a sì dolce alba arrivi il sole.*

His mind circling within its orbit, unable to transcend the obsessively fixed terms of his meditation, the lover imagines the only transcendence that is continuous with it—an eternal night of love. He knows it is impossible, and the poem ends with the only alternative within the obsessive circle, death. But the poem must be understood in the light of its ultimate implications. The time when the lover will be underground and the day will be full of stars is not only that of his own death: it is the end of the world.[13] Furthermore, though the lover does not understand it in this poem, his idolatrous eternity of love, his eternal night, is a parody of the eternal noon of Heaven, that ultimate Sabbath of rest.[14] The lover eventually comes to understand his idolatry, but the grace he prays for never comes to free him from it. He remains in the pinfold of his natural being, subject to time.

It is at this level that the theme of idolatry and the theme of metamorphosis coincide. It is because his love is turned outward, toward the external world, that the lover is subject to abrupt changes. Petrarch is adapting the Augustinian conception of the

---

* Before I return to you, bright stars, or fall down into the amorous wood, leaving my body that will be powdered earth, would that I might see pity in her, for in but one day it could restore many years and before the dawn enrich me from the setting of the sun. Might I be with her from when the sun departs, and no other see us but the stars, just one night, and let the dawn never come! And let her not be transformed into a green wood to escape from my arms, as on the day Apollo pursued her down here on earth. But I will be under the earth in dried wood, and the day will be full of tiny stars, before the sun arrives at so sweet a dawn.

ontological instability of natural, or carnal, man. Unless sustained
by God's hand over the waters of the flood, man flows into multiplicity. Man's life in time is, according to Augustine, essentially
an extension, a distension, as opposed to the eternal *in-tension*
that is God. Succession and time are by definition the mark of
man's imperfection. Thus the theme of metamorphosis in the
Canzoniere is also that of natural time not upheld, not gathered
and stabilized by eternity.[15]

This is, as Petrarch himself pointed out in the first poem of
the *Canzoniere*, the thematic significance of the *vario stile*, his
changing style. His letter to Pandolfo Malatesta said, "Opusculi
varietatem vagus furor amantium, de quo statim in principio
agitur, ruditatem stili aetas excuset" (let my age excuse the
rusticity of my style, and let the wandering furor characteristic
of lovers, which it treats from the very beginning, excuse the
variety of the little work).[16] This also accounts for the remarkably original and innovative structure of the *Canzoniere*, with
its mixture of elaborate symmetries and looseness, with its fundamental method of setting groups of longer poems among the
sonnets and madrigals, longer poems that gather and develop
more fully what is scattered among the short poems. Petrarch's
own title for the collection is *Rerum vulgarium fragmenta* (fragments of vernacular poetry); the first poem offers an alternative
title, *rime sparse* (scattered rhymes).[17] Both phrases refer to
the essentially provisional nature of the unification of the work.
Perfect integration of man's life and art comes only when the
mutable and imperfect is caught up into eternity. That ultimate
gathering, that binding of the book, comes only on the seventh
day, on the anagogical Sabbath of the vision of God. Such a
poem as the *Divina Commedia* can indeed pretend to some ultimate integration and unification precisely because it derives, like
all things, from that ultimate source of unity:

> Nel suo profondo vidi che s'interna,
> legato con amore in un volume,
> ciò che per l'universo si squaderna.*
> (*Par.* XXXIII. 85-87)

* In its depths I saw internalize itself, bound with love in one volume, what
through the universe is scattered unbound.

The very originality of Petrarch's conception of an artistic form expressive of the plight of natural man is closely related to, and perhaps in some sense was suggested by, Dante's conception of the *Commedia*.

Petrarch is traditionally thought of as an inventor of the modern idea of personality, and with some justice. It is not merely that he is introspective; introspection is a dominant theme of Christian writing from St. Paul on. Rather, his is an introspection which, while making use of traditional Christian schemas, remains resolutely natural. For Chaucer and Dante, as typically for medieval writers, the bond with the audience is established on the basis of a publicly recognized, shared openness to the transcendental.[18] Petrarch heralds the modern world, in which the sense of kinship among men is based instead on the shared plight of being natural.

Part Two

FOUR RENAISSANCE EPICS

IV

Boiardo

W ith characteristic inventiveness, the Renaissance developed many kinds of poetry it considered to be epic—historical, chivalric, Biblical, hagiographic, mythological, geographical, and so forth. The tradition of chivalric epic, to which belong all the poems I shall discuss in Part Two, unites elements from Homeric and Virgilian epic, medieval courtly and popular romance, and *chanson de geste*. The form developed by Boiardo and Ariosto derives from an essentially popular genre. The matter of France had been a favorite subject in Italian poetry long before these learned court poets took it over; in the thirteenth and fourteenth centuries the story of Charlemagne's invasion of Spain, which culminated in the slaughter at Roncesvalles, was adapted to narratives in *ottava rima* by the *cantastorie*, jongleurs who wandered about singing at fairs and festivals.

The manner of the *cantastorie* reflects the circumstances of oral delivery for which the poems were composed. The usual pattern is as follows: Each *cantare* begins with a one- or two-stanza prayer followed by a brief summary of the previous *cantare*, the announcement of the subject of the present one, and the request for silence and attention. In the more skillful poems, such as the mid-fourteenth-century *Spagna in rima*,[1] the prayers are given some relevance; in others they consist often of the mere stringing together of tags from the liturgy. The *cantare* ends with a brief indication of the subject of the next one, followed by a one- or two-line prayer for the audience. From certain passages in the *Spagna in rima* we can infer that more than one *cantare* was recited at a time; for instance, in one closing *congedo*, the Poet says he will pause to rest and have a drink before continuing

(VI.46). The poem as a whole ends with a more elaborate *con-gedo*, in which he thanks his listeners for their attention, exhorts them to be virtuous, apologizes for the roughness of his verse, prays for everyone, and identifies himself by name (XL.41-43). The Poet of the *Spagna* often appeals to the authority of the "book" he claims to be following; his appeals are always serious, and in fact every episode in the poem is traditional. He does not, like Chaucer and the later court poets, spoof the genre by such appeals. He claims that his story is true and that he is simply "adorning" it with "pleasant rhymes" (XXI.1, XVI.1). He hopes that his listeners will be pleased each time they hear him (XIX.1), that no one will criticize his handling of the subject (XL.2), and that his listeners will enable him to make a living (XIX.1, XXI.1) and make him famous (XVII.2).

This traditional manner lies behind the manner adopted by Pulci, Boiardo, and Ariosto. Pulci adopted the manner directly, in a sophisticated, slangy, usually dryly humorous mockery of the conventions I have just described. Boiardo's experiment was more fruitful in its influence, since it is essentially a courtly version of the popular manner. In the *Orlando innamorato* Boiardo deliberately attempts—not only in the introductions and endings of his cantos, but throughout—to create the illusion of a series of recitations of the poem, but they are supposed to take place at court, not in the marketplace.

> Signori e cavallier che ve adunati
> Per odir cose dilettose e nove,
> Stati attenti e quïeti, et ascoltati
> La bella istoria che 'l mio canto muove.*
>
> (I.1.1)

The Poet is thus represented as speaking to a group of gentlemen and ladies, who are often described as sitting around him. At each of these gatherings, which are apparently thought of as occurring on successive days (with some intervals, as between Books II and III), the Poet recites one canto.[2]

With few exceptions, the cantos open and close with some reference to this imagined situation. In Book I the Poet usually

---

* Lords and knights who come together to hear delightful new things, be attentive and quiet, and listen to the lovely story that my song tells.

limits himself, at the beginnings of each canto, to inviting his
audience to listen and reminding them of where he had broken
off the last canto. For example:

> Stati ad odir, segnor, la gran boattaglia,
> Che un'altra non fu mai cotanto oscura.
> Di sopra odisti la forza e la taglia
> De Zambardo, diversa creatura,
> Ora odireti con quanta travaglia
> Fu combattuto.*   (I.6.1)

> Segnori e cavallieri inamorati,
> Cortesi damiselle e grazïose,
> Venitene davanti et ascoltati
> L'alte venture e le guerre amorose
> Che fer' li antiqui cavallier pregiati,
> E fôrno al mondo degne e glorïose;
> Ma sopra tutti Orlando et Agricane
> Fier' opre, per amore, alte e soprane.

> Sì come io dissi nel canto di sopra,
> Con fiero assalto dispietato e duro
> Per una dama ciascadun se adopra.†
>   (I.19.1-2)

The second example represents a more subtle and developed
technique, leading from compliment and invitation of the audience, through a general characterization of the subject matter,
to the specific point of the story where the narrative is to resume.
Indeed, beginning with Canto 16 of Book I, Boiardo's practice
changes gradually, until in Books II and III the direct plunge
into the narrative, exemplified in the first quotation, becomes
the exception, and the representation of the relation between
Poet and audience becomes quite elaborate.

Cantos almost invariably end with a direct address to the
audience. They are often asked to return to hear the next canto

---

* Stay to hear, lords, the great battle, than which none was ever more cruel.
Above you heard of the strength and shape of Zambardo, that strange creature;
now hear with how much difficulty he was fought.

† Lords and knights in love, courteous and gracious damsels, come forward
and listen to the high adventures and amorous wars waged by the honored
knights of olden time, which were glorious and honored in the world. But above
all Orlando and Agricane performed works for love that were high and noteworthy. As I told you in the last canto, each struggles for a lady with fierce, pitiless, and harsh assault.

(as in I.1.91, 22.62, 26.64; II.1.77, 4.86, 6.65); sometimes a vague prediction of what the next canto will contain is made (I.3.81, 7.72, 10.53). The most frequent closing remarks are the claim that the next canto will be well worth hearing and that the tale now broken off will be continued:

> Ne l'altro canto dirò la travaglia,
> E de nove baroni un tale ardire,
> Che mai nel mondo più se odette dire.*
>
> (I.14.66)

> Questo canto al presente è qui finito;
> Segnor, che seti stati ad ascoltare,
> Tornati a l'altro canto, ch' io prometto
> Contarvi cosa ancor d'alto diletto.†
>
> (II.1.77)

Sometimes the endings are more extended. The *commiato* of Book I is naturally so, since it marks the end of a large section of the poem:

> Dirovi tutta quanta poi la cosa,
> Qual gli incontrò, quando fu gionto al gioco,
> E serà di piacere e dilettosa;
> Ma poi la contaremo in altro loco,
> Perché il cantar della storia amorosa
> E' necessario abandonare un poco,
> Per ritornare a Carlo imperatore,
> E ricontarvi cosa assai maggiore.

> Cosa maggior, né di gloria cotanta
> Fu giamai scritta, né di più diletto,
> Ché del novo Rugier quivi si canta,
> Qual fu d'ogni virtute il più perfetto
> Di qualunche altro che al mondo si vanta.
> Sì che, segnori, ad ascoltar vi aspetto,
> Per farvi di piacer la mente sazia,
> Se Dio mi serva al fin la usata grazia.‡
>
> (I.29.55-56)

* In the next canto I shall tell of the trouble and of a feat of nine barons so bold that no greater was ever heard of in the world before.

† This canto is now finished here; lords who have been listening, come back to the next canto, for I promise to tell you more things of high delight.

‡ Later I shall tell you all about the matter—who met him when he got to the action—and it will be pleasant and delightful; but we shall tell it later in another place, for it is necessary to leave singing this lovely tale and to return to Charles the emperor and to tell you something much greater. No greater thing, nor so glorious nor so delightful, was ever written, for there I sing of young Rug-

But for the most part the leave-takings are brief, sometimes consisting of only one line: "Ma ciò riserbo in l'altro canto a dire" (but that I shall keep to tell you in the next canto—III.2.60).

The topoi of these canto endings are varied, but all serve to continue and signalize the fundamental, imagined situation of recitation. A number of cantos end with a farewell which implies that the whole group disbands until the next day (I.19.65, 25.61; II.6.65); sometimes the dramatic illusion goes so far as to present the audience as unhappy that the canto should end (II.25.58). It is interesting to find the Poet occasionally giving a reason for breaking off where he does. Once he humorously claims that the next canto will be so strenuous that he must rest before singing it:

> Dura battaglia fu sopra quel piano.
> Ma in questo canto più non dico avante,
> Ché quello assalto è tanto faticoso,
> Che, avendo a dirlo, anch' io chiedo riposo.*
> (I.5.83)

Expressions of the Poet's need or desire for rest occur frequently (as in I.7.72; II.13.66, 23.78). Once it is the audience's desire for rest that is given as the reason for ending:

> Ma già son gionto a l'ultimo confino
> Del canto consueto; onde io me aviso
> Che alquanto riposar vi fia diletto:
> Poi serà il fatto a l'altro canto detto.†
> (II.29.65)

Here we find the Poet verging on a statement of the basic relation between his practice and the tastes and desires of the imagined audience. This becomes clearer in such cases as the following:

> Or, bei signori, a voi mi racomando,
> Compìto ha questo canto le sue carte,

---

giero, who was the most perfect in every virtue of all heroes the world boasts of. So that, lords, I shall wait for you to come and listen, in order to make your minds sated with pleasure, if God maintains to the end his wonted grace.

* It was a hard battle on that plain. But in this canto I shall not tell any further; for that assault is so laborious that, having to tell of it, I too need rest.

† But already I have reached the accustomed limit of the canto; wherefore it seems to me that you would like to rest somewhat: then the deed will be told in the next canto.

Et io per veritate aggio compreso
Che il troppo lungo dir sempre è ripreso.*
(II.10.61)

Ma non vi vo' tenir tanto a disconcio,
E nel presente canto io ve abandono,
Ché ogni diletto a tramutare è bono!†
(III.3.60)

In the passages commenting upon transition from one thread of the story to another, we might expect to find more explicit comment on the conduct of the narrative. Boiardo presents a marked contrast to Ariosto in this respect, for there is nothing systematic about his practice. The narrating "I" always does appear to signalize the shift (except that in a few cases Boiardo echoes the traditional "Ores dist li histoires que . . ." of the medieval romances, as in II.5.24), but usually with a minimum of comment. The most common device is simply to announce the intention of shifting by the use of such traditional terms as "voglio," "lassiam," "torniam," and so forth:

Lassiam costor che a vella se ne vano,
Che sentirete poi ben la sua gionta;
E ritornamo in Francia a Carlo Mano.‡
(I.1.8)

Although the promise to return to the abandoned story line is frequent, as well as the assurance that the tale will be told in its entirety, it is only rarely that a reason of any kind is given for the change, except the arbitrary *volere* of the Poet. In Ariosto, as we shall see, the network of transition and reprise is intricate and contributes a large measure of the formal interest of the work. But Boiardo's Poet almost never makes any comment on the formal significance of his transitions:

Or lasciamo costor tutti da parte,
Ché nel presente ne è detto a bastanza,
Però che il conte Orlando e Brandimarte
Mi fa bisogno di condurli in Franza,

---

* Now, fair lords, I commend myself to you. This canto has its pages full, and in truth I have understood that speaking too long is always criticized.

† But I do not wish to keep you too long, and for the present canto I leave you, since it is good to vary any pleasure.

‡ Let us leave them sailing on, for you will hear all about their arrival later; and let us go back to Paris to Charlemagne.

Accioché queste istorie che son sparte,
Siano raccolte insieme a una sustanza;
Poi seguiremo un fatto tanto degno
Quanto abbia libro alcuno in suo contegno.*
(II.17.38)

This is a far cry from Ariosto's "il vario telo che io ordisco." Indeed, in another passage the audience is asked to think, not of formal balance or intricate design, but simply of the excitement of bringing the most valiant characters together (the "worthy event," for which the bringing together of the stories in "one substance" is necessary):

La bella istoria che cantando io conto,
Serà più dilettosa ad ascoltare,
Come sia il conte Orlando in Franza gionto
Et Agramante, che è di là del mare.†
(II.16.1)

The Poet almost seems to be apologizing for what seems an awkward change of focus. The reader is surprised to learn, after a series of cataclysmic wars, that:

Come colui che con la prima nave
Trovò del navicar l'arte e l'ingegno,
Prima alla ripa e ne l'onda suave
Andò spengendo senza vella il legno;
A poco a poco temenza non have
De intrare a l'alto, e poi, senza ritegno
Seguendo al corso il lume de le stelle,
Vidde gran cose e glorïose e belle;

Così ancora io fin qui nel mio cantare
Non ho la ripa troppo abandonata;
Or mi conviene al gran pelago intrare,
Volendo aprir la guerra sterminata.‡
(II.17.1-2)

* Now let us leave all of them to one side, for enough has been said about them for now; I need to conduct Count Orlando and Brandimarte to France so that these stories that are scattered may be gathered together into one substance; then we shall follow an event as worthy as any book has in its contents.

† The beautiful story that singing I tell will be more delightful to listen to when Count Orlando gets to France, and Agramante who is across the sea.

‡ As he who with the first ship found the art and skill of sailing first by the shore and in calm water pushed his boat without sails; little by little he loses his fear of going out on the deep, and then, without holding back, following in his course the light of the stars, he saw great things and glorious and beautiful; so I, too, in my singing, up to now have not gone too far away from shore; now I must go out upon the vast sea, wishing to open that bitter war.

When one stops to consider the nature of the poem's structure, a certain broad plan is evident: the poem will center on the invasion of France by the Saracen Agramante. But within the scheme that traces the origins and moves toward the culmination of the war, there is an extraordinary freedom of episodic development, and most of the episodes are lingered over with extensive detail and have little connection with one another.

Occasionally we do find the Poet invoking a principle to justify the arrangement of the material—that of variety:

> Già molto tempo m'han tenuto a bada
> Morgana, Alcina, e le incantazioni,
> Né ve ho mostrato un bel colpo de spada,
> E pieno il cel de lancie e de tronconi;
> Or conviene che il mondo a terra vada,
> E 'l sangue cresca insin sopra a l'arcioni,
> Ché il fin di questo canto, s' io non erro,
> Seran ferite e fiamme e foco e ferro.*
>
> (II.14.1)

It is indeed this principle that, more than any plan, motivates the confusing proliferation of incident. The complex interlocking of episodes of the *Orlando furioso* is entirely foreign to the *Orlando innamorato*. Thus while he continually asserts his presence and his whims in the arrangement of the poem, Boiardo's practice is a far cry from Ariosto's attitude of absolute domination of the world of the poem.

So far we have been considering the Poet's comments on certain aspects of his arrangement of the material—his manner of opening and closing cantos, of making transitions from one thread of the story to another, and of invoking simple structural principles to explain his procedure. We now turn to the most interesting and original aspect of Boiardo's use of the figure of the Poet: the representation of the relation between Poet and audience. We have already glanced at the quasi-dramatic situation that remains as the permanent backdrop of

---

* For a long time now Morgana, Alcina, and their enchantments have kept me busy; nor have I shown you a good swordblow or the sky filled with spears and shattered lances. Now the world must be destroyed, and the blood must rise up to the saddle bows, for the end of this canto, if I am not mistaken, will be wounds and flames and fire and iron.

the narrative: the friendly gathering of gentlemen and ladies who have assembled to hear the Poet recite the poem. Pulci had echoed the traditional prayer of the *cantastorie* at the beginning of each canto of the *Morgante,* thus evoking the familiar scene of the motley crowd surrounding the professional storyteller on the streets of Florence. In the *Orlando innamorato,* however, the poet is not a *cantastorie,* and the audience is not the vulgar herd. It is composed of the "segnori e cavallieri inamorati, cortesi damiselle e graziose" of the Court of Ferrara.[3] The atmosphere is one of culture, refinement, and ease. The audience is clearly thought of as composed predominantly of young people (II.12.1): young cavaliers burning with the thirst for glory, and ladies who are gracious and witty as well as beautiful. Above all, they are "anime gentili" (II.24.2), distinguished from commoners by their innate spiritual superiority, which shows itself in their love of chivalry (II.10.1). They are all in love in the finest courtly manner (II.31.50, III.9.1-3), and when they make war they do so out of a disinterested desire to win honor and to be worthy of their ladies. They are thus on a moral plane far superior to that of most of the warriors of the day—especially the French (II.31.50).

It is no accident, therefore, that stories of love and derring-do appeal to this audience. The Poet is sure that they know the stories of Tristan and Lancelot (II.18.1-2, II.26.1-3) and expects them to be surprised at the idea of Orlando's being in love (I.1.2). They listen with delight to the stories the Poet tells them, responding to them eagerly. He can see by their faces how much they enjoy listening (II.27.2, III.9.1). They become so enthralled by the story as to imagine they are taking part in it (II.24.1-2) and object that a canto should end (I.28.54, II.25.58) or that the narrative should shift from one thread to another (I.19.22, II.3. 16). They have put aside their cares and for the moment are in the hands of the Poet (II.31.1).

It is with continual reference to this audience that the figure of the Poet is presented. We learn very little about him except this relation to his hearers and his attitude toward the work. He is a carefully selective, idealized, and strictly functional Narrator. References to events outside the poem or the situation of recital are very few. Apart from allusions to the war that interrupts the composition and recitation of the poem, the Poet almost never tells us about his personal life, and even those few cases we can find are clearly related to the basic narrative situation. The most important of these instances occurs in II.4.1:

> Luce de gli occhi miei, spirto del core,
> Per cui cantar suolea sì dolcemente
> Rime legiadre e bei versi d'amore,
> Spirami aiuto alla istoria presente.
> Tu sola al canto mio facesti onore,
> Quando di te parlai primeramente,
> Perché a qualunche che di te ragiona,
> Amor la voce e l'intelletto dona.*

Here he speaks of his love and of his love poetry in the language of courtly love—in specifically Petrarchan terms, in fact.[4] He offers a conventionalized picture of himself as lover and, not least important, identifies himself as a member of the same cultured and leisurely class of gentlemen and ladies to which his audience belongs. Indeed, the tone in which he addresses his listeners throughout the poem is that of a social equal. He is not the servant of a patron;[5] he is composing the poem, not because the duty has been laid upon him, but because he enjoys it. The very fact that he is in love—indeed, has been serving the same lady faithfully for some years, as the passage implies—is another link between him and his hearers.

In fact, the Poet and his audience are clearly made for each other. The group comes to hear "new and delightful things," which are just what he claims to give. They listen for the sheer delight, and it is his own pleasure that motivates him to write (II.8.2, II.26.1, III.3.1). They share their love of the old romances, of exploits, love, glory, honor, and valor. The poem is written "a vostro onore" (II.3.50); "per dar diletto a cui piaccia di odire" (to please those who delight to hear, II.4.3); "per darvi zoia e diletto" (to give you joy and delight, I.22.62); "a dilettarvi alquanto" (to delight you for a while, II.23.2). He asks no thanks but the knowledge of having pleased them (III.1.4). This desire

---

* Light of my eyes, spirit of my heart, for whom I used to sing so sweetly gay rhymes and lovely verses of love, breathe help to me now for the present story. You alone brought honor to my song when first I spoke of you, for Love gives voice and intellect to whoever speaks to you.

is based on the Poet's intense admiration for his audience; as he
says again and again, they are an honor to the court, to chivalry,
and to *gentilezza* (II.8.2, II.13.2). Their very reactions to the
poem are proof of their nobility of soul:

> Quando la tromba alla battaglia infesta
> Suonando a l'arme sveglia il crudo gioco,
> Il bon destrier superbo alcia la testa,
> Battendo e piedi, e par tutto di foco;
>
> . . . . .
>
> Così ad ogni atto degno e signorile,
> Qual se raconti, di cavalleria,
> Sempre se allegra lo animo gentile,
> Come nel fatto fusse tuttavia,
> Manifestando fuore il cor virile
> Quel che gli piace e quel ch' egli disia;
> Onde io di voi comprendo il spirto audace,
> Poi che de odirme vi diletta e piace.*
>
> (II.24.1-2)

And so the Poet—out of his own disinterested love of *gentilezza*,
his own *cortesia*—feels impelled to serve them as well as he can:

> Non debbo adunque a gente sì cortese
> Donar diletto a tutta mia possanza?
> Io debbo e voglio, e non faccio contese,
> E torno ove io lasciai ne l'altra stanza.†
>
> (II.24.3)

Hence he is often represented as eager to recite the poem. Sometimes, however, his realization of his limitations makes him dif-
fident:

> Ché, cognoscendo quel ch' io vaglio e quanto,
> Mal volentieri alcuna fiata io canto.
>
> Ma tutto quel che io vaglio, o poco o assai,
> Come vedeti, è nel vostro comando,

---

* When the trumpet, sounding the alarm to cruel battle, starts the harsh game,
the good warhorse proudly raises his head, beating his feet and seeming all fire;
. . . So the noble spirit is pleased with any worthy and princely act of chivalry
that is related, as if he were in the event itself, his manly heart showing forth
what pleases him and what he desires; therefore I know that your spirit is
audacious, since it pleases and delights you to hear me.

† Must I not then to folk so courteous give delight with all my power? I
must and I wish to, I make no objections, and I return to where I left off in
the last canto.

E con più voglia e più piacer che mai
La bella istoria vi verrò contando.*
                                  (II.19.2-3)

Thus the audience's pleasure and eagerness increase the Poet's and spur him on to greater efforts:

Poi che il mio canto tanto a voi diletta,
Ché ben ne vedo ne la faccia il signo,
Io vo' trar for la citera più eletta
E le più argute corde che abbia in scrigno.
Or vieni, Amore, e qua meco te assetta,
E se io ben son di tal richiesta indigno,
Perché e mirti al mio capo non se avoltano,
Degni ne son costor che intorno ascoltano.

Come nanti l'aurora, al primo albore,
Splendono stelle chiare e matutine,
Tal questra corte luce in tant' onore
De cavallieri e dame peregrine,
Che tu pôi ben dal cel scendere, Amore,
Tra queste genti angelice e divine;
Se tu vien' tra costoro, io te so dire
Che starai nosco e non vorai partire.

Qui trovarai un altro paradiso;
Or vieni adunque e spirami, di graccia,
Il tuo dolce diletto e 'l dolce riso.†
                                  (III.9.1-3)

Poet and audience are, then, bound together by spontaneous admiration and love, just as the court itself is. It is interesting to compare this invocation of Love with the invocation of the Poet's lady that was quoted in part earlier:

---

* For, knowing what and how much I am worth, unwillingly at times I sing. But all that I am worth, whether much or little, is at your command, as you see, and with more good will and more pleasure than ever I shall go on telling you the lovely story.

† Since my singing delights you so much, for I can plainly see the sign of it in your faces, I shall bring forth the noblest lyre and the highest strings in my case. Now come, Love, and sit down here with me; though I am unworthy of such a request, since myrtle does not bind my head, those who are listening here are well worthy. As before the dawn, at the first glimmer of whiteness, the bright morning stars shine, so this court shines with such honor of knights and wondrous ladies that you may well come down from heaven. Love, among these angelic, divine persons; if you come among them, I can tell you that you will stay with us and will not wish to leave. Here you will find another paradise; come then and breathe into me, by your grace, your sweet delight and sweet smile.

Luce de gli occhi miei, spirto del core,
Per cui cantar suolea sì dolcemente
Rime legiadre e bei versi d'amore,
Spirami aiuto alla istoria presente.
Tu sola al canto mio facesti onore,
Quando di te parlai primeramente,
Perché a qualunche che di te ragiona,
Amor la voce e l'intelletto dona.

Amor primo trovò le rime e' versi,
I suoni, i canti et ogni melodia;
E genti istrane e populi dispersi
Congionse Amore in dolce compagnia.
Il diletto e il piacer serian sumersi,
Dove Amor non avesse signoria;
Odio crudele e dispietata guerra,
Se Amor non fusse, avrian tutta la terra.

Lui pone l'avarizia e l'ira in bando,
E il core accresce alle animose imprese,
Né tante prove più mai fece Orlando,
Quante nel tempo che de amor se accese.*

(II.4.1-3)

The love that knits together the court, and also Poet and audience, is essentially the same as the Love that is the source of all
beauty and the basis of social existence.[6] That the Poet is able
to give his listeners pleasure thus seems to him "del cel . . . in
summa graccia" (II.27.1).

The invocation of the Poet's lady has other important implications. It contains an important statement about the nature of
his art and about the themes of the poem. From it and from
similar pronouncements we can derive a theory of the poem.[7]
One of the most frequent criticisms is that the poem is weak in
structure; Boiardo, it is said, lacked the gift of form—or lacked
the energy and concentration necessary to produce a thoroughly

* Light of my eyes, spirit of my heart, for whom I used to sing so sweetly
gay rhymes and lovely verses of love, breathe help to me now for the present
story. You alone brought honor to my song when first I spoke of you, for Love
gives voice and intellect to whoever speaks of you. Love first found rhymes and
verses, playing of instruments, songs, and every melody; and strange peoples and
dispersed peoples Love joined in sweet company. Delight and pleasure would be
lost wherever Love were not master; cruel hate and pitiless war, if Love were
not, would possess all the earth. He banishes avarice and anger, and makes
the heart grow to brave endeavors; nor did Orlando ever perform so many exploits as when he was enflamed by love.

shaped poem—was, in fact, a mere improvisor, albeit a highly gifted one. There is, of course, some justice in these charges, but we ought to ask whether Boiardo wanted to write a tightly organized poem. The poem contains a rationale of its peculiar nature, and, indeed, the fact that Boiardo should be accused of being an improvisor is ironic evidence of the success of the rhetorical self-representation of the Poet, as we shall see.

"Amor primo trovò le rime e' versi, / I suoni, i canti et ogni melodia." After appealing to his lady for inspiration, and noting that Love produced his earlier poetry, the Poet shows that the Love which inspires him is the very fountainhead of art. The implication is that his poem is of a very high order and that it, too, is capable of joining men "in dolce compagnia." As we have just seen, this is just what it does in the case of the Poet's recitations.

> Lui pone l'avarizia e l'ira in bando,
> E il core accresce alle animose imprese,
> Né tante prove più mai fece Orlando,
> Quante nel tempo che de amor se accese.

Love is not only the source of all poetry; it is the basis of all virtue, and particularly of valor—hence of glory and honor. From this fact derives the conjunction of the two major themes of the poem.[8]

> Stella de amor, che 'l terzo cel governi,
> E tu, quinto splendor sì rubicondo,
> Che, girando in duo anni e cerchi eterni,
> De ogni pigrizia fai digiuno il mondo,
> Venga da' corpi vostri alti e superni
> Grazia e virtute al mio cantar iocondo,
> Sì che lo influsso vostro ora mi vaglia,
> Poi ch' io canto de amor e di battaglia.

> L'uno e l'altro escercizio è giovenile,
> Nemico di riposo, atto allo affanno;
> L'un e l'altro è mestier de omo gentile,
> Qual non rifuti la fatica, o il danno;
> E questo e quel fa l'animo virile.*
> (II.12.1-2)

* Star of love, who govern the third heaven, and you, fifth splendor so rubicund, who, rounding in two years the eternal circle, rid the world of all sloth: send down from your high, supernal bodies grace and power to my pleasant song, so

The ultimate justification of the poem, then, is found in the fact that it pleases its noble audience, that it is fit entertainment for a noble soul:

Se onor di corte e di cavalleria
Può dar diletto a l'animo virile,
A voi dilettarà l'istoria mia,
Gente legiadra, nobile e gentile,
Che seguite ardimento e cortesia,
La qual mai non dimora in petto vile,
Venite et ascoltati lo mio canto
De li antiqui baroni il pregio e il vanto.*

(II.10.1)

To translate into such solemn terms what is said in a tone of gracious compliment is no doubt to falsify somewhat: the poem has no heavily insistent moral tone. The psychology of the characters is of the most rudimentary sort, and any moral conflicts that arise are quickly resolved in terms of the chivalric code Boiardo refers to. What the poem presents is a brilliant but almost purely external spectacle of superhuman feats of valor, marvelous enchantments, and frankly sensual loves, all informed by an unsubtle but rich humor. It is offered as entertainment; as I have already said so often, its aim is to give *diletto*, a word whose meaning for Boiardo requires some attention.

We have already seen that it is on love that this *diletto* depends. Although the Poet speaks of love in terms of the Celestial Eros, it is clear that what he has in mind is no mystical *Askese*, but what he regards as a healthily sensual courtly love. The language of the Poet's invocation to his lady clearly suggests, that *diletto* is the end of love: "Il diletto e il piacer serian sumersi / Dove Amor non avesse signoria." And when the Poet invokes Love, it is to ask for "il tuo dolce diletto e 'l dolce riso" (III.9.3). We have in another connection already glanced at part of the lovely passage describing the Poet's pleasure at hearing a young girl sing:

that your influence may now help me, since I sing of love and battle. Both are activities of youth, enemies to rest, full of struggle; each demands a gentleman who will not refuse struggle or loss; both make the spirit manly.

* If the honor of court and of chivalry can give delight to the manly spirit, my tale will delight you, noble, gentle, gay folk who follow daring and courtesy, which never dwells in vulgar breast. Come and listen to my singing, the praise and vaunt of the ancient barons.

Già me trovai di maggio una matina
Intro un bel prato adorno d'ogni fiore,
Sopra ad un colle, a lato alla marina
Che tutta tremolava de splendore;
E tra le rose de una verde spina
Una donzella cantava de amore,
Movendo sì soave la sua bocca
Che tal dolcezza ancor nel cor mi tocca.

Toccami il core e fammi sovenire
Dal gran piacer che io presi ad ascoltare;
E se io sapessi così farme odire
Come ella seppe al suo dolce cantare,
Io stesso mi verrebbi a proferire,
Ove tal volta me faccio pregare;
Ché, cognoscendo quel ch' io vaglio e quanto,
Mal volentieri alcuna fiata io canto.

Ma tutto quel che io vaglio, o poco o assai,
Come vedeti, è nel vostro comando,
E con più voglia e più piacer che mai
La bella istoria vi verrò contando.*
(II.19.1-3)

We notice first the delicate evocation of the setting of the experience. The girl's singing is made to seem a spontaneous response to the beauty of the season: she is in tune with it and her heart overflows in music. Boiardo carefully avoids any suggestion of technical discipline in the singer or of formal elaboration in the song. The pleasure of the Poet as he listens depends, in fact, on the girl's singing being natural, artless, spontaneous, and fleeting—like the red of the roses (and she is almost made to seem one of them) or the trembling of the sea.[9]

It is significant that spring is the only season mentioned as the time of composition or recitation of the poem.[10]

---

* Once I found myself, on a May morning, in a beautiful plain adorned with every flower, on a hill beside the sea, which was all trembling with brightness; and among the roses of a green thornbush a damsel was singing of love, so sweetly moving her mouth that my heart is still touched. My heart is touched and makes me remember the great pleasure that I took in listening; and if I could make myself heard thus, as she did with her sweet singing, I would come forward myself to offer to sing, whereas sometimes I wait to be asked. For, knowing what and how much I am worth, unwillingly at times I sing. But all that I am worth, whether much or little, is at your command, as you see; and with more good will and more pleasure than ever I shall go on telling you the lovely story.

Quando la terra più verde è fiorita,
E più sereno il cielo e grazïoso,
Alor cantando il rosignol se aita
La notte e il giorno a l'arboscello ombroso;
Così lieta stagione ora me invita
A seguitare il canto dilettoso,
E racontare il pregio e 'l grand' onore
Che donan l'arme gionte con amore.*

(II.8.1)

The implication of this passage is that the poem is just as spontaneous an outpouring of the Poet's joy as is the song of the
nightingale or the young girl. The idea is even clearer in a later
passage which suggests (falsely, of course) that the Poet writes
without his audience in mind—spontaneously, in fact:

Tra bianche rose e tra vermiglie, e fiori
Diversamente in terra coloriti,
Tra fresche erbette e tra soavi odori
De gli arboscelli a verde rivestiti,
Cantando componea gli antichi onori
De' cavallier sì prodi e tanto arditi,
Che ogni tremenda cosa in tutto il mondo
Fu da lor vinta a forza e posta al fondo;

Quando mi venne a mente che il diletto
Che l'om se prende solo, è mal compiuto.
Però, baroni e dame, a tal conspetto
Per dilettarvi alquanto io son venuto;
E con gran zoia ad ascoltar vi aspetto
L'aspra battaglia de Grifone arguto
E de Aquilante.†

(III.3.1)

Thus the Poet represents his own poetic activity as a kind of
improvisation. Certain qualities of the poem are logical neces-

---

* When the earth is most flowering and green and the sky most clear and
gracious, then the nightingale gives vent to her singing night and day in the
shady bush; so happy a season now invites me to continue my delightful song
and tell the worth and the great honor that arms joined with love give.

† Among white roses and red, and diversely colored flowers on the earth, amid
fresh new grass and sweet odors of the bushes newly clothed in green, I was
singing and composing the ancient honors of those knights, so valiant and bold,
whose valor vanquished and put down all fearsome things in all the world; when
it came to my mind that the delight that one takes alone is incomplete. Therefore, barons and ladies, to your presence I have come to delight you for a
while; and with great joy I wait for you to come and listen to the bitter fight
of fierce Grifone and Aquilante.

sities, once we understand the particular kind of pleasure the Poet is trying to convey. First of all, it must be easily attainable. The faculties of the ladies and gentlemen of the court are not to be taxed: they are to hear one canto at a time, and the cantos must not be too long. Even the song of the nightingale becomes tiresome if we listen to it too much. The structure of this tale is to be loose: strenuousness of form is foreign to the effect of spontaneity and to the free indulgence in the moment that the courtly audience seeks.

The emphasis on the spring as a setting for the song of the young girl and for the composition of the poem has its equivalent in the conditions of the audience's response. This is no poem that ministers to hearts burdened with uncertainties and griefs. The audience must bring to it an uncomplicated ability to participate in the play of fancy: they must be able to respond to it spontaneously, as to the "soavi odori de gli arboscelli a verde rivestiti." Any really serious demand on the listener—like any serious critique of our instinctive joy at the return of spring—will detroy the essential nature of the intended pleasure.

So it is that the recitation of the poem takes place in an ideally harmonious social setting. Should anything disturb the peace of the court, the poem itself is interrupted. The romantic idealization of an impossible past withers in the wind (see III.1.1) of the exigencies of real life. Ariosto and Milton may have been spurred on by what they regarded as the social disasters of the time to cope with fundamental issues in their poems. But when war comes to Italy and the very existence of the court is endangered, Boiardo is forced to discard the poem:

> Alor con rime elette e miglior versi
> Farò battaglie e amor tutto di foco;
> Non seran sempre e tempi sì diversi
> Che mi tragan la mente di suo loco;
> Ma nel presente e canti miei son persi,
> E porvi ogni pensier mi giova poco:
> Sentendo Italia de lamenti piena,
> Non che or canti, ma sospiro apena.*
>
> (II.31.49)

* Then with chosen rhymes and better verses I will make battles and loves all of fire; not always will the times be so strange as to distract my mind. But for the present my songs are lost, and it little profits to apply all my thoughts to them: hearing Italy full of laments, I can hardly sigh, let alone sing.

Only when the war is over and life is once again harmonious will the Poet be able to sing again or his audience be willing to listen.

> Come più dolce a' naviganti pare,
> Poi che fortuna li ha battuti intorno,
> Veder l'onda tranquilla e queto il mare
> L'aria serena e il cel di stelle adorno;
> E come il peregrin nel caminare
> Se allegra al vago piano al novo giorno,
> Essendo fuori uscito alla sicura
> De l'aspro monte per la notte oscura;
>
> Così, dapoi che la infernal tempesta
> De la guerra spietata è dipartita,
> Poi che tornato è il mondo in zoia e in festa
> E questa corte più che mai fiorita,
> Farò con più diletto manifesta
> La bella istoria che ho gran tempo ordita.*
>
> (III.1.1-2)

The return of tranquillity after a storm, the emergence of a traveler from the mountains to the plain—these images, like the return of peace itself, have obvious kinship to the motif of the return of spring after winter, "Tornato è il mondo in zoia e in festa": such a statement is really an exhortation to the audience to believe, or to indulge, in the illusion that all is well with the world. The device occurs earlier, in II.1.1ff:

> Nel grazïoso tempo onde natura
> Fa più lucente la stella d'amore,
> Quando la terra copre di verdura,
> E li arboscelli adorna di bel fiore,
> Giovani e dame et ogni creatura
> Fanno allegrezza con zoioso core;
> Ma poi che 'l verno viene e il tempo passa,
> Fugge il diletto e quel piacer si lassa.
>
> Così nel tempo che virtù fioria
> Ne li antiqui segnori e cavallieri,

---

* As to voyagers it is sweeter, when fortune has beaten them about, to see the wave tranquil and the sea calm, the air clear and the heavens adorned with stars; and as the pilgrim in his journeying rejoices at the lovely plain in the newness of the day, having come safely through the harsh mountains in the dark night; so, after the infernal tempest of pitiless war has departed, now that the world has returned to joy and festivity and this court flowers more than ever, with more delight I shall make manifest the lovely story that I have for a long time put in order.

Con noi stava allegrezza e cortesia,
E poi fuggirno per strani sentieri,
Sì che un gran tempo smarirno la via,
Né del più ritornar ferno pensieri;
Ora è il mal vento e quel verno compito,
E torna il mondo di virtù fiorito.

Et io cantando torno alla memoria
Delle prodezze de' tempi passati,
E contarovi la più bella istoria
(Se con quïete attenti me ascoltati)
Che fusse mai nel mondo, e di più gloria.*

Again we find the familiar motif of spring, here used to describe a supposed renascence of virtue in the world that the Poet, when faced by harsh reality, is often forced to deny (as in II.12.2-3 or II.22.1-3). It is almost essential to the enjoyment of the poem that its reading or recitation be conceived as continually interrupted and taken up again. The demands of real life must first de dealt with on their own terms, whether day by day or in a time of crisis. Then the group can reassemble and regain for a moment the haven of spontaneous and uncomplicated joy.

The *Orlando innamorato* was written for publication. Boiardo himself supervised the publication of the first two books, which were released for public sale in Ferrara in 1484. A second edition was published in Venice in 1486. The third book was published separately after the author's death, in 1495. But even if the poem had not been written with a large public in mind, the rhetorical method of shaping the audience's attitude toward the work would still be evident in the thematically determined representation of the relation between Poet and listeners. It is interesting that Boiardo's awareness of the relation between his poem and real

---

* In the gracious time when nature makes brighter the star of love, when she covers the earth with green and adorns the shrubs with lovely flowers, then young men and ladies and all creatures are gay with joyous heart; but when that season passes and winter comes, delight flees and that pleasure takes flight. Thus in the time when valor flowered in the ancient lords, gayety and courtesy were with us; and then they fled by strange paths, so that for a long time they lost their way, nor thought any more of coming back. Now that evil wind and that winter are over, and the world begins again to flower with valor. And I singing turn to the memory of the exploits of olden times, and I will sing to you the loveliest story (if quiet and attentive you listen to me) that was ever heard, and the most glorious.

life seems to have grown in the course of the writing. The reader
may have noticed that most of the passages discussed are from
the second and third books. While the fundamental situation of
recitation is dominant from the beginning, it is only fairly late
that the Poet becomes discursive about the nature of the poem.

The last canto in Book II opens with what is almost a plea to
the audience. Until this point we have been given almost no indication that the audience had any worries:

> Il sol girando in su quel celo adorno
> Passa volando e nostra vita lassa,
> La qual non sembra pur durar un giorno
> A cui senza diletto la trapassa;
> Ond' io pur chieggio a voi che sete intorno,
> Che ciascun ponga ogni sua noia in cassa,
> Et ogni affanno et ogni pensier grave
> Dentro ve chiuda, e poi perda la chiave.
>
> Et io, quivi a voi tuttavia cantando,
> Perso ho ogni noia et ogni mal pensiero.*
>   (II.31.1-2)

Here we do find the implication that the poem may be an *escape*
from reality. It is as if Boiardo were struggling to keep the im-
minence of war from disrupting the fragile surface of this
diletto. But that was in vain, and, indeed, Boiardo was not an
escapist. Elsewhere the goal, the pleasure, of the poem is presented not as an escape from reality, but as the elevation of a
deserved and noble relaxation to a state of harmony.[11]

---

* Circling up in that beauteous heaven, the sun passes flying and leaves our
life behind, which seems not to last a day for anyone who lives through it without delight; wherefore I ask you who are here each to put his cares all in the
chest, and every worry and every heavy thought close up in it and then lose the
key. And I, going on singing to you here, have lost all sorrow and every painful
thought.

V

Ariosto

U SING many of Boiardo's devices and methods, but developing them with a complexity undreamed of by his predecessor, Ariosto created in the *Orlando furioso* (1516, 1521, 1532) one of the most brilliant narrative styles in European literature. His Narrator not only forms one of the chief attractions of the poem, but has had great influence on writers as diverse as Spenser and Fielding. It is the most elaborate and in many ways the most important of those considered in this study. If I treat the *Orlando furioso* at considerable length, then, it is because its historical and intrinsic importance demands thorough discussion and because, in this country and in England, it is generally less well known than Tasso's or Spenser's poem.[1]

1

Although Ariosto's Poet-Narrator is clearly based on Boiardo's, he modifies it in a number of important respects. For one thing, we no longer find in Ariosto the insistence upon the illusion of public recitation that is so pervasive in Boiardo. References to a concrete narrative situation do occur in the *Orlando furioso*, but they are scattered and for the most part extremely brief. Only one or two canto openings make explicit reference to re-citation or even imply it (as in XXXVIII.1, XXX.1-3, XXXII), and, among the closing *congedi* that speak of the poem as listened to, only a few speak of the audience as coming to hear the Poet (IX.94, XVI.89, XIX.108, XXII.98, XXXVI.84). Never is any specific group identified as the hearers of the poem, as Boiardo identified the members of the court of Ferrara. Instead the poem is addressed to Ariosto's patron (Ippolito d'Este), like such classical models as the *Georgics* or the *Pharsalia*, and some *congedi* and transitional comments are addressed to the patron.

Not that Ariosto does not make us aware that he thinks of himself as writing for a larger audience; he does indeed, and he identifies many of its members by name. The last canto begins with a long complimentary list of all the friends who will be happy that he has finished the poem; they are imagined as waiting for him on shore as his ship nears port. These friends are not the members of one court, however; they live in many parts of Italy, and among them are patrons, relatives, and personal friends. Furthermore, they are spoken of in the third person. Only three persons are directly addressed by name in the poem: Ippolito and Alfonso d'Este and Federigo Fregoso (the last only in XLII.20-22). The Poet's lady is the only other individual addressed, and she is never addressed by name (there is nothing to establish that she is supposed to be Alessandra Benucci, about whom Ariosto did not expect his readers to know).[2] She is simply and generically "his lady."

The Poet most often addresses his audience with an undifferentiated *voi*, which may be understood as addressed to Ippolito d'Este, whom he always does address with this relatively respectful form, or it may be understood as referring to the supposed hearers or readers of the poem, since the form can be either singular or plural. When it is understood as a plural, it never refers to any specific group. Even when the Poet addresses the ladies in his audience, they are not the ladies of any particular court but "the ladies" in general. (A particularly good example of this is the opening of Canto XXII—"Cortesi donne . . . come che certo sia . . . che rarissime siate," where "cortesi donne" must be understood as referring to *all* courteous ladies wherever they may be, even to those the Poet has never met.)

Ariosto's Poet maintains a conversational tone with his readers, and he gathers from different traditions devices suited to that purpose. The references to singing, reciting, or hearing as often as not are meant to be recognized as merely conventional metaphors for writing and reading. The poem presents itself as a literary product designed to be read, and several passages, such as the joke of XXXVIII.1-3, depend upon and make explicit the idea (see also I.3, VIII.9, XIV.108). The metaphor of recitation is there in the background—submerged, as it were, ready to be brought to the fore if the poet wishes. On several occasions Ariosto does bring it out and, as we shall see, derives splendid effects from it, effects that depend upon its very lack of emphasis in other parts of the poem.

The most striking quality of the Poet's many comments on the conduct of the narrative is their expression of an attitude of absolute control. Perhaps most frequent are the comments on transitions from one thread of the story to another. Sometimes these comments are brief, in the manner of Boiardo: "Lasciánlo andar, ché fara buon cammino, / E torniamo a Rinaldo paladino" (let us let him go, for he will have a good trip, and let us return to Rinaldo the Paladin).[3] More frequently we find characteristically Ariostan remarks. For example, many transitions include the assurance that the interrupted story will be duly completed (or not) as and when the Poet sees fit:

> Ch' ordine abbian tra lor, come s'assaglia
> La gran Biserta, e da che lato e quando,
> Come fu presa alla prima battaglia,
> Chi ne l'onor parte ebbe con Orlando;
> S'io non vi seguito ora, non vi caglia;
> Ch' io non me ne vo molto dilungando.*
> (XXXIX.65)

Sometimes the Poet's assertion of control takes the form of frustration of the reader's expectations. When Ruggiero is hurriedly stripping off his armor and the reader is on the edge of his seat to know whether or not Angelica will at last lose that long-preserved virginity, the Poet ironically pretends that the canto is becoming tedious:

> Frettoloso, or da questo, or da quel canto
> Confusamente l'arme si levava:
> Non gli parve altra volta mai star tanto,
> Che s'un laccio scioglieva, dui n'annodava.
> Ma troppo è lungo ormai, Signor, il canto,
> E forse, ch' anco l'ascoltar vi grava;

---

* What order they followed among themselves, how great Biserta is stormed, and from what side and when, how it was taken in the first onslaught, who shared the honors with Orlando, if I do not pursue all this now, do not mind; for I am not going to go very far from it.

Sì ch' io differirò l'istoria mia
In altro tempo, che più grata sia.*
(X.115)

Here the Poet is playing the same trick on the reader as on
Ruggiero, in whose way he puts those troublesome lacings.

Play upon the reader's expectations is frequent in the manner
of the transitions as well as in the moment (almost always one
of crisis or at least of aroused curiosity) chosen for the shift.
Some of the more elaborate examples occur at the beginnings
of cantos:

Soviemmi, che cantare io vi dovea—
Già lo promisi, e poi m'uscì di mente—
D'una sospizion, che fatto avea
La bella Donna de Ruggier dolente,
De l'altra più spiacevole, e più rea
E di più acuto, e venenoso dente,
Che, per quel ch'ella udì da Ricciardetto,
A devorare il cor l'entrò nel petto.

Dovea cantarne, et altro incominciai,
Perché Rinaldo in mezzo sopravenne;
E poi Guidon mi diè che fare assai,
Che tra camino a bada un pezzo il tenne.
D'una cosa in un' altra in modo entrai,
Che mal di Bradamante mi sovenne.
Soviemmene ora; e vo' narrarne inanti
Che di Rinaldo e di Gradasso io canti.

Ma bisogna anco, prima ch'io ne parli,
Che d'Agramante io vi ragioni un poco.†
(XXXII.1-3)

* Hastily, now on this side, now on that, confusedly, he was taking off his
armor. It seemed to him he had never been so slow; for if he untied one knot,
he tangled two. But this canto by now is much too long, my Lord, and perhaps
listening is wearisome to you; so that I shall defer my story to another time that
it may be more pleasing.

† I remember that I was supposed to sing (I promised it some time ago, but
then I forgot it) about a suspicion conceived by the lovely lady who sorrows
for Ruggiero, a suspicion much more displeasing and cruel, with a much sharper
and poisonous tooth, than that other one; a suspicion that entered her breast to
devour her heart on account of what she heard from Ricciardetto. I was supposed
to sing about it, and I began something else, because Rinaldo happened along
in the middle of it; and then Guidon kept me very busy, who occupied Rinaldo
for a while along his way. I went from one thing to another in such a way that
I ill remembered Bradamante: now I have remembered her, and I wish to tell
you about her before I sing of Rinaldo and Gradasso. But still it is necessary,
before I speak of her, to tell you a little about Agramante.

This elaborate pretense that the Poet has forgotten himself gives an occasion for reviewing some of the brilliant shifts and re-combinations of the poem; we are taken through them all again and think that now, at last, we are going to hear about Brada-mante, when the Poet ironically turns to another delay. (In the *Orlando innamorato*, however, we believe the Poet when he claims to have been forgetful, as in III.5.48.)

The same device of pretending to embark on an elaborate account of one of the narrative strands, only to break off and turn to another, is often used. At the beginning of Canto XXII, for instance:

> Ma tornando al lavor che vario ordisco,
> Ch'a molti, lor mercé, grato esser suole:
> Del cavalier di Scozia io vi dicea,
> Ch'un alto grido appresso udito avea.
>
> Fra due montagne entrò in un stretto calle,
> Onde uscia il grido, e non fu molto inante,
> Che giunse dove in una chiusa valle
> Si vide un cavallier morto davante.
> Chi sia dirò; ma prima dar le spalle
> A Francia voglio, e girmene in Levante,
> Tanto ch'io trovi Astolfo paladino,
> Che per Ponente avea preso il camino.*
>
> (XXII.3-4)

Not only does Ariosto delight in frustrating the reader's ex-pectations or his natural desire to hear a story through; some-times the implicit demand that the reader subordinate his will to the will of the Poet becomes explicit:

> Ma voglio questo canto abbia qui fine:
> E di quel che voglio io, siate contenti,
> Che miglior cose vi prometto dire,
> S' a l'altro canto me verrete a udire.†
>
> (XXXVI.84)

---

* But returning to the work that I am laying out in variety, which is wont to please many—thanks to them—I was telling you about the Scottish knight who heard a loud cry from nearby. Between two mountains he entered a narrow pass from which the cry had come forth, and he had not gone far before he reached a closed valley where he saw a knight lying dead before him. I will tell who it is; but first I wish to turn my back on France and go to the Levant until I find Astolfo the Paladin, who had taken the road to the West.

† But I wish this canto to end here, and with what I wish, you be content; for I promise to tell you something even better, if you will come to hear me in the next canto.

A particularly striking and important difference between Ariosto's and Boiardo's comments on the course of their poems is that, unlike Boiardo's, Ariosto's Poet repeatedly asserts that the structure has a rationale. He invokes an aesthetic principle —that of variety—to give the impression not of more or less haphazard execution (like Boiardo's appeals to the same principle), but of a systematic and deliberate plan:

> Ma perché non convien che sempre io dica,
> Né ch'io vi occupi sempre in una cosa;
> Io lascierò Ruggiero in questo caldo,
> E girò in Scozia a ritrovar Rinaldo.*
>
> (VIII.21)

I shall have more to say later on about the significance of this principle of variety. For the moment it is enough to note that it is advanced with great frequency, often in terms of analogies with other arts:

> Signor, far mi convien come fa il buono
> Sonator sopra il suo instrumento arguto,
> Che spesso muta corda, e varia suono,
> Ricercando ora il grave, or l'acuto:
> Mentre a dir di Rinaldo attento sono,
> D'Angelica gentil m'è sovenuto.†
>
> (VIII.29)

Other significant passages compare the poem to a great web or tapestry woven of many threads, an image Ariosto would have known from Petrarch's sonnet "S'Amore o Morte non dà qualche stroppio," among other places. The image is given prominence by Ariosto's use of it to signalize the first major shift from one narrative thread to another (II.30):

> Or a poppa, or a l'orza hanno il crudele,
> Che mai non cessa, e vien più ognior crescendo:
> Essi di qua di là con umil vele
> Vansi aggirando, e l'alto mar scorrendo.
> Ma perché varie fila a varie tele

---

* But since I must not always be telling of the same thing or keeping you occupied with one thing, I shall leave Ruggiero in this heat, and go to Scotland to find Rinaldo.

† My Lord, it is necessary for me to do as does the good musician on his harmonious instrument; for he often changes strings and varies the sound, seeking now the low, now the high. While I have been concentrating on telling about Rinaldo, the thought has come to me of the gentle Angelica.

> Uopo mi son, che tutte ordire intendo,
> Lascio Rinaldo e l'agitata prua,
> E torno a dir di Bradamante sua.*

This passage calls attention to two things—first, the fullness of the variety the Poet intends to embody in the poem ("varie fila a varie tele"); second, his confidence that he can manipulate them all skillfully enough to create and maintain order among them ("che tutte ordire intendo"). Another important passage combines these notions with the idea of VIII.29—the Boiardesque rhetorical principle of not fatiguing the audience:

> Ma lasciam Bradamante, e non v'incresca
> Udir che così resti in quello incanto;
> Che quando sarà il tempo ch' ella n'esca,
> La farò uscire, e Ruggiero altretanto.
> Come raccende il gusto il mutar esca,
> Così mi par che la mia istoria, quanto
> Or qua or là più variata sia,
> Meno a chi l'udirà noiosa fia.
>
> Di molte fila esser bisogno parme
> A condur la gran tela ch' io lavoro.†
> (XIII.80-81)

These many threads, as several of these passages point out, must be kept in some sort of balance, and we often find the Poet alleging this consideration as a reason for shifting from one to another. None of them is to be concentrated on at the expense of the others:

> Ma differendo questa pugna alquanto
> Io vo' passar senza naviglio il mare.
> Non ho con quei di Francia da far tanto,
> Ch'io non m'abbia d'Astolfo a ricordare.‡
> (XXXIX.19)

---

* The cruel wind is now astern, now aport, and it never pauses but keeps growing: now here, now there with lowered sails they go turning about and scouring the deep sea. But because I need diverse threads for diverse weaves, all of which I mean to combine in order, I leave Rinaldo and his agitated prow and return to tell of his Bradamante.

† But let us leave Brandamante, and let it not bother you to hear that she remains thus in that enchantment; for when it is time for her to come out of it, I shall make her come out, and Ruggiero as well. As changing foods rekindles appetite, so it seems to me that my story will be the less wearisome to whoever listens to it the more it is varied now here, now there. It seems to me I need many threads to weave the great tapestry that I am working on.

‡ By putting this battle off for a while, I'll cross the sea without a ship. I do not have so much to do with those of France that I can afford to forget Astolfo.

Ma non dirò d'Angelica or più inante,
Che molte cose ho da narrarvi prima;
Né sono a Ferrau né a Sacripante
Sin a gran pezzo per donar più rima.
Da lor mi leva il Principe d'Anglante.*
(XII.66)

Several of the passages we have been looking at include a frequent, even habitual play of wit derived from taking literally the
metaphor of the Poet's *leaving* one character to talk about
another. The characters always stay in the fix in which they are
left, until the Poet rescues them:

Ma lasciam Bradamante, e non v'incresca
Udir che così resti in quello incanto.†
(XIII.80)

Or si ferma [Olimpia] su un sasso, e guarda il mare;
Né men d'un vero sasso un sasso pare.

Ma lasciánla doler fin ch' io ritorno,
Per voler di Ruggier dirvi pur anco.‡   (X.34-35)

Sometimes the joke becomes rather elaborate, as when the Poet
comments that he must not leave Ruggiero swimming too long
in the ocean (XLI.46):

Ma mi parria, Signor, far troppo fallo,
Se, per voler di costor dir, lasciassi
Tanto Ruggier nel mar, che v'affogassi.§

On another occasion, it is the characters themselves who remind
the Poet to return to them:

Di questo altrove io vo' rendervi conto;
Ch' ad un gran Duca è forza ch' io riguardi,
Il qual mi grida, e di lontano accenna,
E priega ch' io no'l lasci ne la penna.§§
(XV.9)

---

* But I shall not tell any more Angelica now; for I have many things to tell
you first: nor am I going to give any rhymes to Ferrau or Sacripante for quite
a while. The Prince of Anglante takes me away from them.
† But let us leave Bradamante, and let it not bother you to hear that she thus
remains in that enchantment.
‡ Now she stands still on a rock and looks out to sea; nor does she seem
any less a stone than the real stone does. But let us let her suffer until I come back
to her, for I wish also to tell you about Ruggiero.
§ But it would seem to me, my Lord, that I would commit too grave a fault if,
wishing to tell about them, I left Ruggiero in the sea so long that he drowned.
§§ Of this I wish to tell you elsewhere, for I must look to a great duke, who is
shouting to me and signaling from afar to beg that I not leave him in the pen.

Like the humorous leaving of characters in their fixes, the various disclaimers of control serve to emphasize the absolute subjection of the poem to the Poet. One of the more frequent kinds of disclaimer of control is the pretense of fidelity to historical truth, which often takes the form of appeal to the authority of Turpin and his history of Charlemagne.[4] For example, to justify the inclusion of the indecent story of Fiammetta, the Poet claims that he has to include it because Turpin does (XXVIII.-1-2) But what the passage serves to emphasize is that Ariosto wanted to include it, that there is nothing in the poem but what he planned. At times Ariosto indulges in a kind of play with the notion of fidelity to truth that seems (and surely is designed to seem) the result of a kind of Schillerian superabundance of vitality. For instance, after the somber and gripping account of the duel on Lipadusa, in which Brandimarte, Agramante, and Gradasso are killed, he inserts the following:

> Qui de la istoria mia, che non sia vera,
> Federigo Fulgoso è in dubbio alquanto;
> Che con l'armata avendo la riviera
> Di Barbaria trascorsa in ogni canto,
> Capitò quivi, e l'isola sì fiera
> Montuosa e inegual ritrovò tanto,
> Che non è, dice, in tutto il luogo strano,
> Ove un sol piè si possa metter piano:
>
> Né verisimil tien, che ne l'alpestre
> Scoglio sei cavallieri, il fior del mondo,
> Potesson far quella battaglia equestre:
> A la qual obiezïon così rispondo:
> Ch'a quel tempo una piazza de le destre,
> Che sieno a questo, avea lo scoglio al fondo:
> Ma poi, ch' un sasso, che 'l tremuoto aperse,
> Le cadde sopra, e tutta la coperse.
>
> Sì che, o chiaro fulgor de la Fulgosa
> Stirpe, o serena, o sempre viva luce,
> Se mai mi riprendeste in questa cosa,
> E forse inanti a quello invitto Duce,
> Per cui la vostra patria or si riposa,
> Lascia ogni odio, e in amor tutta s'induce;
> Vi priego che non siate a dirgli tardo,
> Ch' esser può che né in questo io sia bugiardo.*
>   (XLII.20-22)

* Here Federigo Fulgoso is a bit in doubt whether or not my story is true; who, having sailed along every angle of the Barbary shore, arrived there also, and

Not only is the heroic pretension to historicity being parodied in this graceful badinage; for the reader who demands verisimilitude, the Poet will create a *vero* to which the poem can refer. He will adjust "actual history" to the needs of his fiction. Whether or not Federigo Fregoso actually made this objection to Ariosto (the passage appears first in the second edition of the poem), we are made to imagine him humorously suggesting the objection and wondering how Ariosto would be able to get out of that one. The Poet rises to the occasion superbly—he rewrites history.

One of the most interesting kinds of disclaimer of control is the pretense that the Poet is overcome by emotion of some kind—sorrow, grief, jealousy, fear, indignation—at the spectacle of the events of the poem. For instance, when Angelica chooses Medoro as her lover, the Poet himself is outraged:

> O Conte Orlando, o Re di Circasia,
> Vostra incluta virtù, dite, che giova?
> Vostro alto onor dite in che prezzo sia?
> O che mercé vostro servir ritruova?
> Mostratemi una sol cortesia
> Che mai costei v'usasse, o vecchia, o nuova,
> Per ricompensa, et guidardone, e merto
> Di quanto avete già per lei sofferto.
>
> O se potessi ritornar mai vivo,
> Quanto ti parria duro, o Re Agricane!
> Che già mostrò costei sì averti a schivo
> Con repulse crudeli et inumane.
> O Ferraú, o mille altri, ch' io non scrivo,
> Ch' avete fatto mille pruove vane
> Per questa ingrata, quanto aspro vi fôra,
> S' a costu' in braccio voi la vedeste ora!*
>   (XIX.31-32)

---

found the island to be so savage, so mountainous and uneven, that there is not, he says, in the whole wild place anywhere you can put your foot down flat: nor does he hold it likely that in that mountainous rock six knights, the flower of the world, could do mounted battle. To which objection I thus reply: that at that time the rock had at its foot a very good place for mounted fighting; but that later a rock that the earthquake loosened fell upon it and covered it all up. So that, o bright effulgence of the Fulgosan stock, o clear, o always living light, if you ever reproached me with this, and perhaps even in front of that unvanquished duke because of whom your fatherland now enjoys peace, leaves all hatred, and is led altogether to love: I beg you not to be slow to tell him that it is possible that I am not a liar in this either.

* O Count Orlando, o King of Circassia, say, of what use is your famous valor? Say what value is set on your high honor and what guerdon your service finds. Show me one courtesy that girl ever did you, a recent one or an old one, as a recompense and guerdon and merit, in return for all that you have suffered

The passage has several functions, not the least important of which is to emphasize the thematic significance of the failure of Orlando's hopes. The form of the comment is of course that of a reaction to an event over which the Poet supposedly has no control; the effect is to emphasize the controlling hand of the plot constructor, who has arranged events so that they will have this ironic outcome. And the tone hovers ambiguously between a pretended sense of outrage and an enjoyment of the irony and even pride in having produced it. I shall have more to say later about the thematic significance of the passage.

Another striking instance of pretended emotion also involves Angelica. When, early in the poem, she is chained to the rock as an offering for the sea monster, the Poet is so overcome that he leaves her there:

> Chi narrerà l'angoscie, i pianti, e i gridi,
> L'alta querela che nel ciel penètra?
> Maraviglia ho che non s'apriro i lidi,
> Quando fu posta in su la fredda pietra,
> Dove in catena, priva di sussidi,
> Morte aspettava abominosa e tetra.
> Io no'l dirò; che sì il dolor mi muove,
> Che mi sforza voltar le rime altrove,
>
> E trovar versi non tanti lugúbri,
> Fin che 'l mio spirto stanco si rïabbia.*
> (VIII.66-67)

Now we have just been watching Ariosto subject Angelica to a whole series of misfortunes. The Poet has had to narrate at great length, and with much ironic enjoyment, the indignities she suffers (in her sleep, to be sure) at the hands of the impotent necromancer. We know, furthermore, that he is breaking off her story at this point, first, for the sake of suspense and, second, in

---

for her. O, if you could come back to life, how hard it would seem to you, o King Agricane! For with cruel and inhuman repulses she showed so much dislike for you. O Ferrau, o a thousand others that I do not write down, who have performed a thousand useless exploits for this ungrateful girl, how bitter it would be for you if you saw her now in the arms of this fellow!

* Who will narrate the anguish, the weeping, the cries, the high complaining that penetrates heaven? I marvel that the shores did not open when she was put out on the cold stone, where in chains, deprived of all help, she awaited abominable dark death. I shall not say it; for sorrow so moves me that it forces me to turn my rhymes elsewhere, and to find verses less lugubrious, until my wearied spirit recovers.

order to prepare some fantastic coincidence—two fundamental patterns of the poem we have come to delight in. The Poet's pretense of ungovernable emotion serves, like a cadenza, to emphasize Ariosto's astonishing bravura.

In his comments about his conduct of the narrative, then, the Poet adopts a stance of absolute control over the material of the poem. He asserts repeatedly that the enormous richness and variety of the poem have a plan and that his narrative procedures have a rationale. He reminds us repeatedly of his presence as manipulator. This attitude of control of an extremely complex work of art is an example of the analogy between the poem and the cosmos and between the artist and God—that "fundamental motive," as Cassirer put it, of the Renaissance.[5] The idea itself has a long history, which goes back at least as far as the allegorical interpretation of Homer, in which Achilles' and Agamemnon's shields were interpreted by Neoplatonic and earlier commentators as symbolic of the cosmos, and in which the song of Demodocus was compared with the music of the spheres.[6] The Renaissance adapted a number of ancient and medieval ideas into a doctrine of poetry that was often self-consciously, deliberately ontological.

Poems may be seen to be analogous to the cosmos in several different ways, of course. They may be generically like the universe in that all art forms are governed by numerical proportion and harmony, quite apart from any particular content or subject matter. The notion that the universe itself was a musical harmony had been given its classic statements by Plato, Cicero, Plotinus, Augustine, and Boethius, which dominated both cosmology and musical theory well into the sixteenth century.[7] There are several variants of the idea, from Plato's unchanging music of the spheres to the idea of the universe as a *canticum*, a song, the syllables of which are the successive moments of time.[8] In the twelfth century, Alanus of Lille speaks of the universe as a great palace or temple, of which God is the "elegans architectus."[9] The songs and music of men, Boethius taught, imitate the harmony of the universe, just as, for the Gothic architect, the cathedral imitated the harmony of the universe and prefigured the glory of the afterlife.

The analogy between the work of art and the universe can be quite detailed and precise. The harmony of the universe was usually thought of as a reconciliation of opposites—the mingling of odd and even, cold and hot, wet and dry. So Ficino describes the composition of music as a kind of chemistry that blends light and heavy sounds. He clearly has the cosmic harmony in mind, which both music and chemistry imitate.[10]

> Just as expert doctors [chemists] mix together certain liquids, according to the case, by a certain principle by which many different materials may combine together into one new form . . . similarly artful musicians mix together very low tones (as it were cold substances) and very high tones (as it were hot substances), or, again, moderately low tones (moderately humid) and moderately high (moderately dry)—mix them together according to a principle by which one form is made of many.

A poem could be thought of as including and reconciling not only such opposites as unity and variety, but also differing types of subject, such as sorrowful and happy or military and pastoral. Poems were thought of as microcosms when their scope was particularly broad—when, in an even more literal sense, they contained the universe as a whole as their subject matter.[11]

These two points of comparison—harmony and universality—both go back ultimately to the topics of praise of Homer and Virgil developed in antiquity.[12] Macrobius, for instance, compares the rich variety of Virgil's eloquence to the variety of the cosmos, in a passage that underlies many Renaissance statements of the idea.[13]

> Do you see how his eloquence is beautified with the variety of all things? which variety Virgil seems to me to have put together designedly, not without that sagacity he brought to all his undertakings, and to have envisaged it all with divine rather than mortal understanding: and thus not having followed any guide but Nature herself, the mother of all things, he wove this variety together, like a harmony deriving from discordant sounds in music. For if you carefully inspect the world itself, you will find a great similarity between that divine handiwork and this poetic one. For just as the eloquence of Virgil is perfectly adequate to portray the natures of all men, now brief, now copious, now spare, now flowery, now all these at once, and meanwhile mild or vehement: so the earth herself is here glad with crops and meadows, there bristles with woods and cliffs, here is arid with sands, there is watered by springs, and a part is open to the vast sea. Pardon me, and do not think me excessive, if I have compared Virgil with Nature. For it would seem to me insufficient praise if I were to say that he alone has combined the differing styles of the ten orators of Athens.

This passage is clearly the source of Poliziano's account of the works of Virgil in his *Manto* (1482), where he repeats it image by image and device by device.[14]

And who, oh youths, perusing the miracles of this great eloquence, would not suppose that he was looking out over the immense tracts of the land and the sea? Here the grain richly flourishes; here the herd grazes on the soft grass; here the elm is married to the slender vines; on that side the oaks rise up with mossy trunks; on this side the vast sea lies open; here the shore lies with its thirsty sands; from these mountains the chilly rivers flow down; over here tower huge cliffs, and here great caves open their folds, while over there lie hidden valleys; and in all this a variegated [discors] beauty tempers the lovely world. So his rich eloquence takes on differing aspects: and like a river is now carried rushing with great impetus, now shrinks in its dry bed; now it is relaxed, now stepping proudly forth it is compelling; now negligence befits it, now it shines filled with lovely flowers; and sometimes it beautifully mingles all.

Tasso's famous description of the variety in the epic is closely related to the Poliziano passage, proceeding as it does from an enumeration of the variety of the universe (conceived as a land-scape—note the shortness of the part referring to the celestial bodies) to the enumeration of events or effects in the poem.[15]

Però che, sì come in questo mirabile magisterio di Dio, che mondo si chiama, e 'l cielo si vede sparso o distinto di tanta varietà di stelle; e, discendendo poi giuso di mano in mano, l'aria e 'l mare pieni d'uccelli e di pesci; e la terra albergatrice di tanti animali così feroci come mansueti, nella quale e ruscelli e fonti e laghi e prati e campagne e selve e monti si trovano; e qui frutti e fiori, là ghiacci e neve, qui abitazioni e colture, là solitudini ed orrori; con tutto ciò, uno è il mondo che tante e sì diverse cose nel suo grembo rinchiude, una la forma e l'essenza sua, uno il nodo, dal quale sono le sue parti con discorde concordia insieme congiunte e collegate, e non mancando nulla in lui, nulla però vi è di soverchio o di non necessario: così parimente giudico, che da eccellente poeta (il quale non per altro divino è detto, se non perchè al supremo Artefice nelle sue operazioni assomigliandosi, della sua divinità viene a partecipare) un poema formar si possa, nel quale, quasi in un picciolo mondo, qui si leggano ordinanze d'eserciti, qui battaglie terrestri e navali, qui espugnazioni di città, scaramucce e duelli, qui giostre, qui descrizioni di fame e di sete, qui tempeste, qui incendii, qui prodigii; là si trovino concilii celesti ed infernali, là si veggiano sedizioni, là discordie, là errori, là venture, là incanti, là opere di crudeltà, di audacia, di cortesia, di generosità; là avvenimenti d'amore, or felici or infelici, or lieti or compassionevoli; ma che nondimeno uno sia il poema.*

---

* For, just as in this wonderful masterpiece of God's that is called the world, the sky is sprinkled and marked out with such variety of stars; and, coming down little by little, the air and the sea are full of birds and fish; the land harbors so many animals, both fierce and tame, and in it are found rivers and fountains and lakes and meadows and fields and woods and mountains; and here fruits and flowers, there ice and snow, here habitations and agriculture, there solitude

We note in both these passages the emphasis upon fullness (plenitude) and variety. The same note occurs in Castiglione's application of the cosmic analogy to painting. The dispute over the relative merits of painting and sculpture is resolved by Count Ludovico Canossa in favor of painting, because of its greater variety, versatility, and self-sufficiency.[16]

All of the various ways in which the analogy between a poem and the universe was understood in the sixteenth century are echoed in the Poet's comments on his manipulation of the narrative. The poem is a musical harmony that combines the *grave* and the *acuto* (VII.29); like the cosmos, the poem evinces order (II.30, XIII.80-81), plenitude (XIII.80), variety (II.30), and unity (*la grande tela*). Even more literally, the poem will include, like Achilles' shield, the entire universe—all geographical space, the planets, the cities of men, and, as one sixteenth-century critic put it in drawing the analogy, "più specchi della vita umana."[17] Futhermore, on this literal level—on the level of the metaphor according to which the Poet can enter the same world that the characters inhabit—the poem is governed by the providence of the manipulating Poet, and the poem presents a dramatization of the analogy between Poet and Providence. In the first place, as we have already seen, the reader of the poem is asked to accept without complaint the judgment of the Poet about when to break off stories. Just so, man in his imperfect knowledge should realize that, in His disposition of worldly events, God knows best:

> [God] knows much better than man what in every moment of time should be brought about; knows what and when to bestow, add, take away, increase, diminish, being the immutable moderator, as He is the creator, of

and wilderness. But nevertheless the world is one, which gathers in its lap so many and so different things—one is its form and essence, and one the knot by which its parts are joined and bound together in discordant harmony. In just the same way, it seems to me, an excellent poet (who for no other reason is called divine than because, resembling the supreme Artificer in his operations, he comes to participate in His divinity) could form a poem in which, as if in a little world, one would read here of the formation of armies, here of terrestrial and naval battles, here of the capture of cities, of skirmishes and duels, here of jousts, here descriptions of hunger and thirst, here of tempests, here of fires, here of marvels; and over there would be heavenly and infernal councils, there would be seen sedition, there discord, there wanderings and error, there adventures, there enchantments, there works of cruelty, of courage, of courtesy, of generosity; there vicissitudes of love, now lucky now unlucky, now happy, now pitiable. But nevertheless the poem would be one.

mutable things; until the universal beauty of the world, whose parts are those things which are all fitted to their times, like a great piece of music by some ineffable musician, shall be over. (Augustine, in Migne, *Patrologia latina* 33, 537; cited in Spitzer, p. 29)

> . . . non v'incresca
> Udir che così resti in quello incanto;
> Ché quando sarà il tempo ch'ella n'esca,
> La farò uscire, e Ruggiero altretanto.*
>   (XIII.80)

> Ma voglio questo canto abbia qui fine:
> E di quel che voglio io, siate contenti.
> Ché miglior cosa vi prometto dire,
> S'a l'altro canto mi verrete a udire.†
>   (XXXVI.84)

Futhermore, like God in His regulation of the world, the Poet produces a harmony in which everything has its due importance, in which nothing is neglected or omitted. No thread of the narrative is concentrated on at the expense of others, as we have seen.

Wherefore if a man who makes a song knows what length to allow to each note so that what is sung will run and go by most beautifully with its transient, successive sounds; by how much more will God not permit any spaces of time in natures that come to be and pass away—spaces of time that are their parts, like syllables and words in this wonderful music of mutable things—God will not permit any of these spaces of time to be either shorter or longer than in His foreknown and foreordained modulation He has decided. (Augustine, *Epistle* 166.33; cited in Spitzer, p. 31)

Furthermore, the Poet contemplates the action from a point of view that is sometimes analogous to God's in the Empyrean, as we have seen in the instance of one character's calling out to him for inclusion in the poem:

> Di questo altrove io vo' rendervi conto;
> Ch' ad un gran Duca è forza ch'io riguardi,
> Il qual mi grida, e di lontano accenna,
> E priega ch' io no'l lasci ne la penna.

> Gli è tempo ch'io ritorni ove lasciai
> L'aventuroso Astolfo d'Inghilterra. (XV.9-10)

---

* Let it not bother you to hear that she remains thus in that enchantment; for when it is time for her to come out of it, I shall make her come out, and Ruggiero as well.

† But I wish this canto to end here, and with what I wish, you be content; for I promise to tell you something even better, if you will come to hear me in the next canto.

Just before these lines, the Poet has been telling of Agramante's general assault on Paris, and from Paris Astolfo is very *lontano* indeed—he is off beyond the Arabian Sea. From where the Poet is, however, he can see both Paris and the gesturing Astolfo. It is as if the geographical space of the poem, for the most part realistically identified and kept in mind (however fast the characters may travel over it), were suddenly shrunk. Astolfo also seems very small, perhaps partly because he is referred to as "un gran Duca," and as he shouts he is none too dignified. Part of the joke here is that the demand is quite in character for Astolfo, who never turns a hair when he voyages to the moon with John the Evangelist; none of the other characters in the poem has quite his aplomb.

On the literal level of the plot, the Poet is analogous to God not only because he controls events, but also because he distributes justice among the characters. Most frequently, the rewards or punishments are the traditional praise or blame that epic poetry was supposed to share as an aim with epideictic rhetoric.[18] A fairly typical example is this comment on the story of Olimpia:

> Fra quanti amor, fra quante fedi al mondo
> Mai si trovâr, fra quanti cor constanti,
> Fra quante, o per dolente o per giocondo
> Stato, fêr prove mai famosi amanti:
> Più tosto il primo loco che 'l secondo
> Darò ad Olimpia: e se pur non va inanti,
> Ben voglio dir che fra gli antichi e nuovi
> Maggior de l'amor suo non si ritruovi.* (X.1)

There is one particularly important instance in which the Poet decides to intervene in the events of the poem because of his anger at the behavior of one of the characters, Rodomonte:

> Donne gentil, per quel ch' a biasmo vostro
> Parlò contra il dover, sì offeso sono,
> Che sin che col suo mal non gli dimostro
> Quanto abbia fatto error, non gli perdono.
> Io farò sì con penna, e con inchiostro,
> Ch' ognun vedrà che gli era utile e buono

---

* Among all the loves, all the faithfulness that ever was in the world, among all the ladies who either for happy or sorrowful state have given proof of their love: I would give to Olimpia rather the first than the second place: and if she does not in fact surpass all, I can tell you that no greater than her love was ever found among the ancients or the moderns.

Aver taciuto, et mordersi anco poi
Prima la lingua, che dir mal di voi.*
(XXIX.2)

The passage follows the familiar rhythm of disclaimer of control
followed by assertion of control: the Poet is surprised at Rodomonte's conduct, as if he himself were not responsible for it, and
he will punish him—by manipulating future events in the poem.
And manipulating these events is going to involve, as we see,
manipulating Rodomonte's actions. This will show Rodomonte
the error of his ways, but it will be done with pen and ink.
Furthermore, the event that will teach Rodomonte the inadvis-
ability of speaking out against women is the heroic death of
Isabella, as if the poet were bringing it about merely to teach
Rodomonte a lesson. The subsidiary play in the passage is
complex, but the most important part of the joke is clear enough:
it is the humorous assumption by the Poet of the function of the
god—dispenser of justice—of this little world. We shall return
to this important episode later.

Ariosto's attitude as dominator of the world of the poem has
seemed crucial to many readers, and their efforts to account for
it have produced several notable interpretations of the poem.
To Hegel and to De Sanctis, who adapted Hegel's aesthetic
method, Ariosto's irony seemed corrosive and destructive. Hegel
produced the formula of Ariosto's being the destroyer of chivalry,
De Sanctis that of his being the poet of pure form, of art for art's
sake; for both, the incessant of play of wit destroyed the imaginative reality of the events of the action and emptied the poem of
any serious content.[19] This is, of course, a serious misreading of
the poem, as recent Italian criticism has been coming to see.[20]
Unfortunately it still survives in this country.[21]

In one sense, it is true that this kind of humor dissolves, as
Hegel maintained, the "objective substantiality" of the narrated
events, or at least it would if they had any substance to begin
with. The only "essential nature"[22] narrated events can have,
however, is what the narrator gives them: they are the *imagined*

---

* Gentle ladies, I am so incensed by what he said in blame of you, contrary
to how one should speak, that until with his own ill I have shown how great an
error he committed, I shall not pardon him. I shall do so much with pen and ink
that everyone will see that it would have been useful and good for him to have
been silent, or even to have bitten his tongue, rather than speak ill of you.

subjects of his predications. Our aesthetic absorption in narrative never involves any literal confusion about the reality of the fictional universe, as Hegel's and De Sanctis' readings of the poem ultimately presuppose. The Poet's comments do not violate our absorption in the poem, as a persistent doorbell might; rather his comments and his abrupt shifts of tone modify our vision of the fictitious universe. We had never believed Angelica to be real in the first place; the Poet's joke will not prevent us from following her story with great absorption the next time she comes on stage.

As readers of fiction, we regularly perform highly complicated mental processes of which we are not always aware. The Narrator of the *Orlando furioso* demands that we be aware of them. He demands that we keep distinctions sharply before us and re-examine them if need be. The analogy of the Poet and God is thus no merely incidental play of wit. It is at the core of almost all of the Poet's references to his handling of the poem, and it serves the highly important function of defining and keeping before the reader the nature of the poem in comparison with the real world. In order to get the jokes, the reader must repeatedly see the ways in which the world of the poem is unlike the real world, but also—and this is just as important—the ways in which it is like the real world, is a serious mimesis of it.

At this point it is necessary to make an important distinction, one upon which much of my later discussion will rest. If the poem is analogous to the cosmos, the poet is analogous to God, and we have seen Ariosto acting as the Providence of the little world of the poem. As M. H. Abrams has pointed out, however, the choice of the particular doctrine of creation that underlies the analogy of the poet and God has considerable consequences for the theory of poetry.[23] It is the image of the Platonic demiurge, the craftsman, that Ariosto has in mind. Speaking of the various story lines being woven into a story implies the rhetorical distinction between *invention* and *disposition;* it suggests that the threads have some kind of existence before being combined into the weave.[24] Ariosto never refers to the doctrine of creation *ex nihilo*, although there was a variant of the analogy between the poet and God based on that doctrine.[25]

Nor does Ariosto's Narrator represent himself as owing his powers to any supernatural inspiration or assistance. He regularly refers to himself as existing and discoursing on the natural plane, as composing his poem with his own natural powers, his *ingegno* and *fantasia*, by *fatica* and *studi* (III.3-4). As we shall see, in the only passage in the poem in which he invokes a deity or muse (Apollo) and refers to a *furor poeticus* (III.1-2), he is recognizably adopting a conventional pose and he means the reader to recognize it as such. Everywhere else he refers to himself as the learned natural man. It is necessary to distinguish sharply the analogy between the poet and God, which is introduced into the poem by Ariosto, and the assertion of divine inspiration. The Poet who seriously speaks of inspiration is not representing himself primarily as an analogue of the Creator, but as His spokesman.

The analogy based upon the doctrine of creation *ex nihilo* involves an exaltation of the poet of a kind that is foreign to Ariosto's poem. It is perhaps best exemplified in Sidney's eloquent statement of the notion that the works of the poet are superior to those of nature:

Onely the Poet, disdayning to be tied to any such subiection, lifted vp with the vigor of his owne inuention, dooth grow *in effect another nature*, in making things either better than Nature bringeth forth, or, quite a newe, formes such as neuer were in Nature . . . Her world is brasen, the Poets onely deliuer a golden . . .

Neyther let it be deemed too sawcie a comparison to ballance the highest poynt of mans wit with the efficacie of Nature: but rather giue right honor to the heauenly Maker of that maker, who, hauing made man to his owne likenes, set him beyond and ouer all the workes of that second nature, which in nothing he sheweth so much as in Poetrie, when, with the force of a diuine breath he bringeth things forth far surpassing her dooings.[26]

Whatever Ariosto would have thought of this doctrine as a theory of poetry in general, it is quite different from the stance he adopts in the poem, where the continuous play of wit upon the surface of the fiction safeguards the reader from sentimentally reacting to the poem as if the events were real. Ariosto continually reminds the reader that the poem is to be *discourse* about an imagined world that does not pretend to have substantial reality, but only to be such a likeness of the real world as human powers can fashion. The reader is continually reminded that he is not to rest in the world of the poem, but to look through it at the real world.[27] One is reminded of the terms in which Nicholas of Cusa defined the analogy of man to God. God possesses *vis entificativa,* the power of creating entities; man possesses the similar but limited *vis assimilativa,* the power of making concepts or likenesses of the created universe and thus, by analogy, in the act of knowing, creating it a second time.[28] Ariosto's Narrator is an analogue of the Creator, but he is still a finite being. If he is a god he is, to use Cusanus' term, a *deus occasionatus,* a contingent god.[29] This is the point that connects Ariosto's joyful pride in his own poetic powers, which has been commented on by so many readers, and his deep sense of the limits of human endeavor.

2

We now turn to a consideration of the passages in which the (supposed) personal individuality of the Poet is presented, as distinct from the underlying poetic purpose or will. In these references to "himself," the Poet deliberately assumes several different roles, all more or less distinct from each other and sometimes even inconsistent. As we shall see, the references to himself are an integral part of the complex thematic statement of the poem. The most important occur in the famous exordia to the individual cantos of the poem; their topics range from the moral implications of the story to the similarity of the events of the poem to actual historical events and the supposed personal experience of the Poet.[30]

As has often been pointed out, most of the canto openings present the Poet in the role of a graceful and good-humored but fundamentally serious moralist. They usually offer moral reflections suggested by the action of the preceding or the present canto. The topics are varied: the right conduct of princes, the prevalence of deception and hypocrisy, the evils of anger or avarice or lust, the nature of true nobility, the value of true friendship, the evils of war, the causes of the oppression of Italy, and so forth. They are elegant, eloquent, and serious. Except on one occasion, their tone never rises to indignation. Ariosto presents his reflections in a tone of *disinvoltura,* in the urbane tone of a man of the world who shuns affectation or self-righteousness. This easy tone has misled some readers into supposing that the attitudes it expresses are not serious. But the mixture of moral earnestness and an unwillingness to seem too preacherly is substantially the same as what we find in several of the interlocutors in Castiglione's *Cortegiano*.[31] Ariosto has a fundamental moral concern, and to its overt, sententious expression the social and literary usages of the day gave much wider scope than do our own. Nevertheless, he and his society share the modern dislike of preaching. His is a calm practical wisdom, unblinded by worldly glory, rather pessimistic about the nobility of most human beings but also without rancor or bitterness, holding firmly to the fundamental chivalric ideals of courtesy, faithfulness, generosity, and honor. None of the moral *sententiae* the Poet utters are especially original; they are the current formulas of his time, and some are based on Boiardo.[32]

Now, although most of the historical exordia speak of the events of the poem as if they were real, their effect depends upon the reader's having clearly in mind the distinction between the poem and the real world. For instance, in one of the most amusing parts of the poem, the placid Astolfo, armed with his magic horn, goes to Abyssinia to enlist the help of its Christian king against the Saracens. He finds the king a victim of harpies, and wins his help by driving the harpies back to Hellmouth. There follows the delightful parody of the *Divina Commedia*, in which Astolfo visits hell, the earthly paradise, and the moon, whence he brings back Orlando's lost wits (Cantos XXXIV and XXXV). Canto XXXIV begins:

> O famelice, inique e fiere arpie
> Ch' a l'accecata Italia, e d'error piena,
> Per punir forse antique colpe rie,
> In ogni mensa alto giudicio mena!
> Innocenti fanciulli e madri pie
> Cascan di fame; e veggon ch' una cena
> Di questi mostri rei tutto divora
> Ciò che del viver lor sostegno fôra.
>
> Troppo fallò chi le spelunche aperse,
> Che già molt' anni erano state chiuse;
> Onde il fetore e l'ingordigia emerse,
> Ch' ad ammorbare Italia si diffuse.
> Il bel vivere allora si summerse,
> E la quïete in tal modo s'escluse,
> Ch' in guerre, in povertà sempre, e in affanni,
> È dopo stata, et è per star molt' anni.
>
> Fin ch' ella un giorno ai neghitosi figli
> Scuota la chioma, e cacci fuor di Lete,

Gridando lor:—Non fia chi rassimigli
A la virtù di Calai e di Zete?
Che le mense dal puzzo e dagli artigli
Liberi, e torni a lor mondizie liete,
Come essi già quelle di Fineo, e dopo
Fe' il Paladin quelle del Re Etïopo.—*

(XXXIV.1-3)

This passage is fairly characteristic. Its complex effect depends upon the reader's taking adequate stock of the difference between the poem and the world: for Italy's sufferings are real. Nor are the events of the poem serious—no deep emotions are in play in this section of the poem, although they are elsewhere; but the misery of Italy is profound. Faced with the spectacle of the French invasion, Boiardo stopped writing his poem, but these are the words of a later generation, one that has to live with the reality of servitude. Ariosto's poem differs from Boiardo's in being an attempt to assimilate the lessons of recent history. What is the result or, at least, how far is it visible in this passage? One of the striking things about the passage is the discontinuity between the motif in the story and the symbolic use made of it in the exordium. This does not purport to be an allegory of the story of Senapo. It purports to be a more or less spontaneous reflection suggested by a common metaphorical use of *harpy*. The allegorical significance of Senapo and his harpies, if they have any, is something else. The passage does not pretend that the Italians are not to blame for their own misfortunes; nor does it pretend that the effects of foreign domination are anything but corrupting. It accurately foresees that conditions in Italy will be miserable for "many years," until some patriotic spirit arouses the

---

* Oh ravenous, wicked, fierce Harpies whom, perhaps to punish blinded, error-ridden Italy for ancient sins, high Judgment brings to every table! Innocent children and unselfish mothers fall from hunger, and they see that one banquet of these wicked monsters devours altogether what would maintain their lives. He sinned greatly who first opened the grottoes, which for many years had been closed; from which the stench and the greediness came forth that spread to sicken Italy. Then delightful living was destroyed, and quiet was so banished, that she has been ever since in wars, in poverty, and in troubles, and she will be for many years: until one day she shakes her locks and drives her lazy sons forth from Lethe, shouting to them: "Will no one resemble the valor of Calais and Zetes? will no one free our tables of this stink and these claws, and return them happy to their former purity, as once they did the table of Phineus, and later the Paladin did the tables of the Ethiopian king?"

people to drive the *barbari* out.[33] After this uncompromisingly honest and moving appeal, there comes the typical Ariostan shift of tone: the personified Italy cites Astolfo's chasing away of Senapo's harpies as if it were a historical event. Is the seriousness of the comment destroyed by this clever transition back to the story? I think not. What happens is simply that the serious out-burst ends: it has to end, naturally, if we are going to return to the story. The cleverness of the transition shows the Poet's urbanity—he will not hold forth for too long even on such a sub-ject as this.[34] The point of the twist, of course, is precisely to focus attention on the disparity of poem and reality. The ultimate point of this focusing of attention may be that the reader is supposed to define for himself the relation of his reading of the poem to his own practical life, and this would have to be defined in terms of the poem's total thematic seriousness. Any other view—any view that sees the transition back to the story as a merely frivolous destruction of seriousness—mistakes the delicate modulations of the tone and denies the very mark of seriousness distinguishing Ariosto from Boiardo.

It seems to me, then, that the moralizing of the exordia is pre-served from any "corrosion"[35] by the famous Ariostan irony. There are several categories of reference to the Poet that are not exempt from it, however, the most important of which are his attitudes toward patrons, women, and love. The *Orlando furioso* purports to be an epic celebrating the heroic virtues of the House of Este, and the opening lines of the poem include, in good classical fashion, the dedication to Ippolito d'Este:

> Piacciavi, generosa Erculea prole,
> Ornamento e splendor del secol nostro,
> Ippolito, aggradir questo che vuole
> E darvi sol può l'umil servo vostro.
> Quel ch'io vi debbo, posso di parole
> Pagare in parte e d'opera d'inchiostro:
> Né che poco io vi dia da imputar sono,
> Che quanto io posso dar, tutto vi dono.*
>
> (I.3)

---

* May it please you, noble offspring of Hercules, ornament and splendor of our century, Ippolito, to look with favor on this, which only your humble servant can and will give to you. What I owe you, I can pay in part with words and the

We have here the conventional posture of courtly compliment
to one's patron—a matter of social as well as literary decorum.[36]
But the stanza occurs just after the boast that the Poet will tell of
Orlando "things never said in prose or rime," and following the
proud assertion of power the posture of humility seems conventional indeed.[37] But both topics were familiar to the public
Ariosto was addressing, and the tone is still well within the
prescriptions of good manners.

   The third canto of the poem is devoted to a Virgilian celebration of the House of Este, in which Bradamante, like Aeneas,
sees pass before her the whole line of descendants down to the
Poet's own day. The canto opens with a passage I have already
referred to in another connection:

> Chi mi darà la voce e le parole
> Convenïenti a sì nobil suggetto?
> Chi l'ale al verso presterà, che vole
> Tanto ch' arrivi a l'alto mio concetto?
> Molto maggior di quel furor che suole,
> Ben or convien che mi riscaldi il petto:
> Che questa parte al mio Signor si debbe,
> Che canta gli Avi onde l'origine ebbe.
>
> Di cui fra tutti li Signori illustri
> Dal ciel sortiti a governar la terra,
> Non vedi, o Febo, che 'l gran mondo lustri,
> Più glorïosa stirpe, o in pace o in guerra;
> Né che sua nobiltade abbia più lustri
> Servata, e servarà, s'in me non erra
> Quel profetico lume che m'inspiri,
> Fin che d'intorno al polo il ciel s'aggiri.
>
> E volendone a pien dicer gli onori,
> Bisogna non la mia, ma quella cetra
> Con che tu dopo i gigantei furori
> Rendesti grazia al regnator de l'Etra.
> S'instrumenti avrò mai da te migliori,
> Atti a sculpire in così degna pietra,
> In queste belle imagini disegno
> Porre ogni mia fatica, ogni mio ingegno.
>
> Levando intanto queste prime rudi
> Scaglie n'andrò con lo scarpello inetto:

---

work of my pen; nor is it to be thought that I give you little, for as much as I
can give, I give it all to you.

Forse ch' ancor con più solerti studi
Poi ridurrò questo lavor perfetto.*
(III.1-4)

This is again the tone of courtly literary compliment. Yet, as I
have already noted, the Poet here describes his poetic activity
in terms altogether different from those he customarily uses. This
is the only place in the entire poem where he invokes the
assistance of any muse or god; this is the only occasion on which
he ascribes his poetic powers to a furor of inspiration; and it is
the only time he lays claim to a prophetic light. Furthermore,
we find him here deprecating both his powers and the poem.

Still, that the Poet is simply being complimentary is clear. The
doctrines of *furor* and *techné* are both laid under contribution in
this passage, in spite of their inconsistency. For instance,
although the Poet is invoking Phoebus, it is only for help in
elocution, not for knowledge.[38] The Poet has an *alto concetto*
—he does not need help in understanding the greatness of his
patron, only in expressing it. Futhermore, stanzas 3 and 4 revert
from the vocabulary of *furor* to something more like Ariosto's
habitual way of referring to his own poetic activity—to the metaphor of sculpture, in which *instrumenti* and *ingegno* refer to his
natural powers of mind, and hard work and studies (III.3 and 4)
to the process of forming the work by art. The passage is of
course an admirable, finely phrased one. The tension between the
notions of furor and art is no more than one customarily finds in
complimentary verse. Their presence here is one of the signals
to the attentive reader that the Poet is assuming the role of
formal celebrator of patrons. The disparity between the Poet's

---

* Who will give me a voice and the words that befit so noble a subject? Who
will lend wings to my verse, that it may fly so high as to reach my high conception? A much greater furor than usual must now enflame my breast; for this
part is my Lord's, which sings the ancestors from whom he takes his birth: than
whom you do not see, O Phoebus, you who scan the great world, among all
the illustrious lords chosen by heaven to rule the earth, a line more glorious
either in peace or in war; nor one that has kept its nobility for more years and
will keep it (if in me that prophetic light that inspires me does not err) as long
as the sky turns about the pole. And if I should wish to tell its honors fully,
I should need not my lyre, but that with which after the raging of the Titans you
gave thanks to the ruler of the aether. If I ever have from you better instruments, ones worthy to carve such worthy marble, I intend to put all of my pains,
all of my wit, into these lovely images. In the meanwhile, I shall continue to
take off these rough fragments with my inept chisel: perhaps later, with more
skillful studies, I shall still make this work perfect.

usual tone and this one is another form of control that the total context of the poem imposes upon the implications of this passage.

Sometimes the Poet's praise of the House of Este and of Alfonso and Ippolito is quite general, as it is in the opening of Canto III. They are the height of "nobiltade"; they are lights of "cortesia" and have "ogni laudabile costume" (XLI.3); each of their actions is praiseworthy (XVIII.1). Just as often, however, particular actions or qualities are singled out for praise. Ippolito's fairmindedness, his reluctance to believe slander, and his slowness to pass judgment are the subject of one exordium (XVIII.1-3). The most frequent topic of praise, however, is the part the two brothers played in the Italian wars, and here again we find Ariosto taking explicit account of recent events.

In considering the comments the Poet makes on the long struggle for the political control of Italy, one should remember several things. First, of course, Ariosto does not view the wars with modern eyes. He does not see in them the emergence of the modern army or a revolution in medieval military tactics. He is a member of the nobility, furthermore, and like other members of his class in this period he still retains much of the medieval chivalric conception of war, as it appears in Froissart, let us say. He tends to formulate the events of battles as the result of the personal heroism of the leaders, and the generally accepted chivalric code makes it possible for him to admire valor wherever he sees it and to associate happily with captured enemies.[39] These wars were very different, nevertheless, from the elaborate ballets of war in fifteenth-century Italy; they were waged with an altogether new ferocity, which vented itself also on the civilian population in a series of notorious sacks of captured cities.[40] In Ariosto's commentary on the wars, horror and disgust at the new cruelty are combined with the older chivalric attitudes.

Second, whatever our judgment may be of Alfonso and Ippolito d'Este, who were both guilty on several occasions of a personal cruelty only too common in their age and who, like the other rulers of the time, blithely exploited the populace to keep up their expensive elegance, it must be remembered that they were eminently successful in their difficult task as rulers of a minor state caught in the struggle of world powers. They managed to keep their possessions more or less intact and to protect Ferrara throughout the period of Ariosto's lifetime. With the dukes of Mantua, they were the only rulers of smaller states who were not driven out of their lands for long either by conquest or rebellion, as were, at one time or another, the dukes of Urbino (1502, 1516), Genoa (1497, 1522) and Milan (1498, 1505, 1516), the Medici (1494, 1527), the tyrants of Bologna and Perugia and of scores of other smaller cities, the king of the Two Sicilies (1495, 1500), and the pope (1527), many of whom were permanently deposed or died in captivity. Only the Republic of Venice withstood the storm as well. Now the *Orlando furioso* was first published in 1516. By 1532, when the last edition during Ariosto's lifetime was published, the alignment of forces in the struggle had changed considerably. During the first thirty years of the wars, the dukes of Ferrara had remained faithful to the traditional alliance with France, often at considerable risk. After the disasters to the French cause in 1525-1530, which culminated in the crowning of Charles V as emperor and as king of Italy, Ferrara was of course forced to make its peace with Spain.

Ariosto's efforts to grapple with contemporary history determined some important additions to the edition of 1532, the most important of which is the extended treatment of the whole sequence of French invasions of Italy in the paintings of the Rocca di Tristano (XXXIII.1-58). The panorama of the wars is on the whole a dispassionate account of the important events. It focuses much laudatory attention on the marchesi of Pescara and Avalos, Charles V's principal generals, and in general attributes most of Italy's troubles to the French. But one of the noteworthy aspects of Ariosto's commentaries on recent Italian history is their consistency. He did not change the comments on politics that he had included in the earlier editions of the poem. In other words, during the period of the French alliance, Ariosto had been just as critical of the French as he was now in 1532. Furthermore, the description of the paintings in the Rocca di Tristano includes some extremely harsh commentary against the imperial side. In short, Ariosto recognizes and repeatedly praises Alfonso and Ippolito for the preservation of Ferrara, while suggesting that the French alliance has been pernicious for Italy as a whole. Let us look at some of the comments included in the poem from the beginning.

These comments are usually represented as reflections suggested by the similarity of the events of the story to actual ones. At the beginning of Canto XXXVI, for example, Bradamante's clemency to the knights she has unhorsed suggests the general topic of generosity and leads to the contrast between the forbearance of Ippolito during the siege of Padua (War of the League of Cambrai, 1508), when he prevented the sacking of outlying villages, and the murder of prisoners of war by Venetian mercenaries(XXXVI.1-10).[41] Of the battles that Alfonso and Ippolito took part in, the most frequently referred to in the poem are those of Polesella (December 22, 1509)[42] and Ravenna (April 11, 1512).[43] The reasons are not far to seek—both were notable triumphs of the leadership and methods of Alfonso and Ippolito, and both saved the city of Ferrara at moments when it was in particular danger of being taken.[44]

Let us examine the most important of the passages on the battle of Ravenna, at which the French forces under Gaston de Foix overcame the combined armies of Spain and the Empire. The artillery of Alfonso d'Este was principally responsible for the victory.[45] The passage in Canto XIV introduces the first important military events of the poem, the assault of Paris by the Saracens.

> Nei molti assalti et nei crudel conflitti,
> Ch' avuti avea con Francia, Africa e Spagna,
> Morti erano infiniti, e derelitti
> Al Lupo, al Corvo, a l'Aquila grifagna;
> E ben che i Franchi fossero più afflitti,
> Che tutta avean perduta la campagna,
> Più si doleano i Saracin, per molti
> Principi e gran Baron ch' eran lor tolti.

> Ebbon vittorie così sanguinose,
> Che lor poco avanzò di che allegrarsi:
> E se alle antique le moderne cose,
> Invitto Alfonso, denno assimigliarsi;
> La gran vittoria, onde a le virtuose
> Opere vostre può la gloria darsi,
> Di ch'aver sempre lacrimose ciglia
> Ravenna debbe, a queste s'assimiglia:

Quando cedendo Morini e Picardi,
L'esercito Normando e l'Aquitano,
Voi nel mezzo assaliste li stendardi
Del quasi vincitor nimico Ispano:
Seguendo voi quei giovени gagliardi,
Che meritâr con valorosa mano
Quel dì da voi per onorati doni
L'else indorate e gl'indorati sproni.

Con sì animosi petti che vi foro
Vicini o poco lungi al gran periglio,
Crollaste sì le ricche Ghiande d'Oro,
Sì rompeste il baston giallo e vermiglio,
Ch' a voi si deve il trionfale Alloro,
Che non fu guasto né sfiorato il Giglio.
D' un' altra fronde v'orna anco la chioma
L'aver servato il suo Fabrizio a Roma.

La gran Colonna del nome Romano,
Che voi prendeste, e che servaste intera,
Vi dà più onor, che se di vostra mano
Fosse caduta la milizia fiera,
Quanta n'ingrassa il campo Ravegnano,
E quanta se n'andò senza bandiera
D'Aragon, di Castiglia, e di Navarra,
Veduto non giovar spiedi né carra.

Quella vittoria fu più di conforto
Che d'allegrezza: perché troppo pesa
Contra la gioia nostra il veder morto
Il Capitan di Francia e de l'impresa:
E seco avere una procella absorto
Tanti Principi illustri, ch' a difesa
Dei Regni lor, dei lor confederati,
Di qua da le fredde Alpi eran passati.

Nostra salute, nostra vita in questa
Vittoria suscitata si conosce;
Che difende che 'l Verno e la tempesta
Di Giove irato sopra noi non crosce.
Ma né goder potiam, né farne festa,
Sentendo i gran ramarichi e l'angosce,
Ch' in vesta bruna e lacrimosa guancia
Le vedovelle fan per tutta Francia.*

(XIV.1-7)

* In the many assaults and cruel conflicts that Africa and Spain had had
with France, infinite numbers had been killed and left for the wolf, the crow,
the clawing eagle; and although the French suffered more, for they had lost

We may pause to notice several things. Beginning with a synoptic view of the Saracen losses, the passage proceeds, like so many others, by drawing a parellel between the events of the poem and modern events. One reason for this, of course, is to compliment Alfonso. But is the passage entirely complimentary? Certain things naturally are, such as the description of Alfonso's valor and his immediate, chivalrously generous recognition of that of his followers in his knighting of them on the field. Alfonso's chivalrous treatment of his foe Fabrizio Colonna is given most emphatic praise—this generosity, the preservation of the honorable customs of war (so contrary to the habits of the French[46]), is more glorious than the slaughter of every Spaniard on the field would have been. An entire stanza is devoted to this ranking of clemency and mercy to the enemy above valor and technological genius (Alfonso's famous cannon being a chief cause of the victory). Do not be too proud of your valor and your cannon, he is saying to Alfonso, since all they can do is kill men. There are better things to be than a butcher, though one does have to be a butcher in order to save one's city. As it is, those Spanish butchers who were killed at Ravenna are making the field fat— "n'ingrassa il campo Ravegnano."

The tone in which this greatest of Alfonso's victories is

---

all their territory, the Saracens sorrowed more, because of the many princes and great barons that had been taken from them. They had such bloody victories that there was little reason left for them to rejoice. And if modern things are to be compared with ancient ones, unvanquished Alfonso, that great victory, for which your valorous works can claim the glory, for which Ravenna must always have a tearful brow, is similar to those: When, the Morini and the Picards retreating, and the Norman and Aquitanian armies, you attacked at the center the standards of the almost victorious Spanish enemy, and those gallant youths followed you who earned from you that day, with their valiant hands, the golden hilts and spurs of knighthood. With such brave breasts that you were close to death, you so shook the rich Acorns of gold, you so broke the red and yellow staff, that to you is due the laurel of triumph that the Lily was not soiled or destroyed. And having preserved for Rome her Fabrizio adorns your brow with another leaf. The great Colonna, column of the fame of Rome, whom you captured and preserved intact, gives you more honor than if all those fierce soldiers had fallen at your hand, all those who make fat the field of Ravenna and all those who fled without banners, Aragonese, Castilians, and Navarrese, seeing that spears and chariots did not avail. That victory brought comfort rather than joy; for against our joy weighs seeing dead the captain of the French and of the field; and that a storm has whirled away with itself so many illustrious princes, who had descended to this side of the cold Alps in defense of their realm and their allies. Our safety, our lives are seen to be revived by this victory, which prevents the wintry storms of angry Jove from falling on our heads; but we cannot rejoice or celebrate, hearing the great anguished weeping that the widows make throughout France, in black clothes and with tearful cheeks.

discussed, then, expresses sheer horror at the slaughter. It explicitly shows sympathy for the French widows and suggests considerable pity for the Spanish dead also, who are not even
identified as gentlemen. The very next exordium, furthermore, is
devoted to the topic of the superiority of the kind of victory in
which one saves one's own men. We ask again, why draw the
parallel? If we look back to the story, we see that the Pyrrhic
victories of the Saracens are a stage in their inevitable defeat.
They have, as the *propositione* of the poem tells us, come to
France "seguendo l'ire e i giovenil furori D'Agramante" (following the wrath and the youthful furor of Agramante). Agramante's
mad adventure is foredoomed. It is perhaps attributing to Ariosto
excessive clairvoyance to suggest that he foresaw the ultimate
defeat of Francis I's Italian adventures in 1516, when the in-
credible series of them had hardly begun. He had, however,
already seen the folly of Charles VIII and Louis XII come to
naught. In any case, the story might suggest some disturbing
thoughts about the parallel historical events.

One of the most disturbing thoughts comes up in the very lines
that identify the battle—"that great victory for which Ravenna
must always have a tearful brow." Stanzas 8 and 9 bring the topic
up again:

> Bisogna che proveggia il Re Luigi
> Di nuovi Capitani alle sue squadre;
> Che per onor de l'aurea Fiordeligi
> Castighino le man rapaci e ladre,
> Che suore, e frati, e bianchi, e neri, e bigi
> Vïolato hanno, e sposa, e figlia, e madre;
> Gittato in terra Cristo in sacramento,
> Per torgli un tabernaculo d'argento.

> O misera Ravenna, t'era meglio
> Ch' al vincitor non fessi resistenza:
> Far ch' a te fosse inanzi Brescia speglio,
> Che tu lo fossi a Arimino, e a Faenza.
> Manda, Luigi, il buon Traulcio veglio,
> Ch' insegni a questi tuoi più continenza.
> E conti lor quanti per simil torti
> Stati ne sian per tutta Italia morti.*
> (XIV.8-9)

---

* King Louis must provide new captains for his squadrons, who, for the
honor of the golden Fleur-de-lis, must chastise the rapacious, thieving hands that
have violated nuns and friars, white, black, and grey, and wives and daughters

This is harsh and daring language. The atrocious sack of Ravenna is a dishonor to France. Some of the indignation is softened by the suggestion that the rape of Ravenna would not have been so bad if so many French officers had not been killed. Nevertheless, the mention of the fate of Brescia reminds the reader that the presence of its officers had not restrained the French army earlier. Not only that, the concluding lines are an open threat. In the first edition of the poem, published when the French alliance was still strong, the warning was even more explicit: "e cōti lor dil sangue che fu spanto/al uespro ch' intonò 'l horribil canto," (and let him tell them of the blood shed at the Vespers that intoned the horrible chant),[47] a reference to the Sicilian Vespers, a rebellion directed not merely against the common soldiers of the French army, but also—principally—against the ruling class, that is, against what Ariosto calls the *Capitani*.

Ariosto's most extended comment on the battle of Ravenna thus sets forth, still within the bounds of social decorum, an outspoken and complicated judgment of the public significance of his masters' conduct. The judgment has to be complicated, for this is a complicated world. What in Alfonso's achievement is praiseworthy is singled out for praise; what in the event was disastrous is called disastrous. Something of the same pattern can be seen in the brief account of the battle of Ravenna in Canto XXXIII, added in 1532. The last three lines are noteworthy for their terrifying and merciless concision:

> Di qua la Francia, e di là il campo ingrossa
> La gente Ispana; e la battaglia è grande.
> Cader si vede e far la terra rossa
> La gente d'arme in amendua le bande.
> Piena di sangue uman pare ogni fossa:
> Marte sta in dubbio u' la vittoria mande.
> Per virtù d'un Alfonso al fin si vede
> Che resta il Franco, e che l'Ispano cede,
>
> E che Ravenna saccheggiata resta.*
>   (XXXIII.40-41)

---

and mothers; that have thrown Christ in the Sacrament to the ground to steal from Him a silver tabernacle. Oh wretched Ravenna, it would have been better for you not to have resisted the victor; for Brescia to have taught you rather than for you to teach Rimini and Faenza. Send, Louis, your good old Trivulzio, that he may teach these soldiers of your more restraint, and let him tell them how many, for similar wrongs, have been killed throughout Italy.

* On this side the French crowd the field, on that side the Spaniards; and

That puts it exactly. *Resta il Franco*—the synechdoches express
the detachment, the merciless clarity. Ravenna, however, is
named unmetaphorically, as is her fate. The *virtù* of Alfonso is
made responsible for all three grammatical members—*Che
resta, e che . . . cede,* and *E che Ravenna saccheggiata resta.*
Not that it would have been preferable for Ferrara to have been
sacked. This late mention of the miseries attendant upon victory
thus suggests the same judgment, with the same sharpness and
the same complexity, as the earlier passage.

It is not that Ariosto has been all along a covert partisan of
Spain. The exordium to Canto XXXIV might have applied
especially to France in 1516, but in 1532 it could only be understood as referring to both France and Spain. The sack of Rome is
described in precisely the same tone as the sack of Ravenna
(XXXIII.55). The exordium to Canto XVII refers to both the
French and the Spaniards as divine scourges sent down upon
Italy for her sins. The most extended treatment occurs later in
the same canto, when Ariosto addresses one by one the peoples
and rulers of Europe:

> Voi, gente Ispana, e voi, gente di Francia,
> Volgete altrove, e voi, Svizzeri, il piede,
> E voi, Tedeschi, a far più degno acquisto:
> Che quanto qui cercate è gia di Cristo.
>
> Se Cristianissimi esser voi volete,
> E voi altri Catolici nomati,
> Perché di Cristo gli uomini uccidete?
> Perché de' beni lor son dispogliati?
> Perché Ierusalem non rïavete,
> Che tolto è stato a voi da' rinegati?
> Perché Constantinopoli e del mondo
> La miglior parte occupa il Turco immondo?
>
> Non hai tu, Spagna, l'Africa vicina,
> Che t'ha via più di questa Italia offesa?
> E pur, per dar travaglio alla meschina,
> Lasci la prima tua sì bella impresa.
> O d'ogni vizio fetida sentina,
> Dormi, Italia imbrïaca; e non ti pesa

---

the battle is great. In both bands one sees the gens-d'armes falling and making
the earth red. Every ditch by now seems full of blood; Mars is in doubt where
to send victory. Through the valor of an Alfonso, at the end, one sees that the
Frank remains and that the Spaniard retreats, and that Ravenna is sacked.

Ch'ora di questa gente, ora di quella
Che già serva ti fu, sei fatta ancella?*
(XVII.74-76)[48]

War itself, then, except against the infidel, is an object of
horror to Ariosto. He emphasizes its impiousness, its cruelty, its
motivation in greed. Its wastefulness and the sufferings of the
helpless especially arouse his compassion and indignation. He
repeatedly demands that the reader take stock of all the disasters
of recent Italian history. Even in 1532 he is reminding Alfonso
that his great victory led to the sack of Ravenna, by putting in
an additional reference to it. It is not surprising that Ariosto
uses some conventional complimentary language; nor would it
have been surprising if he had been thoroughly confused amid
the shifting ambiguities of the politics of the time and had simply
avoided committing himself. But he thought and felt his way
to a hard-minded, honest, and consistent position from which he
did not have to waver, no matter what the changes in the political
scene, and he insistently demanded that his reader do the same.
No simple or dogmatic view of things could withstand the
pressure of the times.[49]

The Poet's direct serious commentary on contemporary events,
then, qualifies his courtly praise of his patrons and demands that
the reader make manifold distinctions among levels of reserva-
tion. There are less serious parts of the poem that are also set
against the attitude of praise. The most important of these is
the allegory on fame in Canto XXXV. While on the moon with St.
John the Evangelist, Astolfo watches as an old man throws pieces
of metal engraved with names into a turgid, rushing river. Most
of the names sink, but a few are picked out of the water by two
groups of birds. The larger group is that of the crows and

* You, people of Spain, and you, people of France, and you, Switzers, and
you, Germans, turn your feet elsewhere to more worthy acquisitions; for everything you are seeking here already belongs to Christ. If you wish to be called
Most Christian, and you others Catholic, why do you kill the men of Christ?
Why are they robbed of their goods? Why do you not capture Jerusalem again,
which has been taken from you by the apostates? Why does the filthy Turk
occupy Constantinople and the better part of the world? Do you not, Spain,
have Africa nearby, which has harmed you much more than Italy? But still,
to torture the wretch, you leave your first beauteous undertaking. O stinking
alleyway of all vice, you sleep, drunken Italy, and does it not sorrow you that
you are made the handmaid now of this people, now of that one, who were
formerly your slaves?

vultures; they are unable to carry the names for long and soon let them fall again into the river. There are also two white swans on the scene, who succeed in saving certain names, which they carry to the temple of immortality (XXXV.11-16). As St. John explains to Astolfo, the old man is time, the river is oblivion, and the crows and vultures are

> Ruffiani, Adulatori,
> Buffon, Cinedi, Accusatori, e quelli
> Che viveno alle corti e che vi sono
> Più grati assai che 'l virtuoso, e 'l bono,
>
> E son chiamati Cortigian gentili,
> Perché sanno imitar l'Asino e 'l Ciacco.*
> (XXXV.20-21)

They flatter their lord while he is alive but forget him as soon as he is dead.[50] The swans, who are rare, are the true poets:

> Ma come i Cigni, che cantando lieti
> Rendeno salve le medaglie al tempio;
> Così gli uomini degni da' Poeti
> Son tolti da l'oblio, più che morte empio.
> Oh bene accorti Principi, e discreti,
> Che seguite di Cesare l'esempio,
> E gli scrittor vi fate amici: donde
> Non avete a temer di Lete l'onde!
>
> Son, come i Cigni, anco i Poeti rari,
> Poeti che non sian del nome indegni:
> Si perché il ciel degli uomini preclari
> Non pate mai che troppa copia regni:
> Sì per gran colpa dei Signori avari,
> Che lascian mendicare i sacri ingegni;
> Che le virtù premendo, et esaltando
> I vizii, caccian le buone arti in bando.†
> (XXV.22-23)

---

* Pimps, flatterers, buffoons, faggots, informers, and those who live at courts and are much more pleasing than the good and virtuous, and are called noble courtiers because they know how to imitate the ass and the hog.

† But as the swans, joyously singing, bring the medals safe to the temple, so the poets rescue worthy men from oblivion, which is more cruel than death. O princes wise and discreet indeed, who follow Caesar's example, and make writers your friends, and thus do not have to be afraid of the waves of Lethe! Like swans, the poets are rare—poets who are worthy of the name; both because heaven never allows too great an abundance of noteworthy men and because of the great fault of stingy rulers, who let sacred intellects go begging and who, oppressing virtue and exalting vice, drive humane arts into exile.

So far so good. Now it can hardly have failed to occur to the reader that Ariosto is a poet writing in praise of princes, though he never claims *in propria persona* to bestow immortality upon them. We might expect a complimentary reference to Alfonso and Ippolito here—the saint might go on to predict that they will not be *avari*, for instance, or that they will be worthy of a Virgil, or that without a trumpet for their greatness "Seria fiorito il suo valore invano" (*O.I.* II.21.1), since there were many valiant men before Agamemnon whose memory has perished for want of a holy poet.[51] Not at all. With coruscating wit St. John is made to say:

> Non sì pietoso Enea, né forte Achille
> Fu, come è fama, né sì fiero Ettorre;
> E ne son stati e mille, e mille, e mille,
> Che lor si pon con verità anteporre.
> Ma i donati palazzi e le gran ville
> Dai descendenti lor, gli ha fatto porre
> In questi senza fin sublimi onori
> Da l'onorate man degli scrittori.

> Non fu sì santo né benigno Augusto
> Come la tuba di Virgilio suona.
> L'aver avuto in poesia buon gusto
> La proscrizion iniqua gli perdona.
> Nessun sapria se Neron fosse ingiusto,
> Né sua fama saria forse men buona,
> Avesse avuto e terra e ciel nimici,
> Se gli scrittor sapea tenersi amici.

> Omero Agamennon vittorïoso,
> E fe' i Troian parer vili et inerti:
> E che Penelopea fida al suo sposo
> Dai prochi mille oltraggi avea sufferti.
> E se tu vuoi che 'l ver non ti sia ascoso,
> Tutta al contrario l'istoria converti:
> Che i Greci rotti, e che Troia vittrice,
> E che Penelopea fu meretrice.

> Da l'altra parte odi che fama lascia
> Elissa, ch' ebbe il cor tanto pudico;
> Che riputata viene una bagascia
> Solo perché Maron non le fu amico.
> Non ti maravigliar ch' io n'abbia ambascia,
> E se di ciò diffusamente io dico.

Gli scrittori amo, e fo il debito mio:
Ch' al vostro mondo fui Scrittor anch' io.

E sopra tutti gli altri io feci acquisto
Che non mi può levar tempo né morte;
E ben convenne al mio lodato Cristo
Rendermi guiderdon di sì gran sorte.*
(XXXV.25-29)

This burlesque of the topics of the defense of poetry brings the
reader sharply up against an attitude—assumed humorously and
only for the moment, to be sure—of extreme skepticism and
demands that he entertain the possibility that the Poet, too,
is lying about his patrons. This is done partly for the sheer fun
of it, for the playful indulgence in irreverence. Its serious function
is not to destroy the justified praise of Alfonso and Ippolito, but
to demand again that the reader sift and consider. St. John puts
the whole matter in a way that safeguards the serious aspects of
the poem, it should be noted. For to suppose that Ariosto meant
to suggest that he was lying in praising his patrons is tantamount
to thinking that he meant to suggest that the Evangelist lied about
Christ.

Ariosto is no venal flatterer, as he has sometimes been accused
of being. The attitude toward his patrons displayed in the poem
is complex and sometimes bold. In the direct references to Ippolito and Alfonso, he adheres to the socially prescribed tone of

---

* Aeneas was not so pious, nor Achilles so brave, nor Hector so fierce, as fame
has it; and there have been a thousand and a thousand and a thousand who
could truthfully be put ahead of them: but the palaces and the great villas given
by their descendants have made the honored hands of writers give them this
endlessly sublime honor. Augustus was not so holy nor so benign as Virgil's
trumpet sounds him to be. His having had good taste in poetry buys off his cruel
proscription. No one would know whether or not Nero had been unjust, nor
would his fame be any worse, perhaps, than Augustus', though he had had as
his enemies both earth and heaven, if he had known how to keep the friendship
of the writers. Homer made Agamemnon victorious and made the Trojans seem
cowardly and lazy; and he said that Penelope, faithful to her husband, had
suffered a thousand outrages from the suitors. And if you want the truth not
to be hidden from you, turn the story around just the other way: that the
Greeks were beaten, and that Troy was victorious, and that Penelope was a
whore. On the other hand, listen to what a reputation Dido has left behind, who
had so chaste a heart; for she is thought to have been a slut, just because Virgil
was not her friend. Do not marvel that I concern myself with this and that I
speak at some length about it. I love writers, and I am doing my duty; for in
your world I was a writer, too. And beyond all others I have acquired what
neither time nor death can take from me: and it was quite fitting for the
Christ whom I praised to give me so great a reward.

literary compliment, and he singles out particular actions and qualities for praise. But the total context suggests some disturbing truths about recent Italian history and about rulers in general, in such a way that the compliments to Ippolito and Alfonso, though not necessarily undermined—the passages praising particular deeds, like the deeds themselves, can hardly be canceled—are qualified. The reader is asked *by the context* to winnow the Poet's compliments.

3

The *querelle des femmes* was a staple of polite conversation in the early sixteenth century. Much of the recurrent badinage that makes Castiglione's *Cortegiano* so lively and delightful turns on the irrepressible antifeminism of such interlocutors as Gaspare Pallavicino and the efforts of Cesare Gonzaga and others to defend women. The topics of attack and defense have a very long history, as we have seen earlier. Characteristic of sixteenth-century Italy is the elegant mixture of humorous banter and serious defense. For it is noteworthy that the attacks made on women by Gaspare Pallavicino, Ottaviano Fregoso, and others are at times partly playful and that Castiglione—through his spokesman—still finds it necessary to answer them with a full-scale eulogy of women, complete with classical and modern examples.[52] So it need not surprise us that some of the same concerns and attitudes appear in Ariosto. What is interesting is that, in a series of closely related passages, the Poet oscillates back and forth among conflicting attitudes toward women and toward love. These range from elaborate defense to confidential advice to absolute condemnation.

There are two principal eulogies to the female sex in the *Orlando furioso*, in the exordia to Cantos XX and XXXVII, the latter added in 1532. Canto XX begins:

> Le donne antique hanno mirabil cose
> Fatto ne l'arme et ne le sacre Muse;
> E di dor opre belle e gloriose
> Gran lume in tutto il mondo si diffuse.
> Arpalice e Camilla son famose,
> Perché in battaglia erano esperte et use;
> Safo e Corinna, perché furon dotte,
> Splendono illustri, e mai non veggon notte.

Le donne son venute in eccellenza
Di ciascun' arte ove hanno posto cura:
E qualunque all' istorie abbia avvertenza,
Ne sente ancor la fama non oscura.
Se 'l mondo n'è gran tempo stato senza,
Non però sempre il mal' influsso dura.
E forse ascosi han lor debiti onori
L'invidia o il non saper degli scrittori.

Ben mi par di veder ch' al secol nostro
Tanta virtù fra belle donne emerga,
Che può dare opra a carte et ad inchiostro,
Perché nei futuri anni si disperga;
E perché, odiose lingue, il mal dir vostro
Con vostra eterna infamia si sommerga;
E le lor lode appariranno in guisa,
Che di gran lunga avanzeran Marfisa.*

(XX.1-3)

This short passage gives the schema to which the passage added in 1532 to Canto XXXVII also conforms. Both turn on the question of the fame of women, asserting that they have been deprived of it by the envy and ignorance of writers. Both assert that women deserving of glory have lived in all times, but especially in the present. Both adopt the standard topic of eulogy that asserts the equality of women to men in activities traditionally thought of as the prerogatives of men (here, war and learning). In addition, the later passage enumerates writers of the present age who, unlike writers of other ages, praise women as they deserve as well as several women of the present age who are especially deserving of praise. The later passage also praises the sex by holding up Vittoria Colonna as pre-eminently glorious, not only for her ability as a poetess but for her devotion and

---

* The ladies of antiquity have done marvelous things in arms and in letters; and great fame has spread through all the world of their lovely, glorious deeds. Harpalyce and Camilla are famous because they were experienced and trusty in battle; Sappho and Corinna shine illustrious and never see night because they were learned. Ladies have been excellent in whatever art they have put their efforts to, and whoever pays attention to history still hears their fame, which is far from dark. If the world has been a long time without it, the evil influence will not therefore last forever; and perhaps the envy and the ignorance of writers have hidden their just praises. Surely it seems to me that in our age so much worth is emerging among beautiful ladies that it can give much work to paper and ink in order to be passed on to future years and in order that your calumnies, hateful tongues, may be drowned to your eternal shame: and their praises shall appear in such a way that they shall far surpass Marfisa.

fidelity to her husband. With the exception of the Ariostan theme of the mendacity of writers, the topics and tone of these eulogies are similar to those of the eulogies presented by Castiglione's spokesmen, Giuliano de' Medici and Cesare Gonzaga. Ariosto also presents essentially the same view of the relative culpability of male and female incontinence as does Castiglione (III.37-50), although its vehicle is not the commentary of the Poet, but rather of characters, in particular those of the "sincero e giusto vecchio" of Canto XXVIII and Rinaldo in Canto XXXIII.[53]

Many of the comments of the Poet, both in exordia and elsewhere, are addressed to the ladies. As we have seen, these are not any particular group of ladies; ladies in general are thought of as being an important part of the audience of the poem. The comments addressed to the ladies are of several different kinds. For instance, the exordium of Canto XXXVIII is a defense of Ruggiero's placing his duty to Agramante before his love of Bradamante; it is addressed to an audience of "cortesi donne," who are represented as showing displeasure at the Ruggiero's actions. One of the reasons for addressing to the ladies this assertion of the superiority of duty to love is gently to identify the opposite view as characteristic of women rather than of men, and thus to discredit it slightly. Sometimes, as in X.1-10 (added in 1532), the Poet becomes a confidential Ovidian *praeceptor amoris* warning women against the fickleness of men.[54]

Not all of the comments addressed to the ladies are so simply complimentary as these. Some of the more interesting ones raise the question of whether the Poet is such a friend of ladies as he says he is. For instance, Canto XXII, in which the story of Gabrina's villainous past is recounted, begins:

> Cortesi donne, et grate al vostro amante,
> Voi che d'un solo amor sete contente:
> Come che certo sia, fra tante, e tante,
> Che rarissime siate in questa mente;
> Non vi dispiaccia quel ch' io dissi inante,
> Quando contra Gabrina fui sì ardente;
> E s' ancor son per spendervi alcun verso,
> Di lei biasmando l'animo perverso.
>
> Ella era tale; e come imposto fummi
> Da chi può in me, non preterisco il vero.
> Per questo io non oscuro gli onori summi

D'una, e d'altra, ch'abbia il cor sincero.
Quel che 'l Maestro suo per trenta nummi
Diede a' Iudei, non nocque a Ianni, o a Piero;
Né d'Ipermestra è la fama men bella,
Se ben di tante inique era sorella.

Per una che biasmar cantando ardisco
(Che l'ordinata istoria così vuole),
Lodarne cento incontra m'offerisco,
E far lor virtù chiara più che 'l sole.*
(XXII.1-3)

The passage explicitly says that ladies who are gracious and
faithful to their lovers are very rare.[55] Thus a principal topic of
eulogy is reversed, as when the Poet tells us that Hypermnestra
was the one faithful sister among so many wicked ones. As we
saw in Ovid, a traditional topic is that the whole sex is not to
be blamed for the crimes of a few. Furthermore, by refuting it,
the Poet himself calls attention to the possibility that the inclusion of the story of Gabrina might be regarded as evidence
that he is not a true friend of the ladies. Anxious to dispel that
idea, he offers to praise a hundred for every one he blames—in
other words, since he has just said that the praiseworthy are
very rare, he offers to *falsify* the truth.[56] But what is his reason
for including the story of Gabrina? that it is true and that he
has been commanded not to gloss over the truth. This disclaimer
of control is replaced in the next stanza by his reference to the
ordering of the story—the Poet includes in the poem what *he*
decides to.

An even clearer example is the opening of Canto XXVIII:

Donne, e voi che le donne avete in pregio,
Per Dio, non date a questa istoria orecchia:
A questa che l'ostier dire in dispregio,

* Courteous ladies who are kind to your lovers, you who are content with
a single love, although it is certain that among so many women you who are of
this mind are extremely rare: let not what I said a while ago, when I was so
angry at Gabrina, displease you, nor my spending some more verses on her,
blaming her perverse mind. She was such; and since I have been commanded by
one who has power over me, I do not omit the truth. But for all that I do
not hide the great honor of one and another whose heart was pure. He who gave
his Master to the Jews for thirty pieces of gold did not harm John or Peter; nor
is Hypermnestra's fame any less, though she was the sister of so many wicked
ones. For one whom I dare to blame in my song (for the ordering of the
story necessitates it) I offer to praise a hundred in return and make their virtue
shine brighter than the sun.

E in vostra infamia, e biasmo s'apparecchia;
Benché né macchia vi può dar, né fregio,
Lingua sì vile, e sia l'usanza vecchia
Che 'l volgare ignorante ognun riprenda,
E parli più di quel che meno intenda.

Lasciate questo canto, che senza esso
Può star l'istoria, e non sarà men chiara.
Mettendolo Turpino, anch' io l'ho messo,
Non per malevolenzia né per gara:
Ch' io v'ami, oltre mia lingua che l'ha espresso,
Che mai non fu di celebrarvi avara,
N'ho fatto mille prove; e v'ho dimostro
Ch' io son, né potrei esser se non vostro.

Passi, chi vuol, tre carte, o quattro, senza
Leggerne verso: e chi pur legger vuole,
Gli dia quella medesima credenza
Che si suol dare a finzioni, e a fole.*
(XXVIII.1-3)

The suggestion is even stronger in this passage. The story *is* being told by the host *in vostra infamia*. And he includes it because Turpin does—we could hardly have a clearer signal of the Poet's own intention to include it. Furthermore, it is all very well to say that the innkeeper is one of the *volgare ignorante*; but is the Poet? That is, if the words of the host are in some sense really the words of the Poet, uttered by a tongue that *can* give blame or praise, it is no weakening of the story to denigrate the reliability of the host. The Poet then must be telling it to shame the women. We may notice that in this passage the Poet does not come right out and say that women are not what the story says they are; if the host speaks most of what he does not understand, he may still be telling the truth. What the Poet

---

* Ladies, and you who value the ladies, for God's sake do not listen to this story, this one that the host is getting ready to tell in order to blame and shame you; although so low a tongue can neither detract from nor add to your fame, and although it is an old usage that the ignorant commoner reproaches everyone and speaks most of what he least understands. Skip this canto, for the story can stand and will be no less understandable without it. Since Turpin has put it in, I have put it in, too, not for any ill-will or out of contentiousness. That I love you I have proved a thousand times, besides expressing it with my tongue, which has never been stingy in praising you; and I have shown you that I am yours and could not be anything else. Let her who will skip three or four pages without reading a line of them, and let her who still wishes to read believe them with the faith one gives to fictions and jokes.

says is that he loves the ladies and has always praised them. Is
he one of those mendacious praisers we learned of in the Earthly
Paradise?[57]

At times the Poet comes close to taking over the topics of
the attack on women. One exordium, for instance, asserts that
most women are governed by avarice:[58]

> Cortesi Donne ebbe l'antiqua etade,
> Che le virtù, non le ricchezze, amaro.
> Al tempo nostro si ritrovan rade
> A cui, più del guadagno, altro sia caro.
> Ma quelle che per lor vera bontade
> Non seguon de le più lo stile avaro,
> Vivendo, degne son d'esser contente;
> Gloriose, e immortal poi che fian spente.*
> (XXVI.1)

These different attitudes toward women are expressed as reflections on the events of the story, and much of the central
portion of the poem is concerned with the *querelle des femmes*.
At the very center of the poem (Canto XXIV), Orlando goes
mad from the disappointment of discovering that his beloved
Angelica has accepted another as her lover, and, in a parodic
reductio of Orlando's madness, Rodomonte, betrayed by Doralice, goes off blaspheming against women and declaring himself
their enemy. As we shall see, we are dealing with matters very
close to the thematic heart of the work. Rodomonte delivers a
full-scale invective against the female sex:

> —Oh feminile ingegno (egli dicea),
> Come ti volgi e muti facilmente,
> Contrario oggetto proprio de la fede!
> Oh infelice, oh miser chi ti crede!
>
> Né lunga servitù, né grand'amore
> Che ti fu a mille prove manifesto,
> Ebbono forza di tenerti il core,
> Che non fossi a cangiarsi almen sì presto.
> Non perch'a Mandricardo inferiore
> Io ti paressi, di te privo resto;

* Ancient times had courteous ladies who loved the virtues and not riches:
in our time they are rarely found who love anything more than gain. But those
ladies who in their true goodness do not imitate the greedy style of most, they
are worthy of being happy while they are alive, glorious and immortal after they
die.

Né so trovar cagione ai casi miei,
Se non quest'una, che femina sei.

Credo che t'abbia la Natura e Dio
Produtto, o scelerato sesso, al mondo
Per una soma, per un grave fio
De l'uom, che senza te saria giocondo:
Come ha produtto anco il Serpente rio
E il Lupo, e l'Orso, e fa l'aer fecondo
E di Mosche, e di Vespe, e di Tafani,
E Loglio e Avena fa nascer tra i grani.

Perché fatto non ha l'alma Natura,
Che senza te potesse nascer l'uomo,
Come s'inesta per umana cura
L'un sopra l'altro il Pero, il Sorbo e'l Pomo?
Ma quella non può far sempre a misura;
Anzi, s' io vo' guardar come io la nomo,
Veggo che non può far cosa perfetta,
Poi che la Natura femina vien detta.

Non siate però tumide e fastose,
Donne, per dir che l'uom sia vostro figlio:
Che de le spine ancor nascon le rose,
E d'una fetida erba nasce il Giglio:
Importune, superbe, dispettose,
Prive d'amor, di fede, e di consiglio;
Temerarie, crudeli, inique, ingrate,
Per pestilenzia eterna al mondo nate.—*
(XXVII.117-121)

Rodomonte is of course a comically passionate attacker, entirely

---

* "Oh mind of woman," he was saying, "how you turn and change easily, the exact opposite of faithfulness! Oh unhappy, oh wretched he who relies on you! Neither my long service nor the great love that was plain to you from many proofs had the power to hold your heart or even to prevent it at least from changing so quickly. I am not deprived of you because I seemed to you inferior to Mandricardo; nor can I find any cause of my misfortunes than this one, that you are a woman. Oh wicked sex, I believe that God and Nature have brought you forth into the world to be a burden, a heavy penalty, to man, who without you would be happy: just as they have brought forth the wicked snake and the wolf and the bear, and have made the air fecund with flies and wasps and mosquitoes, and have made chaff and oats grow amid the wheat. Why has not Mother Nature made man so that he could be born without you, as the pear, the crabapple, and the apple are grafted one on the other by human skill? But she cannot always do aright; indeed, if I look how I name her, I see that she can make nothing perfect, since Nature is always called a woman. Then do not be puffed up and proud, ladies, because man is your son; for roses are born from thorns, and the lily is born of a stinking weed: importunate, proud, disdainful, lacking in love, faithfulness, and wits, hasty, cruel, wicked, ungrateful, you were born to the world as an eternal pestilence."

unaware of how ridiculous a figure he cuts as he wanders along
venting his disappointment:

> Con queste, et altre, et infinite appresso
> Querele il Re di Sarza se ne giva,
> Or ragionando in un parlar sommesso,
> Quando in un suon che di lontan s'udiva,
> In onta e in biasmo del femineo sesso.*
>   (XXVII.122)

Any possible seriousness he might possess as a disappointed lover
is also destroyed by the fact that Doralice did in fact desert him
because she found Mandricardo superior. We are invited to look
down with malicious amusement on Rodomonte, identifying
ourselves not with him but with the sexually successful Mandricardo.

Rodomonte's comic invective is rather conspicuous by its
length, and the Poet's comments are quite significant:

> E certo da ragion si dispartiva;
> Che per una, o per due, che trovi ree,
> Che cento buone sien creder si dee.
>
> Se ben di quante io n'abbia fin qui amate,
> Non n'abbia mai trovata una fedele,
> Perfide tutte io non vo' dir, né ingrate,
> Ma darne colpa al mio destin crudele.
> Molte or ne sono, e più già ne son state,
> Che non dan causa ad uom che si querele:
> Ma mia fortuna vuol che s'una ria
> Ne sia tra cento, io di lei preda sia.
>
> Pur vo' tanto cercar prima ch' io mora,[59]
> Anzi prima che 'l crin più mi s'imbianchi,
> Che forse dirò un dì, che per me ancora
> Alcuna sia che di sua fé non manchi.
> Se questo avvien (che di speranza fuora
> Io non ne son), non fia mai ch' io mi stanchi
> Di farla a mia possanza gloriosa
> Con lingua, e con inchiostro, e in verso, e in prosa.†
>   (XXVII.122-124)

---

* With these and other and countless more complaints, the King of Sarza
went along, now speaking in a low voice, now with a loudness that was heard
from afar, all to the shame and blame of the female sex.
† And certainly he had taken leave of reason; since for one or two wicked
ones you find, you must believe that there are a hundred good ones. Though
among all those whom I have loved up to now, I have never found a faithful

Whereas in XXII.1 and in XXVI.1 the Poet explicitly states that women who are faithful or who care for anything but gain are rare, here he suggests that there are a hundred good ones for every one or two wicked ones. We recall that XXII.3 had promised that for each one the Poet blamed he would praise a hundred. Is this passage a fulfillment of the promise? If so, it is remarkably ineffectual. Rodomonte was not speaking reasonably—because one must *believe* that there are more virtuous than vicious women; one must have faith. And the Poet says he has faith, even though the empirical evidence he has gathered in his own experience conflicts with it, even though he has never found a woman who was faithful to him. He will go on looking, however, he says, before his hair gets any whiter—a touch suggesting he has already spent the better part of a lifetime in the fruitless search and that his chances of finding one are rather slight.

A similar contrast between what one may say and what experience suggests underlies the stanzas that announce the Poet's decision to punish Rodomonte, which we have already looked at in another connection:

> Donne gentil, per quel ch' a biasmo vostro
> Parlò contra il dover, sì offeso sono,
> Che sin che col suo mal non gli dimostro
> Quanto abbia fatto error, non gli perdono.
> Io farò sì con penna, e con inchiostro,
> Ch' ognun vedrà che gli era utile e buono
> Aver taciuto, et mordersi anco poi
> Prima la lingua, che dir mal di voi.

> Ma che parlò come ignorante e sciocco,
> Ve lo dimostra chiara esperienzia.
> Già contra tutte trasse fuor lo stocco
> De l'ira, senza farvi differenzia.*

(XXIX.2-3)

---

one, I don't call them all perfidious or ungrateful; instead I blame my cruel destiny. There are many now and there have been more in the past who give no man cause to complain; but my luck has it that if there is one wicked one among a hundred, I become her prey. Still I intend to seek so much before I die, indeed, before my hair gets any whiter, that perhaps one day I shall say that for me too there is one whose faith does not falter. If this happens (for I have not lost all hope yet), I shall never tire in making her glorious, according to my power, with pen and ink, and in verse and prose.

* Gentle ladies, I am so incensed by what he said in blame of you, contrary to how one should speak, that until with his own ill I have shown him

What angers the Poet is the fact that Rodomonte spoke out against women, not, apparently, that he entertained certain opinions but that he voiced them. Rodomonte should have known that it is *utile e buono* not to speak ill of women, no matter how badly one wants to. He spoke *contra il dover: contra il vero* could have been fitted into the line easily enough. The fact that the Poet must intervene in the events of the poem in order to teach Rodomonte his lesson—must change the otherwise "natural" course of events by what, in the analogy of the poet to God and the poem to the world, is a miracle—conveys some suggestion that only in a literary contrivance does experience vindicate women. Still, of course, the Poet, as the reader is well aware, is misrepresenting the poem: Isabella does not die merely because the Poet wishes to punish Rodomonte. The third stanza of the exordium rights the balance, as it were.

The climax of the Poet's own antifeminism comes in a comment upon the one occasion in the poem in which Orlando meets Angelica, when neither recognizes the other because Orlando is both mad and disfigured. Orlando is made to attack Angelica, who is traveling to the East with Medoro, and she escapes only narrowly, when she uses a ring that makes her invisible. The Poet exclaims:

> Deh maledetto sia l'annello, et anco
> Il cavallier che dato le l'avea:
> Che se non era, avrebbe Orlando fatto
> Di sé vendetta e di mill'altri a un tratto.
>
> Né questa sola, ma fosser pur state
> In man d'Orlando quante oggi ne sono:
> Ch'ad ogni modo tutte sono ingrate,
> Non si trova tra lor oncia di buono.*
> (XXIX.73-74)

---

how great an error he committed, I shall not pardon him. I shall do so much with pen and ink that everyone will see that it would have been useful and good for him to have been silent, or even to have bitten his tongue, rather than speak ill of you. But that he spoke like an ignoramus and a fool, plain experience shows you. He drew the blade of his anger against all women, without making any distinctions among them.

* Ah, cursed be the ring and also the knight who gave it to her! for if it had not been, Orlando would have avenged himself and a thousand others all at once. And I wish that not she alone had been in Orlando's hands, but also all the women alive today; for in any case they are all ungrateful, nor is there to be found among them an ounce of goodness.

And the canto abruptly ends.

The spectrum of the Poet's attitudes toward women, then, is quite broad, ranging from rather formal eulogy to violent anger, as in this last example. It is all done with an urbane and charming *disinvoltura*, which may blind us to its thematic and structural importance. Why does Ariosto have his Narrator adopt these conflicting attitudes toward women? The reason is that like Orlando and Rodomonte, the Poet is in love. Like Orlando and Rodomonte, the Poet is unlucky in love. Like Orlando and Rodomonte, finally, he is mad. At every important stage in the narrative, Ariosto stresses the parallelism between the experience of the Poet and that of his characters.

The parallelism of the Poet's and the characters' experience is stressed from the very beginning of the poem, in a tone of Horatian self-mockery:

> Dirò d'Orlando in un medesimo tratto
> Cosa non detta in prosa mai né in rima;
> Che per amor venne in furore e matto,
> D'uom che sì saggio era stimato prima;
> Se da colei che tal quasi m'ha fatto,
> Che 'l poco ingegno ad or, ad or mi lima,
> Me ne sarà però tanto concesso,
> Che mi basti a finir quanto ho promesso.*
>
> (I.2)

Whereas Boiardo ascribed his poetic powers to love, Ariosto here humorously adopts an exactly contrary position. In this passage love is represented as an obstacle to poetic achievement, and the lady's effect on the Poet is ironically represented by an image—that of the file—which was traditionally used of the poet's ceaseless labor over his poem (as in the Horatian "limae labor," *Ars poetica*, 291). If the Poet is as mad as Orlando, we may immediately ask, how can he have the power of mind to say things yet unattempted in prose or verse? Part of the effect of the passage is thus the characteristic Ariostan assertion of control over the poem. Equally important, however, is the fact

---

* At the same time, I shall tell about Orlando things never yet said in prose or rhyme: how for love he went raving mad, from a man who had formerly been thought so wise; if she who has almost made me like that, who keeps filing away at my small wit, will still concede me enough wit to finish what I have promised.

that the very first mention in the poem of Orlando's madness, the central theme, is accompanied by mention of the Poet's own madness.

Another important reference to the parallelism occurs at the beginning of Canto IX. In Canto VIII, after the transition that leaves Angelica exposed on the rock for the sea monster, the narrative turns to Orlando for the first time. He is obsessed by worry about losing Angelica, and, after a powerfully described dream in which he loses her in a wood in a storm, he leaves Paris in search of her. His quest is thus put under way. It will carry him all over Europe through a series of ironic frustrations, to the shepherd's hut where he learns the news that drives him mad. As Orlando starts out, the Poet comments:

> Che non può far d'un cor ch' abbia suggetto
> Questo crudele, traditore Amore,
> Poi ch' ad Orlando può levar del petto
> La tanta fé che debbe al suo Signore?
> Già savio e pieno fu d'ogni rispetto,
> E della Santa Chiesa difensore:
> Or per un vano amor, poco del Zio,
> E di sé poco, e men cura di Dio.

> Ma l'escuso io purtroppo, e mi rallegro
> Nel mio difetto aver compagno tale;
> Ch' anch' io sono al mio ben languido et egro,
> Sano e gagliardo a seguitare il male.*
>
> (IX.1-2)

"Video meliora proboque, deteriora sequor"—here is the witty, self-indulgent, and self-mocking Ovidian tone, the Petrarchan "io fallo e vedo il mio fallir," the Pauline divided man, described in banter. The passage serves to emphasize the abrupt discontinuity between Orlando's usual activities and the conduct to which his futile love for Angelica drives him. The parallel is introduced in more general terms—Orlando is going out on a specific quest, but the particular ways in which the Poet is

---

* What cannot he do with a heart that he has subdued, this cruel, treacherous Love, since he can remove from Orlando's breast all the duty he owes his lord? Formerly he was wise and full of all respect, defender of Holy Church: now because of a vain love he cares little for his uncle, little for himself, and even less for God. But I excuse him, alas, and I am gladdened to find such a companion in my faults; for I too am weak and languid toward the good, healthy and full of vigor in following after evil.

"sano e gagliardo a seguitare il male" are not specified here. The way is thus cleared for a perception of the analogy between the Poet's experience and the reader's. The tone invites us laughingly to admit that we have the same difficulty in doing what we should.

An equally important humorous appearance of the parallel between the Poet and Orlando appears at the opening of Canto XXXV, during the account of Astolfo's trip to the moon to fetch Orlando's lost wits:

Chi salirà per me, Madonna, in cielo
A riportarne il mio perduto ingegno?
Che, poi ch'uscì da' bei vostri occhi il telo
Che 'l cor mi fisse, ognior perdendo vegno.
Né di tanta iattura mi querelo,
Pur che non cresca, ma stia a questo segno;
Ch' io dubito, se più si va sciemando,
Di venir tal, qual ho descritto Orlando.

Per riaver l'ingegno mio m'è aviso
Che non bisogna che per l'aria io poggi
Nel cerchio de la Luna o in Paradiso;
Che 'l mio non credo che tanto alto alloggi.
Ne' bei vostri occhi, e nel sereno viso,
Nel sen d'avorio, e alabastrini poggi
Se ne va errando; et io con queste labbia
Lo corrò, se vi par ch' io lo riabbia.*

(XXXV.1-2)

The marvelously subtle tone of this passage is almost impossible to define. There is an Ovidian sense of disparity in the comparison; the Poet is no titanic Orlando, nor is he even very mad. He is not himself running naked through the sands of the Sahara, nor have his wits taken flight as far as to the moon; what he is obsessed with is of the earth. There is surely a covert jibe here at the fashionable Platonic conception of love. The compliment

* Who will climb up to the sky for me, Lady, to bring back down again my lost wits? which, since the arrow left your lovely eyes to pierce my heart, I keep on losing. Nor do I complain of such a loss, as long as it does not grow greater, but stays at this level; for I am afraid that if they grow any less I shall become such as I have described Orlando. To get my wits back it is my opinion that it is not necessary for me to soar through the air up to the sphere of the moon or to Paradise; for I do not believe mine have lodged so high. In your lovely eyes and bright face, in your ivory breast and alabaster hills they go wandering; and I shall gather them with these lips, if it please you that I regain them.

is urbane and at the same time magnificently impudent in the
exactness with which the parallel is carried out. Furthermore,
there is a slight shift in the Poet's attitude in the course of the
passage, and some of the effect depends upon it. He is losing
his wits for love of the lady, he says. He will regain them if she
will let him make love to her. But his madness is his love for
her; does he mean that if she does he will cease to love her?
Naturally not, but the suggestion lurks slyly in the lines, and
we are reminded of the passage (IX.1-10, added in 1532) in
which the Poet warns the ladies not always to believe lovers
who swear eternal loyalty, for most of them will cease to love
once they have had their way.

The central statement concerning the madness of love interrupts the account of Orlando's loss of sanity, at the exact center
of the poem:

> Chi mette il piè su l'amorosa pania,
> Cerchi ritrarlo, e non v'inveschi l'ale;
> Che non è in somma amor, se non insania,
> A giudizio de' Savi universale.
> E se ben come Orlando ognun non smania,
> Suo furor mostra a qualch'altro segnale.
> E quale è di pazzia segno più espresso
> Che, per altri voler, perder se stesso?
>
> Varii gli effetti son; ma la pazzia
> È tutt' una però, che li fa uscire.
> Gli è come una gran selva, ove la via
> Conviene a forza, a chi vi va, fallire.
> Chi su, chi giù, chi qua, chi là, travia.
> Per concludere in somma, io vi vo' dire:
> A chi in amor s'invecchia, oltr' ogni pena
> Si convengono i ceppi e la catena.
>
> Ben mi si potria dir:—Frate, tu vai
> L'altrui mostrando, e non vedi il tuo fallo.—
> Io vi rispondo che comprendo assai,
> Or che di mente ho lucido intervallo:
> Et ho gran cura (e spero farlo ormai)
> Di riposarmi, e d'uscir fuor di ballo;
> Ma tosto far, come vorrei, nol posso,
> Che 'l male è penetrato infin' a l'osso.*
>
> (XXIV.1-3)

* He who puts his foot on the birdlime of love, let him try to withdraw it,
and let him not get his wings stuck there; for love is finally nothing but mad-

This is a centrally important thematic statement, and we must take adequate account of it. In order to do so I shall devote some attention directly to the themes of the poem. The passage uses the image of a wood (*selva*) in which all who are in love are wandering lost, and it thus explicitly identifies one of the major symbols of the poem. All the characters in the poem are in love —they are heedlessly pursuing some object of desire. They rush through the poem in pursuit of what turn out to be trivial and ultimately illusory goals. It is the placid Astolfo, the most absurd of the paladins, who is granted the vision of the universal madness of mankind in the valley of lost things on the moon (Canto XXXIV). The inventory of lost things is long—here are reputations, prayers, lovers' tears and sighs, time, vain plans and hopes, power, gold presented to princes, adulation, princely favors, treaties, the Donation of Constantine, and women's beauty. The one thing Astolfo does not find much of is insanity, since it is all on earth. There is a mountain of lost wits, however:

> Del suo gran parte vide il Duca franco:
> Ma molto più maravigliar lo fenno
> Molti ch' egli credea che dramma manco
> Non dovessero averne, e quivi dénno
> Chiara notizia che ne tenean poco,
> Che molta quantità n'era in quel loco.
>
> Altri in amar lo perde, altri in onori;
> Altri in cercar, scorrendo il mar, richezze;
> Altri ne le speranze de' Signori:
> Altri dietro alle magiche sciochezze.
> Altri in gemme, altri in opre di pittori:
> Et altri in altro, che più d'altro apprezze.*
> (XXIV.84-85)

---

ness, in the universal judgment of the wise: and although not everyone rages like Orlando, he demonstrates his insanity with some other sign. And what is a plainer sign of madness than, through desiring another, to lose oneself? The effects are various, but the madness that produces them is still all one. It is like a great forest where he who goes must necessarily lose his way; this one goes astray up, this one down, this one here, this one there. To conclude, I tell you: whoever grows old in love needs, beyond all other punishment, shackles and chains. It could well be said to me: "Brother, you go showing others their failings, and you do not see your own." I reply to you that I understand very well, now that I have a lucid interval of mind; and I am taking great pains (and I hope to do it soon) to rest and to get out of the dance: but I cannot do it as quickly as I would like, for the sickness has penetrated to my bones.

* The noble duke saw a great part of his own there, but he wondered much more at many who, he had thought, could not lack a dram of theirs and there

The madness of Orlando is simply the extreme form of what is universal. *La pazzia è tutt' una*—the powerful rhetoric of the last-quoted stanza reduces all men and all their goals to the same level: "et altri in altro, che più d'altro apprezze." Their madness is "per altri voler, perder se stesso" (XXIV.1).[60]

Each character rushes after the will-o'-the-wisp of his fantasy, through the forest of appearances. One of the fundamental patterns of the poem is that of motion in space, and here Ariosto is, of course, taking over a well-established body of symbol. Boiardo had sent Orlando, Rinaldo, Sacripante, and Ferraú to the four corners of the world in pursuit of Angelica, that archetypally fickle object of desire; he had made Mandricardo's aim the acquisition of Durindana, Gradasso's that of Durindana and Baiardo; he had had Brunello steal Sacripante's horse and Marfisa's armor. The most brilliant parts of the *Orlando furioso* regularly involve the intersection of these trajectories and the head-on conflict of desire either with the essential illusoriness of the world of appearances or with the desires of other characters. Much of the action does take place in a forest—the forest of Ardennes, in which so much of the action of Boiardo's poem had taken place. It is a familiar forest, and not only from Boiardo. It is the forest of the opening of the *Divina Commedia*; it is the forest of Arthurian romance, especially in its systematic symbolic development in such works as the *Queste del saint Graal*.[61] The forest traversed by myriad paths was by the time of Ariosto a particularly well-established symbol of man's life, and in a sense Ariosto's forest is all geographical space. Ariosto's lines are an adaptation of Stertinius' description of the madness of mankind in Horace's *Satires* II.3:

> nunc accipe quare
> Desipiant omnes aeque ac tu, qui tibi nomen
> Insano posuere. Velut silvis, ubi passim
> Palantis error certo de tramite pellit,
> Ille sinistrorsum, hic dextrorsum abit, unus utrique
> Error, sed variis illudit partibus; hoc te

give clear indication of having but little; for there was a great quantity of wits in that place. Some lose it loving, others for honors, others in seeking riches by scouring the sea; others lose it hoping to get something from their lords, others throw it away for the nonsense of magic; others for gems, others for the works of painters, and others for some other thing that they prize more than anything else.

Crede modo insanum, nihilo ut sapientior ille
Qui te deridet caudam trahat.*   (46-53)

The theme of universal madness had had a long history before Ariosto made it the central theme of his poem, and the
Orlando furioso sums up and imposes order on these various
traditional views. When Orlando goes literally mad, for instance,
he partly conforms to the medieval tradition of love-madness,
as it appears in Chrétien de Troyes and the Tristan legend. In
these works, madness is conceived essentially as a reduction of
man to a bestial level—the knight tears off his clothes and lives
savagely in the woods.[62] Orlando does not merely go off to the
woods, however; he continues traveling—now entirely without
purpose, just as previously he had traveled with an illusory purpose. A more important conception of madness in the poem is
that inherited from the Stoics through Horace and Erasmus—
behavior that departs from a rational norm, often by attributing
an inflated value to some object.[63]

There is another major conception of madness in the poem,
also derived in part from Horace: madness as inconsistency.
Perhaps the clearest expression of it in Horace occurs in the
description of Tigellius in *Satires* I.3.[64]

Nil aequale homini fuit illi: saepe velut qui
Currebat fugiens hostem, persaepe velut qui
Iunonis sacra feret; habebat saepe ducentos,
Saepe decem servos; modo reges atque tetrarchas,
Omnia magna loquens, modo "sit mihi mensa tripes et
Concha salis puri et toga quae defendere frigus,
Quamvis crassa, queat." Deciens centena dedisses
Huic parco, paucis contento, quinque diebus
Nil erat in loculis. Noctes vigilabat ad ipsum
Mane, diem totum stertebat. Nil fuit unquam
Sic impar sibi.†   (9-19)

---

* Now listen to why everyone who called you insane is just as insane as you
are. As in the woods, where in some places error leads wayfarers from the sure
path, and this one goes off to the left, that one to the right, the same error
leading them both astray, but in different directions; think yourself insane,
in such a way that the fellow who derides you is not a whit wiser and unwitting
is dragging his own tail.

† There was no consistency in the man: sometimes he ran like a man fleeing
the enemy, often he walked like a priest bearing offerings to Juno. Sometimes
he had two hundred, sometimes ten slaves; sometimes he talked all kings and
tetrarchs and everything big, at other times he would say, "Let there be on

The inconsistency of man, even in his most intense feelings and desires, is a central theme of the *Orlando furioso*. There is not a single major character in the poem who does not live through an abrupt psychological change or a series of discontinuities. Not only does Orlando, the chief hero of Christendom, disregard all his duties, but he goes entirely mad; later he is just as abruptly cured of his madness by reinhaling his wits. Ruggiero is carried off to Alcina's island by the hippogriff and forgets all about his beloved Bradamante in his fervid love affair with Alcina. Rinaldo, who in Boiardo's poem had oscillated between love and hatred of Angelica, is abruptly cured of his passion by the monster Sdegno. Sacripante is in one instant the sentimental elegiast, in the next the cynical rapist (Canto I).

One could multiply such examples indefinitely. One of the most important forms of the theme of human mutability is that of betrayal. Ruggiero's situation throughout the poem is that of a conflict between his duty to his lord and to Bradamante; Orlando's faithfulness to Angelica sends him after her like Ceres after Prosperina (Prosperina, the symbol of seasonal change); but both Ruggiero and Orlando are to meet untimely deaths because of the treachery of the House of Mainz. Indeed, there is hardly an episode in the poem that does not revolve around the theme of fidelity and betrayal, whether it be a vassal's betrayal of his lord, a wife's infidelity to her husband, a friend's disloyalty, or a knight's breaking his pledged word. All the characters who claim our sympathy—and they are usually models of fidelity—are the victims of betrayal, often more than once. Zerbino and Isabella are betrayed by Odorico; Zerbino is later betrayed by Gabrina; Brandimarte is killed from behind by Gradasso; Olimpia is deserted by Bireno after giving superhuman proof of her devotion to him; Ariodante and Ginevra are betrayed by Polinesso; Grifone is betrayed by Martano and Orrigille. Gradasso, Marsilio, and Agramante are all oath breakers. Doralice betrays Rodomonte for Mandricardo, and she is ready to be un-

---

my table tripe and a shell with pure salt, and let me have a toga that can keep off the cold, even though it be rough." If you gave a thousand to this frugal fellow who was so content with little, in five days he'd have nothing in his pockets. He would stay up all night to morning, snore out the whole day. There has been never been anything that varied so much from itself.

true to the memory of Mandricardo before he is even buried. Rodomonte deserts his lord. Even the minor episodes and novelle in the poem involve the theme. The desertion of the Cretan women by the Argonauts, for instance, results in the founding of the city of the Amazons; the novelle of Fiammetta, Gabrina, Melissa, and Anselmo all turn on the unfaithfulness of women. Finally, it is the knowledge that Angelica has, as he thinks of it, played him false that drives Orlando mad.

Faced by the spectacle of the universal madness in the poem, the reader is not allowed to become a Stertinius or a Damasippus. It is not true that all forms of madness are equally bad. Like Horace, Ariosto insists that the reader retain his common sense and keep distinctions clear. This is one reason why the Poet has his own, not too serious, form of the universal madness. He is mad, but he knows it, and he is not as mad as Orlando. To live is to desire, and all desire is in some sense infatuation, but there are more and less harmful levels. This is of course an adaptation of the Horatian method of *Satires* II.3 and elsewhere, deeply influenced also by Ovid and Petrarch. The last stanza of the exordium to Canto XXIV, already quoted, is a good example of the complexity of the tone. The Poet has just been explaining that all love is madness:

> Ben mi si potria dir:—Frate, tu vai
> L'altrui mostrando, e non vedi il tuo fallo.—
> Io vi rispondo che comprendo assai,
> Or che di mente ho lucido intervallo:
> Et ho gran cura (e spero farlo ormai)
> Di riposarmi, e d'uscir fuor di ballo;
> Ma tosto far, come vorrei, nol posso,
> Che 'l male è penetrato in fin' a l'osso.
> (XXIV.3)

The stanza is designed to have a function similar to Horace's "quid tu? nullane habes vitia?" (what about you? have you no faults? *Serm.* I.3.19-20),[65] though it avoids the relative bluntness of Horace's lines by its humor. Along with the first two stanzas, however, the proem to XXIV is also a parody of Petrarch's sonnet 99:

> Poi che voi et io più volte abbiam provato
> come 'l nostro sperar torni fallace,

dietr' a quel sommo ben che mai non spiace
levate il core a più felice stato.

Questa vita terrena è quasi un prato
che 'l serpente tra' fiori e l'erba giace;
e, s' alcuna sua vista a gli occhi piace,
è per lassar più l'animo invescato.

Voi dunque, se cercate aver la mente
anzi l'estremo dì queta già mai,
seguite i pochi e non la volgar gente.

Ben si po dire a me:—Frate, tu vai
mostrando altrui la via, dove sovente
fosti smarrito et or se' più che mai.—*

The fact that Ariosto's Poet answers the charge is one of the keys
to the difference between the two passages. Petrarch's sonnet
dramatizes the split between knowledge of the way to a higher
good and inability to pursue it, but it goes no further; it even suggests that there is no way to bridge the gap, and in this respect it
mirrors the themes of the *Canzoniere* as a whole. But the Poet
of the *Orlando* has an answer. In part it is the rich humor and
urbanity of his admission, but there is a more serious aspect.
Just as the accusation is different (*sei smarrito* versus *non vedi
il tuo fallo*), so the answer is different: the Poet does see, in
this lucid interval, and this at least gives him the hope of
leaving the dance.

But the Poet is mad. He is mad in being in love, and he is
mad in his inconsistency. This is the point of his conflicting
attitudes toward love and especially toward women. His attitude
undergoes precisely the same changes as those of his characters,
the most important and emphatic parallel in this respect being
with Rodomonte. We have seen how Rodomonte, infuriated by
Doralice's rejection of him in favor of Mandricardo, deserts his
lord and goes off blaspheming against womankind. He retires to
a deserted church to brood, but when Isabella turns up one day

---

* Since you and I have many times experienced how our hopes turn out to
be mistaken, lift your hearts to a happier state, in pursuit of that highest good
which never fails. This mortal life is like a meadow where the serpent lies amid
the grass and the flowers; and, if any appearance of it pleases the eyes, the result is to lime the soul more deeply. You therefore, if you hope ever to have
quiet minds before the last day, follow the few and not the crowd. Someone
could very well say to me, "Brother, you keep showing others the way, when
you have often been astray, and are now, more than ever."

he promptly falls in love with her, in a characteristically abrupt about-face. But even Rodomonte's fulminations against feminine inconstancy are delivered in a series of abrupt shifts of tone: "Or ragionando in un parlar sommesso, / Quando in un suon che di lontan s'udiva" (XXVII.122). He is like a sick man tossing in his bed—an analogy that will recur.[66]

> Naviga il giorno e la notte seguente
> Rodomonte col cor d'affanni grave;
> E non si può l'ingiuria tor di mente,
> Che da la donna e dal suo Re avuto have;
> E la pena e il dolor medesmo sente,
> Che sentiva a cavallo, ancora in nave:
> Né spegner può, per star ne l'acqua, il fuoco;
> Né può stato mutar, per mutar luoco.
>
> Come l'infermo, che dirotto e stanco
> Di febbre ardente, va cangiando lato;
> O sia su l'uno o sia su l'altro fianco
> Spera aver, se si volge, miglior stato;
> Né sul destro riposa, né sul manco,
> Et per tutto ugualmente è travagliato:
> Così il Pagano al male ond' era infermo
> Mal trova in terra e male in acqua schermo.*
>   (XXVIII.89-90)

When Rodomonte inconsequentially abandons his antifeminism to fall in love with Isabella, the Poet exclaims:

> O degli uomini inferma e instabil mente!
> Come siam presti a variar disegno:
> Tutti i pensier mutamo facilmente,
> Più quei che nascon d'amoroso sdegno.
> Io vidi dianzi il Saracin sì ardente
> Contra le donne, e passar tanto il segno,
> Che non che spegner l'odio, ma pensai
> Che non dovesse intiepidirlo mai.†
>   (XXIX.1)

---

* Rodomonte sails that day and the following night, his heart heavy with trouble; and he cannot get that injury out of his mind which he has received from his lady and from his king; and on the ship he still feels the same pain and sorrow he felt on horseback: nor through being in the water can he put out his fire, nor change his state by changing his place. As a sick man who, broken and tired out with burning fever, keeps changing sides; either on one or the other side he hopes, if he turns over, to feel better; but he finds rest neither on the right nor the left one, and on both he is equally tortured: so Rodomonte shields himself against the evil with which he was sick, poorly on land and poorly on water.

† Oh uncertain and unstable mind of man! how ready we are to change plans! we readily change our thoughts, especially those born of amorous scorn.

The first line picks up the words with which Rodomonte had
earlier accused women: "O feminil ingegno (egli dicea), / Come
ti volgi e muti facilmente" (XXVII.117). The next stanzas of
this exordium we have already examined. They present the
Poet in the role of defender of women and promise to punish
Rodomonte. Now the twenty-ninth canto is a very important one
for the Poet's attitude toward women because, as we have seen,
at the very end of it he wishes Orlando had done Angelica in, and
he asserts that all women are faithless (XXIX. 73-74). In other
words, he has acted out the same pattern of inconsistency as
Rodomonte, only in reverse. The very next stanza is the first of
Canto XXX:

> Quando vincer da l'impeto e da l'ira
> Si lascia la ragion, né si difende,
> E che 'l cieco furor sì inanzi tira
> O mano o lingua, che gli amici offende;
> Se ben dipoi si piagne e si sospira,
> Non è per questo che l'error s'emende.
> Lasso! io mi doglio e affligo invan di quanto
> Dissi per ira al fin de l'altro canto.
>
> Ma simile son fatto ad uno infermo,
> Che dopo molta pazienzia, e molta,
> Quando contra il dolor non ha più schermo,
> Cede alla rabbia, e a bestemmiar si volta.
> Manca il dolor, né l'impeto sta fermo,
> Che la lingua al dir mal facea sí sciolta:
> E si ravvede e pente e n'ha dispetto;
> Ma quel c'ha detto, non può far non detto.
>
> Ben spero, donne, in vostra cortesia
> Aver da voi perdon, poi ch' io vel chieggio.
> Voi scusarete, che per frenesia,
> Vinto da l'aspra passion, vaneggio.
> Date la colpa alla nimica mia,
> Che mi fa star, ch' io non potrei star peggio,
> E mi fa dir quel di ch' io son poi gramo.
> Sallo Iddio, s'ella ha il torto; essa, s'io l'amo.
>
> Non men son fuor di me, che fosse Orlando;
> E non son men di lui di scusa degno. *
>   (XXX.1-4)

A while ago I saw the Saracen so inflamed against women and going so far
beyond the limit, that I thought his anger would never cool, let alone be ex-
tinguished.
* When reason allows herself to be vanquished by the impulse of anger

Because of the similarity of tone to that of the moral exordia, and because the occasion of the moralizing is identified only at the end of the first stanza as the Poet's action rather than, as is usual, a character's, the reader is at first hoodwinked into taking this seriously. It quickly turns into a masterpiece of straight-faced foolery. Its length and emphasis depend upon the centrality of the themes. Like Orlando, the Poet has failed to make proper distinctions:

> Qual lascia morto e qual storpiato lassa:
> Poco si ferma, e sempre inanzi passa.
>
> Avrebbe così fatto, o poco manco,
> Alla sua donna, se non s'ascondea:
> Perché non discernea il nero dal bianco,
> E di giovar nocendo si credea.*
> (XXIX.72-73)

We discover that the Poet, like Rodomonte, has demonstrated the truth of what the *sincero e giusto vecchio* had said of the author of the tale of Fiammetta. They have spoken in anger and repented later:

> A chi tel narrò non do credenza,
> S'Evangelista ben fosse nel resto;
> Ch' opinïone, più ch' esperïenza
> Ch' abbia di donne, lo facea dir questo;
> L'avere ad una, o due malivolenza
> Fa ch' odia e biasma l'altre oltre a l'onesto;
> Ma se gli passa l'ira, io vo' tu l'oda,
> Piú ch' ora biasmo, anco dar lor gran loda.

---

and does not defend herself, and when the blind fury drives hand or tongue so far that we offend our friends; although afterwards we weep and sigh, the error cannot thus be canceled out. Alas! I sorrow and am afflicted in vain about what I said in anger at the end of the last canto. But I have become like a sick man who, after much, much patience, when he no longer has any shield against his pain, gives in to anger and turns to cursing. Then the pain ceases, nor does the impulse remain firm, that made his tongue so loose in speaking ill: and he comes to himself and repents and grieves about it; but what he has said, he cannot unsay. I do hope, ladies, that in your courtesy you will pardon, me, since I beg you to. You will excuse me that in my frenzy, overcome by bitter passion, I rave. Give the blame to my enemy, she who puts me in a state than which there is no worse and makes me say things for which I later grieve: God knows that she is to blame; she knows that I love her. I am no less beside myself than Orlando was; and I am no less worthy of forgiveness than he.

* He leaves one dead and another unconscious; he pauses little and always moves on. He would have done the same, or little short of it, to his lady, if she had not hidden; for he could not distinguish black from white, and he thought he was helping when he was harming.

Non biasmar tutte, ma serbarne fuore
La bontá d'infinite si dovrebbe:
E se 'l Valerio tuo disse altrimenti,
Disse per ira, e non per quel che sente.*
(XXVIII.77-78)

Here is the tension we have noticed before between experience of women and views of their virtues.[67] It is one of the more important patterns involved in Orlando's progress from (supposed) sanity to madness. That whole episode revolves around the tension between the unmistakable evidence Angelica and Medoro have left of their passion and Orlando's natural unwillingness to believe it. He is faced with a series of concrete objects that are increasingly difficult to explain away: first (XXIII.102-104) the names of Angelica and Medoro carved on all the trees of their favorite grove; then (106-115) Medoro's quite explicit inscription in the cave; finally (118-121) the shepherd's tale of the two lovers, with its "conclusion," the golden circlet that Orlando had given Angelica and that she had given the shepherd as payment for their lodgings. The conclusion is the ax that completely takes off his head, as the Poet says, because the split between what desire wishes to believe and what reality demonstrates is now irreconcilable. Orlando has succeeded for half the poem in fooling himself; now he no longer can. Hence his madness, and hence the destructiveness of his madness: his onslaught is first directed precisely against the irreducible facts, the empirical evidence of Angelica's love for Medoro.

There is another profound self-deception in Orlando in addition to his belief that Angelica loves and needs him. Throughout the poem he has set himself up as her protector. We first see him in Canto VIII haunted by the sense that she is in danger, and he leaves Paris in order to find her. There is a noble, self-sacrificing side to his intention, and fortune ironically gives him

---

* I do not believe whoever told it to you, though he spoke gospel truth in everything else; for the opinion he has of women, rather than experience of them, made him say this. His having ill will toward one or two of them makes him hate and blame all the others beyond what is just; but if his anger leaves him, I hope you hear him then, for he will praise them more than now he blames them. One ought not to blame them all, but distinguish the goodness of infinite numbers of them; and if your Valerio spoke differently, he spoke in anger, not in considered judgment.

the opportunity of demonstrating it by putting in his way a series of unfortunate ladies whom he dutifully rescues but who leave his conception of his own generosity intact because they evoke no interest in him. He has no eyes for the naked beauty of Olimpia when he rescues her from the sea monster (XI.58, 72), and his haughty nobility is placed in contrast with the ready lust of Ruggiero for the very Angelica Orlando wishes to rescue (X.112-115). Orlando wishes Angelica to be protected from others in order to be kept for him. His conception of himself as her rescuer is the form into which he sentimentalizes the situation. He thinks of her as a lamb to be saved from the wolves, but it never occurs to him to think of himself as one of the wolves. This other side of the coin is strongly suggested all along, but it is developed most fully in the violence of the mad Orlando. Once the self-styled protector of Angelica, Orlando becomes the destroyer of every memento of her presence. Once a good shepherd searching for his lamb, he becomes the slaughterer of shepherds. Finally, in the incident we began with, the one that occasioned the Poet's sympathetic outburst of indignation against women, Orlando comes close to destroying Angelica herself (XXIX.63-74).

The ambivalence between protectiveness and destructiveness that we see in Orlando also furnishes the two poles—eulogy (protection of reputation) and denunciation (destruction of reputation)—between which we have seen the Poet oscillating. For the lesser madman the extremes are not so far apart as they are for the titanic and paradigmatic Orlando. The madness is all one, however, and the continual dramatization of the Poet's madness, his abruptly discontinuous changes of heart, is a central reinforcement of the richest and most important theme of the poem.

The juxtaposition of conflicting attitudes is a technique we have followed in Ovid, Horace, and Petrarch, all of whom left their mark on Ariosto. Perhaps the influence of Petrarch is the most pervasive. For Ariosto's view of the darkness of human life —"Questa assai più oscura che serena / Vita mortal, tutta d'invidia piena" (IV.1)—is, like Petrarch's hard-won *contemptus mundi*, ultimately Augustinian. He shares with Petrarch and Augustine a sense of the inconstancy of man, and with Petrarch

—one of the most important differences from Augustine and indeed from the entire official medieval tradition—an implicit denial of the viability of the transcendental in everyday life. The world of the poem is resolutely natural, and the teller of the tale exists exclusively on the natural plane. Yet Ariosto retains much of the medieval sense that human inconsistency involves ontological instability. Fielding could be optimistic about the essential integrity and uniformity of the natural. And Emerson could say, "For of one will, the actions will be harmonious, however unlike they seem . . . One tendency unites them all. The voyage of the best ship is a zigzag line of a hundred tacks. See the line from a sufficient distance, and it straightens itself."[68] But Ariosto thinks of man as suspended— like the rest of creation—between being and nothingness. To use the Augustinian phraseology, he cannot altogether be or altogether not be, *nec omnino esse nec omnino non esse*, without grace.[69] Insofar as man really exists, he exists by virtue of some principle of integrity and steadfastness. The darkest form of inconsistency in Ariosto is betrayal, such as Odorico's treachery to his friend Zerbino. This is ultimately similar to the abrupt reversal in Adam before and after the fall; it is the kind of inconsistency by which Criseyde betrayed Troilus—and it involves a basic ontological discontinuity. Ariosto's characters flow into multiplicity on every page. He paints *le passage*.[70]

So it is untrue that women are more changeable than men in the poem; it is man in general who is in flux, like all things. The instability of earthly goods has a principal embodiment in the women of the poem because they are a principal object of desire. The Poet's shifting, contradictory attitudes toward women dramatize the problem of man's understanding the *varium et mutabile* of experience. To be a creature is to live in desire; to live without the intervention of the transcendental is to live in an incessant multiplicity of motion. Yet the final impression left by the Poet's changeability is not one of lack of control; rather it is a sense of the sureness of the author's purposeful control of the appearances of his Narrator. Like Horace, by pretending to be insane and by acting out his insanity, he conveys a strong impression of his real sanity. He at least has the distinctions among things clear in his mind; he is able, at least *qua* poet, to maintain the golden mean to which his essentially Horatian ethic of simplicity of desire refers. The poet in this sense, the author as revealed in the whole, is one who sees clearly and sharply the multiplicity of the universe and mirrors it in the microcosm of the poem. Thus the basic action of the poem, especially as it is embodied in the activity of the Narrator, is that of *seeing clearly*—seeing things in all their complexity, seeing things with as sharp a grasp as possible of the distinctions among them.[71] Ariosto could say with Montaigne, "*Distingo* est le plus universel membre de ma Logique."[72]

4

It may be helpful to test some of these generalizations against a reading of certain passages. References to the conduct of the poem, assertion of the analogy between Poet and God, references to his own supposed experience, acting out of the madness of conflicting attitudes—how are these aspects of the figure of the Poet related to each other and to the effect of the narrative? The seriousness of this poem, we shall see, is not destroyed by the attitude of control the Author assumes, or by his references to himself. The domination of the world of the poem by the intellect of the poet reflects his domination of an experience of reality. The poem itself is meant to be, to use Ariosto's own phrase, a *lucid interval* of mind in the rush of the universal madness. Since we have already examined in detail a number of the narrative instrusions in this particular story line, it will be convenient to examine more fully the account of the meeting of Rodomonte and Isabella.

As a result of Doralice's fickleness, Rodomonte, the titanic figure based upon Virgil's Turnus, has declared himself an enemy of womankind and has retired to a deserted chapel to brood. According to the law of this poem, by which almost every character is bound to meet every other, often in hilariously improbable coincidences, Isabella turns up one day at Rodomonte's chapel. Now Isabella has already established a considerable claim to our sympathy. Rescued by Orlando from a band of robbers, she is reunited to her lover, the gallant and chivalrous Zerbino, only long enough to see him die of wounds received in his hopelessly overmatched fight to prevent Mandricardo from stealing the discarded armor of the mad Orlando. Now, accompanied by the good monk who dissuaded her from committing suicide, she is taking Zerbino's body to a monastery in Provence where she plans to become a nun. Rodomonte falls in love with Isabella as soon as he sees her; when the monk protests this, Rodomonte disposes of him. The desperate Isabella escapes Rodomonte's bed by the ancient stratagem of making Rodomonte believe she can prepare a salve that will make him invulnerable and of having him test its efficacy on her own neck. The drunken Rodomonte chops off her head, and her soul rises to heaven accompanied by the fervent praises of the Poet (XXVIII.96–XXIX.29).

So much for the bare outline of events. The story is an example of the sixteenth-century taste for simple virtue and ferocious violence in tragedy; in some respects it is similar to the story of Isabella and the pot of basil or of Tancred and Ghismonda in the *Decameron*. Trissino, Giraldi Cinthio, or Tasso would have made it the occasion of much fustian. Ariosto's way of telling the story is to maintain an ironically malicious focus upon Rodomonte until the climax of the story. Rodomonte has settled down in the abandoned church with a whole retinue of servants, for one thing. This departure from the traditional solitude of the wandering knight for the supposedly greater plausibility of a king's traveling with attendants has already introduced a slight tension of incongruity. It is similar in effect to the extreme precision of the geography of the poem. Later, when Rodomonte decides to institute a chivalric *passo* in honor of Isabella, he brings all the artisans from the surrounding territory to build her memorial.

Rodomonte is represented as inconsequentially choosing to stay in the church rather than follow his original intention, which was to return home to Algiers, for no other reason than caprice. When Isabella appears on the stage and the fierce Rodomonte falls in love with her, he is made to spout the Ovidian topics of wooing, as if he were a fashionable courtier:

> Ride il Pagano altier, ch' in Dio non crede,
> D'ogni legge nimico e d'ogni fede.

> E chiama intenzione erronea e lieve,
> E dice che per certo ella troppo erra;

> Né men biasmar che l'avaro si deve,
> Che 'l suo ricco tesor mette sotterra;
> Alcuno util per sé non riceve,
> E da l'uso degli altri uomini il serra.
> Chiuder Leon si denno, Orsi, e Serpenti,
> E non le cose belle et innocenti.*
>
> (XXVIII.99-100)

The courtly Ovidian tone does not fit Rodomonte, and Ariosto makes the point deftly. In the first place, it is of course wrong to call Isabella's intention *lieve*—the point here is that she is an example of superhuman constancy and that the episode contrasts her with a particularly *lieve* Rodomonte, who has persevered in no decision for more than a few lines. Second, when Rodomonte proffers the standard contrast between lovely and terrible things in the Ovidian vocabulary of lions, bears, and serpents, we are reminded of the passages on the siege of Paris, where he has been shown to be particularly heartless in war, and of those passages that echo Books II and IX of the *Aeneid*, where he is compared to lions and serpents (XIV.114, 118; XVII.6; XVIII.14-15, 22). We are thus even more forcibly reminded of the incongruity Rodomonte's uttering this amorous speech.

At this point the monk interrupts Rodomonte's persuasions:

> Il Monaco, ch' a questo avea l'orecchia,
> E per soccorrer la giovane incauta,
> Che ritratta non sia per la via vecchia,
> Sedea al governo qual pratico nauta;
> Quivi di spiritual cibo apparecchia
> Tosto una mensa sontuosa e lauta.†
>
> (XXVIII.101)

Now the monk's judgment of the situation is comically inadequate. Isabella is not a *giovane incauta*, but an exemplar of feminine fortitude. The monk, however, sees her in terms of

---

* The proud pagan laughs, he who does not believe in God, who is the enemy of every law and every faith. And he calls her intention mistaken and light, and says that certainly she errs greatly, and is no less to be blamed than the miser who buries his rich treasure in the ground: he receives no utility from it himself and he locks it away from other men's use. Lions should be shut up, bears and serpents, but not things beautiful and harmless.

† The monk, who had lent his ear to all this, in order to succour the inexperienced young woman, to prevent her from being led down the primrose path, there prepares quickly a sumptuous and elegant table of spiritual food.

rigid categories. She is young and beautiful, therefore she must be incautious, liable to go down the *via vecchia*, and in need of him—how much tired worldly wisdom and vanity is suggested by the lines! Furthermore, the monk, fashionable ladies' confessor as he is, does not see past the Ovidian triviality of Rodomonte's wooing; he thinks Rodomonte's brutal lust can be reined in by his own compendious, elegant, self-satisfied eloquence, beautifully evoked by the Latinate "mensa sontuosa e lauta" and "spiritual cibo."[73] The food metaphor serves to reduce Rodomonte's rejection of the moral counsels of the monk to the level of merely physical reaction, and it emphasizes the monk's comic failure to apprehend the situation accurately:

> Ma il Saracin, che con mal gusto nacque,
> Non pur la saporò, che gli dispiacque.
>
> E poi ch' invano il Monaco interroppe,
> E non poté mai far sì che tacesse;
> E che di pazienza il freno roppe;
> Le mani adosso con furor gli messe.*
>   (XXVIII.101-102)

The monk quickly pays the penalty for his bad judgment and his dullness. The first three lines of stanza 102 are a fine, efficient evocation both of the tediousness of the monk and of Rodomonte's growing anger: in three lines connected by anaphora, we have first Rodomonte's interruption of the monk, then the repeated frustration of his efforts to quiet the monk—suggested by the elaborate wordiness of *far sì che tacesse*—and finally the outburst of violence. At this point, just as we are wondering what the poor monk will have to undergo, the Poet breaks off the canto:

> Ma le parole mie parervi troppe
> Potriano omai, se più ne dicesse:
> Sì che finirò il canto; e mi fia specchio
> Quel che per troppo dir accade al vecchio.†
>   (XXVIII.102)

---

* But the Saracen, who was born with a coarse palate, hardly tasted it when it displeased him; and having interrupted the monk in vain, and unable to silence him, and when the bridle of his patience broke, he laid hands on him with fury.

† But my words might seem to you too numerous by now, if I said any more; so that I shall end the canto; and I shall take my cue from the fate of that old man who said too much.

Ariosto knows very well, of course, that he is not being tedious. The humor of the *congedo* depends upon our perceiving the comic contrast between what befits the Poet and what befits the monk, and between the monk's failure to understand his situation and the Poet's pretense of not understanding his.

The action of the next canto begins with a restatement of the contrasts among the three actors, Rodomonte vainly attempting to weaken Isabella's fixed resolve and the monk with his ill-timed "ripari e schermi" (stanzas 4-5). Then the monk meets his fate: Rodomonte throws him as far out toward the sea as he can. The Poet takes time to develop an elaborate joke about the monk's fate; he says he does not know what happened to the monk, for accounts differ; and he gives the conflicting accounts—one for each kind of taste, as it were, both skeptical and religious (stanzas 6-7). This ironic play on the figure of the garrulous, officious monk is partly a means of setting off Isabella's strict constancy.

Now attention focuses on Rodomonte and Isabella. The rest of the episode develops the contrast between Isabella's calm, methodical purposiveness in carrying out her stratagem and the abrupt, arbitrary behavior of Rodomonte. For Isabella's stratagem to succeed, Rodomonte must be made even more inconsistent than he has been up to now. He must show a greed for the promised magical invulnerability, which he would have disdained in Canto XIV when he held off the entire French army single-handed, and he must be befuddled with drink and gullible at the crisis. While Isabella is exalted to heroic stature, Rodomonte is reduced to bestiality (*quel uom bestial*—XXIX.25); his action is essentially on the same plane as Orlando's, and it is successful—he does kill his lady.

Just as the canto began with the poet's decision to punish Rodomonte, the episode ends with the rewarding of Isabella, on whom the Poet bestows immortality:

> Alma, ch' avesti più la fede cara,
> E 'l nome quasi ignoto e peregrino
> Al tempo nostro, de la castitade,
> Che la tua vita, e la tua verde etade,
>
> Vattene in pace, alma beata e bella!
> Così i miei versi avesson forza, come
> Ben m'affaticherei con tutta quella

Arte che tanto il parlar orna e come,
Perché mille, e mill' anni, e più, novella
Sentisse il mondo del tuo chiaro nome.
Vattene in pace a la superna sede,
E lascia a l'altre esempio di tua fede.*
(XXIX.26-27)

The tone is broken off, a few stanzas later, by a characteristic Ariostan obliquity, according to which God is made to decree that all who bear the name Isabella will be beautiful, noble, wise, courteous, and virtuous (XXIX.28-29), a compliment to Isabella d'Este. The peculiar poignancy of the episode of Isabella, and of the lines just quoted, derives in a large degree from the contrast we have seen working on so many different levels between universal lability and heroic constancy. Isabella's reward is a peace that is simply not available in this life; and the incessant rush of the poem, its incessant metamorphoses under our eyes, reflect man's lot in this life. It is important to notice the stance of the Poet in the farewell to Isabella— "vattene in pace alla superna sede," he says, for he is entangled in the world of becoming. If one sees God appear in the poem, it is from below. The *superna sede* is somewhere outside the world of becoming that is the poem.

Canto XXIX opens with the indignant exclamation at Rodomonte's inconsistency and with the announcement of the decision to punish him. The poem becomes at such moments like the stretto passages of a fugue, in which every voice enters closely behind the others with the statement of the theme. The passage is a principal focus of the major themes of the poem as they are reflected in the role of the Narrator—the inconstancy of man, the *querelle des femmes*, the instability of the world of the poem, the stance of the Author as demiurge and as providence—all come to particularly sharp statement here. The poem requires an act of mind that integrates all the complexities of tone and event.

---

* Soul, who loved faithfulness and the name of chastity, in our time almost unknown and foreign, more than your life and your young years, go in peace, blessed, beautiful soul! Would that my verses had power equal to my good will, for I would strive with all that art which adorns and makes beautiful speech, in order that for a thousand and a thousand years and more, the world might hear word of your glorious name. Go in peace to your supernal seat, and leave to other ladies the example of your faithfulness.

VI

Tasso

Tasso was one of the first major poets to be dominated by the neoclassical dream of the correct epic poem. From the 1560s, when he seems to have begun work on the *Gerusalemme liberata* (first authorized edition, 1581), through the extensive rewriting that culminated in the second version of the poem, the *Gerusalemme conquistata* (1593), to his last major effort, *Il mondo creato* (first complete edition, posthumous, 1607), whose composition partly overlapped with the final stages of revision of the *Conquistata*, Tasso's principal literary activity was the writing of epic poetry and of literary theory concerning it; the influence of these poems, especially the *Liberata*, was to be incalculable. He was of course preoccupied by the towering example of Ariosto, and it was perhaps inevitable that he should attempt to lead a reaction against the earlier poet. He regarded himself as writing in the same genre as Ariosto and as trying to outdo him.[1] Thus Tasso's rejection of the Ariostan discursive Narrator is significant, and it is closely connected with his rejection of merely fictional subject matter and multiplicity of plot; it springs from his whole conception of the genre. But it is not merely because of a dogmatic Aristotelianism in literary theory that Tasso rejected Ariosto. This certainly played a part, but it would be more accurate to say that for Tasso, as for his period in general, the emerging neoclassical devotion to the rules answered to profound spiritual exigencies. Artistic styles reflect styles of life and modes of consciousness, and the connection is particularly clear in the case of Tasso.

182

1

The figure of the Poet in the *Gerusalemme liberata* is no longer Ariosto's discursive Narrator, but the traditionally anonymous Singer of classical epic, with his singing robes about him. There is only one reference, at the very beginning of the poem, to the concrete historical identity of the poet (I.4-5). Otherwise, most of the overt appearances of the "I" are directly patterned on passages in Homer and Virgil. They can be roughly classified as invocation, apostrophe, exclamation, and expression of diffidence.

Like Homer and Virgil, Tasso invokes the Muse not only at the beginning of the poem,[2] but also before cataloging heroes or before relating important parts of the action:

> Musa, quale stagion, qual ivi fosse
> stato di cose, or tu mi reca a mente;
> qual' arme il grande imperator, quai posse,
> qual serva avesse e qual compagna gente,
> quando del mezzogiorno in guerra mosse
> le forze e i regi, e l'ultimo Oriente.
> Tu sol le schiere e i duci, e sotto l'arme
> mezzo il mondo raccolto, or puoi dettarme.*
> (XVII.3)

Homer's explicit comments in his own person on the events of both *Iliad* and *Odyssey* (omitting the simile from consideration) had been limited almost entirely to pointing out the irony by which events belied the presumption or heedless expectations of mortals:

> Besotted: had he only kept the command of Peleiades
> he might have got away from the evil spirit of black death.
> But always the mind of Zeus is a stronger thing than a man's mind.
> He terrifies even the warlike man, he takes away victory
> lightly, when he himself has driven a man into battle
> as now he drove on the fury in the heart of Patroklos.
> (*Iliad* XVI.686-691)[3]

With laughter they prepared their dinner—a pleasant meal, such as they

---

* Muse, what season was there, what state of things, now call to my mind: what arms the great emperor had, what powers, what peoples subject and what allied, when he moved in war the forces and the kings of the south and the farthest east: you alone can tell me now the companies and the leaders and half the world gathered under arms.

liked—and many a beast was slaughtered. But how could feast be more unwelcome than the supper which a goddess and a valiant man were soon to set before them? For from the first they had wrought deeds of shame.

(Odyssey XX.390-394)[4]

Virgil greatly extended the range of this kind of comment. He transformed it from a predominantly intellectual, ironic comment to an expression of the Poet's emotions at the events of the story.[5] Brief interjections, such as "miserabile visu," "horrendum dictu," "triste ministerium," "miserum," are scattered throughout, and the austere Homeric signalizing of the infatuation of the doomed becomes, in the passages most like it, a more general comment on the pathos of human ignorance and passion, as in "heu, vatum ignarae mentes" (alas, the ignorant minds of prophets—IV.65).

Tasso clearly has Homer in mind in such passages as:

come sia pur leggiera impresa, ahi stolto!
il repugnare a la divina voglia:
stolto, ch' al Ciel s'agguaglia, e in oblio pone
come di Dio la destra irata tuone.* (IV.2)

The repeated *stolto* is clearly meant as an equivalent of the Homeric *nēpios* (cf. *Aeneid* VI.587-591).

Virgil, on the other hand, is the model for such passages as: "ahi, cieca umana mente, /come i giudizii tuoi son vani e torti!" (ah, blind minds of men, how your judgments are vain and distorted—IV.21), or for such brief outcries as "dura divisïon" (II.55) and "concilio orrendo" (IV.2).

The emphasis on the Poet's emotions toward the characters so characteristic of the *Gerusalemme liberata* is especially clear in the frequent apostrophes to characters.[6] Numerous passages are based on Virgil's manner:

Chiudesti i lumi, Armida: il Cielo avaro
invidïò il conforto a i tuoi martíri.
Apri, misera, gli occhi; il pianto amaro
ne gli occhi al tuo nemico or ché non miri?
Oh s'udir tu 'l potessi, oh come caro
t'adolcirebbe il suon de' suoi sospiri!†
(XVI.61)

---

* As if it were an easy enterprise, ah fool, to resist the divine will: fool, who raises himself up equal to Heaven and forgets how God's right hand thunders in anger.

† You closed your eyes, Armida: greedy Heaven denied any comfort to your

Quis tibi tum, Dido, cernenti talia sensus,
Quosve dabas gemitus, cum litora fervere late
Prospiceres arce ex summa, totumque videres
Miscere ante oculos tantis clamoribus aequor!*
(Aen. IV.408-411)[7]

We might notice that in these the apostrophe also carries forward the narrative. Tasso also follows Virgil in many apostrophes that do not serve any narrative function (as in *G.L.* XVIII.86; cf. *Aen.* XI.446-449).

Even the topos of diffidence before the material is used in a way derived from Homer and Virgil:

Non io, se cento bocche e lingue cento
avessi, ferrea lena e ferrea voce,
narrar potrei quel numero che spento
ne' primi assalti da quel drapel feroce.†
(IX.92)

Non ego cuncta meis amplecti versibus opto,
Non mihi si linguae centum sint oraque centum,
Ferrea vox.†   (*Georgics* II.42-44)

It would be erroneous simply to dismiss such instances as the baggage of neoclassicism. Tasso was one of the most articulate literary theorists of his age, and his theories were not, as is sometimes asserted,[8] merely *ex post facto* self-justifications. His stance as epic Poet had a clear rationale, and we can understand its significance only by taking his theories into account.

2

I shall not review all the details of Tasso's theory of the epic.[9] In relation to the figure of the Poet, the aspects that most directly concern us are the analogy between poetry and rhetoric, the relation between poetry and truth, and the problem of variety

suffering. Open your eyes, wretched one; why do you not look at the bitter weeping of your enemy? Oh, if you could hear him, how you would be softened by the dear sound of his sighs!

* What did you then feel, Dido, as you saw those things, what groans did you give, as you saw from the top of the citadel the shore all busy and saw the sea covered before your eyes, amid so many shouts!

† I could not, if I had a hundred mouths and a hundred tongues, iron breath and iron voice, tell the number who were killed in the first assaults by that fierce band.

‡ I do not hope to include all in my verses, not if I had a hundred tongues and a hundred mouths, a voice of iron.

and unity. For Tasso, as for most of his contemporaries, the function of poetry, which is by definition an imitation of human action, is an emotional one: its end is pleasure, and only through pleasure can it serve a moral purpose. Whereas tragedy achieves its characteristic pleasure through the emotions of pity and fear, epic poetry aims at arousing *maraviglia*, admiration.[10] Tasso conveniently summarizes the doctrine in his Aristotelian definition of the epic poem, in the *Discorsi del poema eroico*,[11] the later of his two important treatises on epic poetry: "We shall say therefore that the heroic poem is an imitation of an illustrious action, great and perfect, made, narrating with high verse, in order to move souls with admiration and to profit them in this way."[12]

Since it is based on the problem of affecting the audience, Tasso's theory of epic poetry is rhetorical, a fact that need not surprise us since Renaissance theories of poetry are almost always rhetorical in this sense. It should be said at once that the audience Tasso has in mind is something very like the "ideal reader" presupposed by many supposedly nonrhetorical modern theories,[13] and the emotional effect Tasso conceives poetry to have is inextricably bound up with the intellectual processes it imposes on the reader. All poetry is like oratory in seeking to produce in the audience a certain state of mind. But in epic poetry, as in narrative poetry in general, the poet speaks in his own person rather than through his characters, as occurs in drama, and in Tasso's mind the distinction of mode is crucial.[14] He repeatedly cites it to define or justify specific characteristics of the genre.[15] The mentality and emotionality of the narrating Poet is the model of the response expected of the reader, and the confidence the reader must have in the Poet is therefore like the *fides* sought, according to traditional rhetorical theory, by the orator.[16] In the most obvious sense, the audience must be moved, and in order to move the audience the Poet must seem moved:

neque fieri potest ut doleat is, qui audit, ut oderit, ut invideat, ut pertimescat aliquid, ut ad fletum misericordiamque deducatur, nisi omnes illi motus, quos orator adhibere volet iudici, in ipso oratore impressi esse atque inusti videbantur.*[17]

---

* Nor can the listener be pained, hate, envy, fear something, be moved to weeping and pity, unless all those motions which the orator wishes the judge to think he feels seem to be in him as if impressed and branded into him.

The principal emotional effect of epic poetry must be admiration, and herein lies the function and the justification of the style of epic, which projects, line by line and stanza by stanza, the sensibility of the Poet. The dominant style of epic is the grand style: "Proprio del magnifico dicitore è il commover e il rapire gli animi, come dell' umile l'insegnare, e del temperato il dilettare" (it is proper to the grand style to move and to carry away the souls of the listeners, as it is proper to the low style to teach and of the middle style to please).[18] This is the traditional doctrine, of course, according to which the grand style finds its justification and decorum in the *intentus animi* of the orator.[19] Tasso also sets forth the traditional distinction between the grand style in prose and in poetry, that in poetry the grand style is "meno proprio."[20] The related contrast between the styles of epic and tragedy depends upon the double distinction of mode and characteristic emotional effect:

nella tragedia non parla mai il poeta, ma sempre coloro che sono introdotti agenti ed operanti; e a questi tali si deve attribuire una maniera di parlare, ch' assomiglia a la favola ordinaria, acciò che l'imitazione riesca più verisimile. Al poeta, a l'incontro, quando ragiona in sua persona, sì come colui che crediamo essere pieno di deità e rapito da divino furore sovra se stesso, molto sovra l'uso comune, e quasi con un' altra mente e con un' altra lingua, gli si concede a pensare e favellare.* (*Prose diverse*, I, 51)

There is a curious and significant ambivalence in this passage. On the one hand, Tasso asserts the centrality of the emotion of the poet to the emotional effect of poetry; yet, when it comes to the justification of details of style, he appeals to the external principle of verisimilitude or appropriateness. In this passage *we believe* (from inside the experience) that the Poet is carried away and that is grounds for *allowing* him (from outside the experience) a certain style, as if, when we are genuinely carried away, we were in any condition to be literary censors. When in the 1590s Tasso revised the passage for inclusion in the *Discorsi del poema eroico*, the last sentence underwent a significant

---

* In tragedy the poet never speaks, but always those who are brought on as agents: and to these must be attributed a manner of speaking that resembles ordinary speech, so that the imitation may be more verisimilar. The poet, on the other hand, when he speaks in his own person, as one whom we believe to be full of divinity and rapt with divine furor above himself, is permitted to think and speak far above ordinary usage, and almost with another mind and another tongue.

change: "parla più altamente il poeta in sua persona, e quasi
ragiona con un' altra lingua, sì come colui che finge d'esser rapito
da furor divino sovra se medesimo" (the poet speaks more
exaltedly in his own person, and almost speaks with another
tongue, as one who pretends [or represents himself] to be carried above himself by divine furor—*Prose diverse*, I, 213).
Here the ambivalence has been resolved. The justification of
the grand style no longer lies in the audience's belief, but rather
in the consistency of the Poet's stance: the Poet may use the
grand style because he pretends to be or represents himself
as inspired; whether or not the audience believes he is inspired is
no longer taken into account.

I shall return later to the problem of Tasso's attitude toward
the doctrine of inspiration. Here I wish to emphasize the duality
in his approach to the problem of the Narrator-Poet. On the one
hand, the projection of the Narrator is internal, a projection of
what is most intimately Tasso's own; on the other hand, the
identity projected is external, one determined by genre, theme,
and tradition, and is consequently invented or constructed, like
the plot of the poem. There is a telling passage in a letter of 1575
to Scipione Gonzaga, in which Tasso says he has deleted from the
poem a suggestion that Olindo and Sofronia might have been
bound face to face because "certo quelle parole non convengono
in persona di grave poeta, quale dev' esser l'epico" (certainly
those words would not be becoming to the person of a grave
poet, such as the epic must be).[21] It is characteristic that Tasso
refers not to a violation of tone but to the *decorum personae*,
what is appropriate to the speaker.

In many respects Tasso's theory of epic poetry is an effort to
reduce the sublime to a system, a *techné*. To the extent to which
the Poet is merely a construction, in terms of a Horatian decorum
of persons, the poem becomes frigid in its effort to sweep the
reader off his feet. One of the dangers of the neoclassical striving
for grandeur is precisely the attempt to project emotions that are
not sustained by the intimate poetic subjectivity of the writer.
The problem is extremely complex in Tasso, however, because
his theory so thoroughly permeates his poetry. Most of the intrusions of the Narrator in both the *Liberata* and the *Conquistata*
are expressions of emotion before the events of the poem; they

are not only imitations of Homer and Virgil, but also theoretically founded attempts to elicit the emotions characteristic of epic. These may include pity, fear, joy, and so forth, but they are to be finally resolved into the *maraviglia* peculiar to epic (*Prose diverse*, I, 18-19, 83-85). "L'illustre dell' eroico è fondato sovra l'imprese d'una eccelsa virtù bellica" (*Prose diverse*, I, 19; cf. I, 273). The purest form of admiration is that aroused by examples of perfect virtue in action: "Oh quai duo cavalier or la fortuna / da gli estremi del mondo in prova aduna!" (Oh what two knights fortune now brings together in combat from the ends of the earth! *G.L.* IX.49; *G.C.* X.51).[22]

> Che di tua man, Clorinda, il colpo uscisse,
> la fama il canta, e tuo l'onor n'è solo:
> Se questo dí servaggio e morte schiva
> la tua gente pagana, a te s'ascriva.*
> (*G.L.* XI.54; *G.C.* XIV.75)

There are other important sources of admiration, of which the most important perhaps is the supernatural (*Prose diverse*, I, 13-14, 83-85):

> Tosto gli dèi d'Abisso in varie torme
> concorron d' ogn' intorno a l'alte porte.
> Oh come strane, oh come orribil forme!
> quant' è ne gli occhi lor terrore e morte!†
> (*G.L.* IV.4; *G.C.* V.4)

> Quercia gli apar, che per sé stessa incisa
> apre feconda il cavo ventre, e figlia:
> e n'esce fuor vestita in strana guisa
> ninfa d'etá cresciuta (oh meraviglia!).‡
> (*G.L.* XVIII.26; *G.C.* XXII.10)

It is primarily the action of the poem which evokes admiration, of course. Plot is the soul of epic just as it is of tragedy, and the basic elements of plot are the same in both—peripety, recogni-

---

* That your hand, Clorinda, dealt the blow, fame relates, and yours alone is the honor of it. If this day your pagan people escape servitude and death, let it be ascribed to you.

† Quickly the gods of the Abyss come together in diverse throngs to the high gates. O what strange and horrible forms! How much is in their eyes of terror and death.

‡ He sees an oak which, cut open by itself, opens fecund its hollow belly and gives birth, and there comes forth from it dressed in strange wise a nymph of nubile years (oh wonder!).

tion, and *perturbazione*, Aristotle's pathos (*Prose diverse* I, 46-48, 157-167; cf. *Poetics* 1452b). At key moments of the story, therefore, the Poet tends to exclaim in order to intensify the emotional effect. One of the most characteristic episodes in the poem is the nocturnal duel of Tancredi and Clorinda (XII.49-71), which neatly exemplifies Tasso's use of the figure of the epic Poet for the development of narrative effect.

The death of Clorinda is an important event, a major peripety, both in the siege of the city and in the personal history of Tancredi. Tasso himself pointed with pride to the episode: "S' egli [Camillo Pellegrino] ricerca piú tosto la maraviglia, la qual nasce da le mutazioni de la fortuna e da' riconoscimenti, la potrá ritrovare ne' casi d'Erminia e di Clorinda" (if he [Camillo Pellegrino] seeks rather the admiration that is born of changes of fortune and of recognition, he can find it in what Erminia and Clorinda undergo).[23] Indeed, the death of Clorinda is a peripety that is combined with recognition (the best kind of peripety, according to Aristotle, *Poetics* 1452a3) and with *perturbazione*. The entire episode was taken over, virtually unchanged, into the *Conquistata*.

It is made clear early in the canto, when Clorinda puts on arms that are "infausto annunzio! ruginose e nere" (*G.L.* XII.18; *G.C.* XV.18), that her fatal hour is at hand. In the development of the episode Tasso empties out his bag of tricks, in order to focus attention on two motifs, the valor of Clorinda, Argante, and Tancredi and the irony of Tancredi's ignorance. As the crisis approaches, the Poet's exclamations become more and more frequent. The duel itself opens with a Virgilian invocation that emphasizes the epic admiration of valor:

> Degne d'un chiaro sol, degne d'un pieno
> teatro, opre sarian sí memorande.
> Notte, che nel profondo oscuro seno
> chiudesti e ne l'oblio fatto sí grande,
> piacciati ch' io ne 'l tragga, e 'n bel sereno
> a le future etá lo spieghi e mande.
> Viva la fama loro; e tra lor gloria
> splenda del fosco tuo l'alta memoria.*
>   (*G.L.* XII.54; *G.C.* XV.68)

---

* Worthy of a bright sun, worthy of a full theater, are deeds so memorable. Night, who in your dark deep bosom have hidden and in oblivion so great an

When during a pause in the duel Tancredi takes joy in the fact that his unknown opponent is bleeding more heavily than he is, the Poet exclaims at his infatuation and apostrophizes him:

> Vede Tancredi in maggior copia il sangue
> del suo nemico, e sé non tanto offeso.
> Ne gode e superbisce. Oh nostra folle
> mente ch' ogn' aura di fortuna estolle!
>
> Misero, di che godi? oh quanto mesti
> fiano i trionfi, ed infelice il vanto!
> Gli occhi tuoi pagheran (se in vita resti)
> di quel sangue ogni stilla un mar di pianto.*
> (*G.L.* XII.58-59; *G.C.* XV. 72-73)

After a brief exchange of dialogue in which Clorinda refuses to reveal her identity, the fight is renewed. Now the Poet's comments express a mixture of admiration and horror:

> Torna l'ira ne' cori e li trasporta,
> benché debili, in guerra. Ah fera pugna!
> u' l'arte in bando, u' giá la forza è morta
> ove, in vece, d'entrambi il furor pugna!
> Oh che sanguigna e spaziosa porta
> fa l'una e l'altra spada, ovunque giugna,
> ne l'arme e ne le carni! e se la vita
> non esce, sdegno tienla al petto unita.†
> (*G.L.* XII.62; *G.C.* XV.76)

Up to this point most of the comments have been moderately extended—a whole or a half stanza. They have been complex in tone, particularly in maintaining a balance between sympathy for the characters' emotions (present or future) and knowledge of what is in store. Immediately after the last-quoted stanza, Clorinda receives her death wound and begs Tancredi to baptize

---

event, let it please you that I draw it forth and under the clear sky spread it forth and hand it on to the future ages. May their fame live; and with their glory may the high memory shine of your darkness.

* Tancredi sees his adversary's blood flowing more copiously, and himself not so much hurt. He is glad and grows proud. O our mad spirit, which every breath of fortune raises up! Wretch, why are you glad? O how sad will be the triumphs and unhappy the boast! Your eyes will pay (if you remain alive) a sea of tears for every drop of that blood.

† Anger returns to their hearts and carries them, weak as they are, to war again. Ah fierce fight! where skill is banished, where force is already dead, and where, instead, the fury of both is fighting! O what a bloody and gaping door both swords make wherever they meet armor and flesh! and if their lives do not come out, it is scorn that keeps them united with their breasts.

her. Tancredi's recognition of her, the moment for which the whole episode is a preparation, is announced in magnificently terse and intense lines:

> La vide, la conobbe; e restò senza
> e voce e moto. Ahi vista! ahi conoscenza!*
> (G.L. XII.67; G.C. XV.81)

The repeated doublet pattern and the weak line-ending on *senza* help to express Tancredi's utter suspension under the shock of the knowledge. It is also a full coalescence of Tasso's poetic sensibility and his theories. There could hardly be a more direct reference to the Aristotelian theory of recognition than this brief interjection, which is also schematic, like the first phrase, in connecting vision and knowledge as well as knowledge and recognition. What may impress us more is the deliberate care with which even the brevity of the outcry has been prepared in the preceding parts of the episode. It is a bold stroke; Tasso carries it off.

3

One of Tasso's major preoccupations throughout his life was the relation of poetry to truth—historical, philosophical, and religious. His conception of the relation was characteristic of his times. That poetry told pleasant lies was the oldest of commonplaces and in the climate of the Counter-Reformation the formula acquired new power. The problem of the truth of poetry is intimately bound up, however, with its rhetorical nature. The emotional effect of epic poetry depends for Tasso directly on the reader's belief in the truth—the historicity—of what is narrated. If the readers believe it false, he says,[24]

non consentono di leggieri a le cose scritte, per le quali or sono mossi ad ira, ora a pietà, or a timore, or contristati, or pieni di vana allegrezza, or sospesi, or rapiti . . . perchè dove manca la fede, non può abbondare l'affetto o il piacere di quel che si legge o s'ascolta.†

> (*Prose diverse*, I, 95-96)

---

* He saw her and knew her: and he remained without either voice or motion. Ah the sight! Ah the knowledge!

† They do not easily consent to writings by which they now are moved to anger, now to pity, now to fear, now made sad, now full of vain gladness, now in suspense, now carried away . . . for where belief is lacking, the emotion or the pleasure of what is being read or heard cannot abound.

This rhetorical necessity is the ground for preferring a subject taken from history rather than a fictional one:

dovendo il poeta con la sembianza della verità ingannare i lettori, e non solo persuader loro che le cose da lui trattate sian vere, ma sottoporle in guisa a i lor sensi che credano non di leggerle ma di esser presenti, e di vederle, e di udirle, è necessitato di guadagnarsi nell' animo loro questa opinion di verità il che facilmente con l'autorità dell' istoria gli verrá fatto.*

(Prose diverse, I, 11)

That is the position in the *Discorsi dell'arte poetica*. One of the most notable changes presented by the *Discorsi del poema eroico* is the entirely new, rigorously argued philosophical definition of the verisimilar as the proper subject of poetry. Following the scholastic classification of the arts of discourse, Tasso ranges poetry alongside rhetoric as a branch of dialectic, devoting considerable space to refuting Mazzoni's recent assertion that poetry is a branch of sophistic. Poetry has as its subject the universal, or the truly probable, as opposed to the apparent probable that is the subject of sophistic.[25]

se i poeti sono imitatori, conviene che siano imitatori del vero, perchè il falso non è; e quel che non è, non si può imitare: però quelli che scrivono *cose in tutto false*, se non sono imitatori, non sono poeti, ed i suoi componimenti non sono poesie, ma finzioni più tosto: laonde non meritano il nome di poeta *o non tanto*.†   (*Prose diverse*, I, 96; italics added)

The hedging of this statement in the italicized phrases points to a central ambiguity in Tasso's position. On the one hand, the poet must imitate what is true, but, on the other, his very office consists in pretense and in the effort to create an illusion of truth about what is false.[26] In imitating the universal truth of events, the poet has almost complete freedom to change particulars as long as he retains the foundation of truth:

però che quello che principalmente constituisce e determina la natura della

---

* Since the poet must with the semblance of truth deceive his readers, and not only persuade them that the things he treats are true but submit them to their senses in such a way that the readers believe they are present and are seeing and hearing them, not reading them, the poet must gain this opinion of truth in their minds, which he can easily do with the authority of history.

† If poets are imitators, they must be imitators of what is true, because what is false does not exist and what does not exist cannot be imitated; therefore those who write *things altogether false*, if they are not imitators, are not poets, and their compositions are not poems but rather fictions; thus they do not merit the name of poet *or not as much*.

poesia . . . è il considerare le cose non come sono state, ma in quella guisa
che dovrebbono essere state, avendo riguardo più tosto a l'universale, che
a la verità de' particolari: prima d'ogni altra cosa dee il poeta avvertire, se
nella materia ch' egli prende a trattare sia avvenimento alcuno, il quale,
altrimente essendo succeduto, fosse più meraviglioso, o verisimile, *o per
qualsivoglia altra cagione portasse maggior diletto;* e tutti i successi che
sì fatti troverà (cioè che meglio in un altro modo potessero essere avvenuti),
senza rispetto alcuno di vero o d'istoria, a sua voglia muti e rimuti, ordini
e riordini, e riduca gli accidenti de le cose a quel modo ch' egli giudica
migliore, mescolando il vero co 'l finto, ma in guisa che 'l vero sia fonda-
mento de la favola.*   (*Prose diverse*, I, 130-131; italics added)

Just what it means to keep the truth as the foundation of the fable
is unclear; in the earlier version of the treatise, it meant keeping
the general outline of events, and in particular the beginning and
the outcome of the action, true to the facts.[27] In any case, what is
described here is obviously not a process of extracting from real
events a philosophical significance. Pleasure is the most important
criterion, and where it is involved the poet can do what he pleases
without any consideration of *vero o d'istoria.*

There is also a further reason why the poet must mix falsehoods
with the truth: pleasant fictions increase the persuasiveness of
the truth.

dovendo il poeta con la sembianza de la verità ingannare il lettore, suol
dilettarlo con la varietà de le menzogne, come dice Pindaro ne la prima
ode de l'olimpiache . . . Imperò che il diletto de la bugia, variando l'aspetto
de la verità, e co' suoi colori quasi dipingendolo, suole ingannare più agevol-
mente.†   (*Prose diverse*, I, 96)

It has been pointed out before that the ambiguity in Tasso's
position rests in part upon a confusion of historicity with truth,

---

* Since that which principally constitutes and determines the nature of
poetry . . . is the contemplation of things not as they have been but as they
out to have been, taking account rather of the universal than of the truth of particulars; before anything else the poet ought to consider whether, in the material
he is going to treat, there is any event which, if it came about in a different way,
would be more marvelous and verisimilar *or for any other reason would cause
greater pleasure;* and all such events that he shall find, that is, events that could
have come about better in another way, let him *without taking any account
whatever of truth or history* change and rechange them, order and reorder them,
and reduce the accidents of things to that mode which he judges best, mixing
the true with the invented, but in such a way that the true is the foundation of
the fable.
† Since the poet must deceive the reader with the semblance of truth, he
often seeks to please him with the variety of his lies, as Pindar says in the first
Olympic . . . For the pleasurableness of lies, varying the face of truth and as it
were painting the face of truth with its colors, makes the deception easier.

by which he is put in the paradoxical position of identifying the universal with the false. We need to be sure that we understand the terms of the argument in such cases, for the error, if it is that, is one Tasso shared with his contemporaries. One fact that may give us pause is that the universal and the verisimilar are not at all identical; a poetic representation may approach the universal as a limit, but the very act of imitation, as Tasso conceives it, means representing events as concrete particulars, especially since it seeks an effect of vividness (*enargeia*).

In any case, it is noteworthy that, although Tasso argues rigorously for a philosophical justification of poetry in general, his discussions of the way in which epic poetry is more philosophical than history make no claims whatsoever for any special philosophical insights into human action on the part of the poet. When he speaks discursively about what epic poetry teaches or about the philosophical content of his own poetry, he always refers to received, traditional doctrine. The *Gerusalemme liberata* grows from the Renaissance ethical and religious tradition in which it is rooted and fed, and the allegories Tasso constructed accurately reflect it.[28] On the other hand, the *Gerusalemme* presents—as has been almost universally recognized and perhaps overemphasized—a highly individual *considerare le cose*, and Tasso was too keenly self-aware and proud of his gifts not to realize it. What is at stake for Tasso, in his struggle with the problem of the truth of poetry, is ultimately the claims of the individual poet's subjectivity against the massive institutionalization and formulation of doctrine that was then taking place in Italy.

One of the most significant parts of this problem is the question of the divine inspiration of the poet, and it will be instructive to examine the opening invocation of the *Gerusalemme*. It is not only scrupulously accurate in its reference to the relation of the poem to truth; it is also firmly grounded in the theory of composition. In the treatises Tasso discusses *inventio, dispositio*, and *elocutio* as both logically and chronologically consecutive. Hence when he comes to discuss the *proposizione* of the epic poem (which is analogous, he says, to the orator's *proemio*[29]), he understands the traditional invocation of the Muse as a prayer for aid in the process of *elocutio*, as well as an evidence of the piety that should make us invoke divine aid on undertaking any activity.[30]

The invocation of the Muse at the beginning of the *Liberata* is the second of a least three versions. In an early sketch, the *Gierusalemme*,[31] the invocation is quite short and addressed to God himself:

> Tu, Re del Cielo, come al tuo fuoco accesa
> La mente fu di quei fedeli tuoi,
> Tal me n'accendi, e se la tua santa luce
> Fu lor ne l'opre, a me nel dir sia duce.*

The prayer that God's holy light guide the poet is as explicit an assertion of the poet's responsibility to truth as one could wish. Indeed, the young Tasso draws a parallel between himself and the faithful crusaders which suggests that the inspiration of the poet is of the same order as holy or saintly zeal. Never again did Tasso venture such a suggestion, and, if the dedication of the *Liberata* draws a parallel between the poet and some of his heroes, it is of an altogether different kind.

The invocation of the *Liberata* (I.2-3) is the most elaborate of the three, and in it we find an explicit statement of the relation of the poem to truth, a statement that agrees exactly with the two *Discorsi*:

> O Musa, tu che di caduchi allori
> non circondi la fronte in Elicona,
> ma su nel cielo in fra i beati cori
> hai di stelle immortali aurea corona,
> tu spira al petto mio celesti ardori,
> tu rischiara il mio canto, e tu perdona
> s'intesso fregi al ver, s'adorno in parte
> d'altri diletti, che de' tuoi, le carte.
>
> Sai che lá corre il mondo ove piú versi
> di sue dolcezze il lusinghier Parnaso;
> e che 'l vero condito in molli versi
> i piú schivi allettando ha persuaso:
> cosí a l'egro fanciul porgiamo aspersi
> di soavi licor gli orli del vaso:
> succhi amari ingannato in tanto ei beve,
> e da l'inganno suo vita riceve.†

---

* Thou, King of Heaven, as the minds of those thy faithful were set aflame by thy fire, so set me aflame with it, and if thy holy light led them in their works, let it lead me in my words.

† Oh Muse, you who do not circle your brow in Helicon with laurels that fade, but up in Heaven among the blessed choirs have a golden crown of immortal stars, breathe into my breast celestial ardors, make bright my song, and pardon if I have woven ornaments with the truth, if I in part adorn my pages with other delights than yours. You know that the world runs to where flat-

The invocation is both the adoption of the traditional attitude of the inspired Poet and a genuine prayer; that Tasso felt it necessary to adapt the traditional epic manner to a theoretically and factually accurate account of the stages of composition is itself an indication of his religious seriousness.[32] He asks of the Muse three things: "celesti ardori," the gift of *elocutio* ("tu rischiara il mio canto") and pardon. The implication is that the processes of invention and disposition (for which Tasso does not invoke the Muse's aid) have already been completed according to a deliberate plan of combining falsehood and truth in order to deceive the reader, and so there is no need to ask the Muse for knowledge, traditionally the principal demand of the epic poet.[33] On the other hand, asking the Muse's pardon for the nature of the completed fable suggests the undertaking has been wrong from the start; indeed, if her pardon must be asked, how can the Muse be expected to infuse into the culprit "celesti ardori"?[34]

The prayer for pardon, of course, reflects Tasso's haunting uneasiness, his fear of the heterodox. The lofty prayer of the early *Gierusalemme* may well have come to seem presumptuous to him, especially in its equation of poetic inspiration with active saintly zeal. If by addressing the Muse rather than God in this particularly conspicuous place he was seeking support in the tradition, at least one critic attacked the invocation because the Muse is nonexistent (*Lettere*, V.211). The invocation of the *Conquistata* represents a further step, from the classical tradition to that of Dante:

> Voi che volgete il ciel, superne menti,
> e tu che duce sei del santo coro,
> e fra giri lá su veloci e lenti,
> porti la face luminoso e d'oro;
> il pensier m'inspirate e i chiari accenti,
> perch' io sia degno del toscano alloro:
> e d'angelico suon canora tromba
> faccia quella tacer ch' oggi rimbomba.*
>
> (*G.C.*I.3)[35]

---

tering Parnassus most pours forth its sweetness, and that the truth hidden in soft verses has with its allurement persuaded the most unwilling: so for the sick child we sprinkle the edge of the cup with sweet liquids: deceived, he drinks bitter juices and from the deception receives life.

* You who turn the heavens, supernal minds, and you who are the leader of the holy chorus and among the swift and slow circles up there carry your luminous golden torch; inspire me with thought and with clear accents that I

Here again the fable has been found and disposed. Now, however, the "altri diletti" of the *Liberata* have been removed, and there is no more need to ask the angels' pardon. In these now tired and redundant accents there recur the same specific demands: the gifts of *elocutio* and inspiration. But how changed is this last metamorphosis of the prayer for a crusader's zeal that had opened the *Gierusalemme!* From the fire of the King of Heaven to "celesti ardori" to the generic and pale "il pensier m'inspirate," there is a progressive diminution of demand, which reflects the gradual ebbing of the poet's confidence.

One of the most characteristic portions of the *Conquistata* is the elaborate invocation preceding the description of heaven in Book XX.4:

> Sommo sol, il cui raggio è luce a l'alma,
> e dolce ardor perché non giaccia e geli;
> e voi che, sciolti da terrena salma,
> rapti volaste ov' egli illustra i cieli;
> qual sia gloria lá su, corona, e palma
> per me, con vostra pace, or si riveli,
> come giá lessi; e i gradi, e i cori, e 'l canto,
> e ciò che in luce involve il regno santo.*

One need only recall the passionate conviction and confidence of the famous invocation of light that opens the third book of *Paradise Lost* to see in how curious a position Tasso has placed the Poet. He has the Poet ask permission to reveal what has already been revealed. Let me now, he says, without offense recount *what I have read* of heaven.[36] This invocation is the emptiest kind of ornamental flourish. It calls attention to the fact that the poet has no special knowledge and even speaks under correction. Its net effect is to emphasize the impression that the poet's office has been merely external (compilation, disposition, elocution).

It is impossible for Tasso, in both the *Liberata* and the *Conquistata*, to adopt wholeheartedly the pose of the divinely inspired Poet. Even in the *Liberata*, Tasso is led, by his rationalistic view

---

may be worthy of the Tuscan laurel: and let my harmonious trumpet with angelic sound make silent the one that echoes today.
   * Highest Sun, whose ray is light to the soul and sweet ardor that it may not freeze and be idle; and you who, freed from the earthly body, have flown, raised up, to where He makes bright the heavens; what glory, crowns, and palms are, up there, suffer me to reveal as I have read of them; and the degrees, and the choruses, and the singing, and that which wraps the holy kingdom in light.

of his own activity and by a lack of belief in the possibility of genuinely supernatural inspiration in his own case (a phenomenon reserved for saints), to call attention at the outset to the element of falsity in his position. The fable has been constructed, as it were, *invita Musa*, and the subsequent Virgilian or Homeric demands for knowledge from the Muse will be literary devices, rhetorical attitudes.

There are many reasons why Tasso's confidence waned, and an important one is the growing skepticism among his contemporaries about the theory of poetic furor.[37] His fear of presumption and heterodoxy is another. But it should be clear, from the very scrupulousness with which he refers to the realities of composition in the invocations, that what is at stake is in fact his whole conception of the activity of the poet in invention and disposition, as well as in elocution. He may have yearned for a *sense* of divine inspiration, but he did not view poetry as a product of this inspiration: his theory is that of a rationalistic, autonomous *techné*. Yet in Tasso, these tendencies are two faces of the same coin; both reflect his yearning for sanctions that do not depend upon any external authority.

Like the sanction of divine inspiration, however, the autonomy of the poet is problematic for Tasso. Tasso's technical conception is Platonic in representing the poet as imposing upon material a form seen first in the mind.[38] In the case of epic poetry, what the poet produces is an analogue of the cosmos and the poet is analogous to God. Now it is striking that while Ariosto, although he left us no extrapoetical statement of the analogy, makes it explicit through his Narrator, Tasso, who repeatedly and passionately asserted the analogy in his theoretical writings,[39] avoids any overt references to it in the *Gerusalemme*. With the exception of the opening invocation, Tasso avoids referring to the process of composition, to his own activity as *maker*. That is of course because there is a fundamentally important split between the processes of invention and disposition, on the one hand, and that of elocution, on the other. The figure of the Poet, which comes into being at the moment of elocution, is designed to make the reader forget that the poem is a construct and thus is limited to referring to the events of the poem as if they were real.[40] This is the reverse of Ariosto's use of the analogy of the Poet and God to *prevent* the reader from mistaking the world of the poem for the real world.

Such a split between what poetry is and what it can say it is, for a poet of Tasso's genius and pride—and anxieties—is a momentous one and goes hand in hand with the paradoxical nature of the analogy between the poet and God as Tasso conceived it. The poet fashions a universe, it is true, but only by taking the real universe and wresting it to his purposes: only by taking God's creation, which exists *in rebus,* and interweaving it with fictions that exist only *in verbis* does the poet make something uniquely his own. But it is merely his own and can be nothing more as long as he insists upon the autonomy of his art.

Ultimately Tasso re-established the integrity of his poetic subjectivity and a continuity in the processes of composition by giving up the autonomy that had been so dear to him. In his last poem, *Il Mondo creato,* he does not fashion his own universe but sings directly of God's fashioning of the real universe; he does not invent falsehoods, but instead follows scrupulously the received theological and scientific doctrines. The very disposition is based upon authority: he follows that of St. Basil's *Hexaemeron.*[41] The contrast with Milton is again instructive. Tasso's *Mondo creato* has none of the highly individualized imaginative vision of *Paradise Lost;* it puts forward not the products of the poet's own insight as such, but only what is traditional and approved. Yet, insofar as the poet has assimilated what is approved, he can become its spokesman. He can expect his audience to accept what he says as coming, if only indirectly, from divine inspiration. He can return at long last to direct and meaningful invocation of God for help in the composition of the poem. Finally, and paradoxically enough, he can become discursive about himself as well as about his material.[42] Whatever the rigidities and faults of the *Mondo creato,* it represents the only possible resolution of the ambiguities of Tasso's position as he himself understood it, and it comes as a natural outgrowth of his entire career.[43]

4

I turn now to the all-important problem of unity and variety. First I shall examine Tasso's theoretical statements and then their relation to the poetry. His theory of disposition is an adaption of Aristotle's discussion of plot and takes over Aristotle's requirement that a plot be complete, of a certain magnitude, and one. Tasso's discussion of the requirement of unity, which is almost identical in both of his treatises on epic poetry, is part of the contemporary debate over the merits of the *Orlando furioso*, in which both sides argued from the position that Ariosto's poem was characterized by a multitude of actions;[44] he follows the formal rhetoric of *confirmatio* followed by *refutatio*. The *confirmatio* consists of five arguments for unity of action. The first is an argument from analogy with other arts and an appeal to the authority of custom. Two of Tasso's arguments regard the nature of the thing made: unity is more perfect than multiplicity; since the fable is the essential form of the poem, multiplicity of actions in fact brings into being a multiplicity of poems. The last two arguments regard the maker: since the fable is the end proposed to himself by the poet, one who proposes multiple actions is proposing multiple ends and will be impeded in his operation; unity is the only possible principle of determinateness, and, unless the poet decides to imitate only one action, he tends toward an infinite number and no principle can tell him where to stop.[45]

The two arguments that regard the nature of the thing made, based as they are on the Aristotelian conception of *substance*, assume that a poem is—or should be—ontologically similar to a thing or being, and clearly involve us from the outset in the analogy between the Maker of things and the maker of poems, which becomes explicit in the *refutatio*. The *refutatio* takes issue with four arguments in favor of the Ariostan multiplicity of action— the *romanzo* was not known by Aristotle and therefore escapes his rules; the *romanzo*, unlike classical epic, is suited to the modern languages; the *romanzo* is sanctioned by custom; multiplicity of action, variety, is more pleasant than unity.[46] Tasso's refutation of the final argument is highly significant. He accepts the principle that variety is more pleasing than unvaried unity, but insists that the most pleasing is variety *in* unity. This, of course, is the eloquent passage asserting that the poem combining unity and variety is like the cosmos and its fashioner like God.

Tasso's statement of the analogy makes it amply clear that the pleasurableness of variety is not the only criterion for its inclusion

in the epic poem. There is an ontological one as well. After the
sentences that outline the diversity of things included in the
poem, the passage continues:

ma che nondimeno uno sia il poema che tanta varietà di materie contegna,
una la forma e l'anima sua; e che tutte queste cose sieno di maniera
composte, che l'una l'altra riguardi, l'una a l'altra risponda, l'una da l'altra
necessariamente o verisimilmente dependa, sì che una sola parte o tolta
via, o mutata di sito, il tutto si distrugga. E se ciò fosse vero, l'arte del
comporre il poema sarebbe simile a la ragion dell' universo, la qual è
composta de' contrari, come la ragion musica: perchè s'ella non fosse
moltiplice, non sarebbe tutta nè sarebbe ragione, come dice Plotino.*

(*Prose diverse*, I, 155)

The reference to Plotinus is to the theory of *nous*, the first hypos-
tasis, which is unified in itself but contains the principle of
multiplicity by containing (knowing) the forms of all things.
Things themselves are later fashioned by the Soul that both
contemplates the forms in *nous* and shapes things out of pure
potentiality.[47] Tasso is saying that since the poem includes
variety, the formal principle (*ragione*) of the poem—by which
he seems to mean the plot (the soul or form of the poem), the
principle of the unity of the plot, and perhaps also the faculty
that conceives the plot—is compound, partakes of multiplicity.
In this context, the principle of multiplicity is asserted as a value
because it makes the formal principle of the poem like that of
the universe.

As the passage points out, it is by the principle of causality
that the complexities of the poem are to be held together. This
is actually a referring of the principle of unity of the poem to a
principle of unity of the real world; it is, *pace* Aristotle, an extra-
poetic criterion of unity, and the fact is not without significance
for Tasso. For the admission of the principle of multiplicity into
the poem also admits that of indeterminacy, to which Tasso
referred in the *confirmatio*, and it is precisely here that the anal-

* But that nevertheless the poem which contains so much variety of subject
matter be one, and one its form and soul, and that all these things be so put
together that each involves the others, each answers to the others, each depends on the others necessarily or verisimilarly, so that if a single part were taken
away or shifted the whole would be destroyed. And if that were true, the art of
composing the poem would be similar to the formal principle of the universe,
which is composed of opposites, like the formal principle of music: for if it were
not multiple, it would not be entire nor would it be a formal principle, as
Plotinus says.

ogy with the cosmos cannot help him. For the fullness of variety
of the cosmos, as soon as it is introduced as a model for the
variety of the poem, brings with it the principle of plenitude.
The variety of the cosmos is virtually if not in fact infinite, and
all things are related by causality; the poet cannot imitate its
fullness absolutely, and how is he to decide where to stop? The
analogy itself, in its pure form, gives no help.

It should be clear that I am pointing out a fundamental fallacy
in Tasso's rejection of Ariosto. For as far as the mere principle of
causality goes, the *Orlando furioso* is fully integrated, and its
variety was also compared by its defenders to that of the cosmos.[48] Tasso finds, however, that the degree of variety of the
Furioso is in fact *confusion,* and so the reasons for Tasso's and his
supporters' preference for the particular kind if unity-in-variety
he calls for—one based upon Aristotelian ontology and literary
theory—must be sought in fundamental psychological and spiritual exigencies.

The principle that tells the poet how much variety he can put
in his poem is his own subjectivity, and we must look at Tasso's
attitude toward the relation between the unity-in-variety of the
thing made, the poem, and the subjectivity of the poet. First of
all, the unity and variety must be in tension, the unity must be
difficult, and this is one of the most important indications of the
poet's power:

Ma questa varietà sì fatta tanto sarà più meravigliosa quanto recherà seco
più di malagevolezza e quasi d'impossibilità . . . E' certo assai agevol cosa
e di niuna industria il far che 'n molte e separate azioni nasca gran varietà
di accidenti; ma che la istessa varietà in una sola azione si trovi, "hoc opus,
hic labor est." In quella che nasce de la moltitudine delle favole per se
stessa, arte o ingegno alcuno del poeta non si conosce, e può essere a' dotti
e a gl' indotti comune; questa in tutto da l'artificio del poeta depende, e
conseguita da lui solo si riconosce, nè può da mediocre ingegno essere
conseguita: quella tanto meno diletterà, quanto sarà più confusa e meno
intelligibile; questa, per l'ordine e per la legatura delle sue parti, non solo
sarà più chiara e più distinta, ma porterà molto maggior novità e meraviglia.*

(*Prose diverse*, I, 45, 155-156)

---

* But this variety will be so much more worthy of admiration as it involves
greater difficulty and almost impossibility . . . It is certainly easy and a thing
requiring no industry to cause a great variety of events to come about in many
and separate actions; but that the same variety be found in a single action,
"this is the work, this the labor." In the former, which is born automatically of

204 FOUR RENAISSANCE EPICS

In such a context the artifice of the poet clearly involves his whole subjectivity, as suggested by the Platonic analysis of the imposition of a formed grasped or created by the mind in the act of intellection of it. Hence the dangers Tasso saw in multiplicity of action are especially significant. Two of his arguments in the *confirmatio,* as we saw, regard the maker of the poem, and they both reject multiplicity of action as endangering the very unity of the poetic subjectivity. I have already pointed out the difficulties of the argument from indeterminacy. The argument itself reflects the need Tasso felt for rational sureness of purpose, and presents the curious image of a hypothetical poet tempted to greater and greater multiplicity and requiring an arbitrary, even an external, rationale to decide how much he should permit himself.

The other argument is even more significant:

presupponendo che la favola sia il fine del poeta . . . s' una sarà la favola, uno sarà il fine; se più e diverse saranno le favole, più e diversi saranno i fini. Ma quanto meglio opera quel che riguarda ad un sol fine, di colui il qual diversi fini si propone, tanto ancora sarà più lodato l'imitatore d'una sola favola e d'una sola azione.*   (*Prose diverse,* I, 141)

Now this is one of the few passages in the entire discussion of unity that Tasso revised when writing the *Discorsi del poema eroico.*[49] In the earlier treatise, the second sentence above read as follows:

ma quanto meglio opera chi riguarda ad un sol fine, che chi diversi fini si propone; *nascendo da la diversità de' fini distrazione nell' animo, ed impedimento nell' operare;* tanto meglio operarà l'imitator d'una sola favola, che l'imitatore di molte azioni.†   (*Prose diverse,* I, 31; italics added)

---

the multiplicity of plots, no art or skill of the poet is recognized, and it can be attained by learned and unlearned alike; the latter depends entirely on the artifice of the poet and is recognized as attained by him alone, nor can it be achieved by a mediocre talent. The former, the more confused and unintelligible it is, delights all the less; the latter will not only be clearer and more distinct because of its order and the binding together of its parts, but it will bring a much greater newness and admiration.

   * Presupposing that the plot is the goal [end] of the poet . . . if the plot is one, his goal will be one; if the plots are many and different, his goals will be many and different. But just as one who looks to a single goal operates better than one who proposes to himself several goals, so the imitator of a single plot and a single action is more praiseworthy.

   † But just as one who looks to a single goal operates better than one who proposes to himself several goals, *since from the diversity of goals comes distrac-*

One wonders why in rewriting the passage Tasso omitted the italicized phrase. Perhaps by then he felt it was too dangerous and painful a personal admission to be kept in, and so limited the argument to the impersonal and purely logical phrases of the later version. *Distrazione nell' animo* is the failure of the poetic subjectivity to maintain its own integrity, a splitting into multiplicity resulting from the impossibility of synthesizing subject matter. Thus when Tasso says that "la varietà è lodevole sino a quel termine, che non passi in confusione" (variety is praiseworthy up to the point at which it passes into confusion—*Prose diverse*, I, 44, 154), the confusion he means is as much in the mind of the poet—or the reader—as in the thing itself: excessive variety "hampers the operation of the soul" of both poet and reader.[50] In this connection, it is significant that Tasso cites an argument for the pleasurableness of variety based upon the inner multiplicity of the soul:

essendo la nostra umanità composta di nature assai fra loro diverse, è necessario che d'una istessa cosa sempre non si compiaccia, ma con la diversità procuri or a l'una or a l'altra delle sue parti sodisfare; essendo dunque la varietà dilettevolissima a la nostra natura, potranno dire ch' assai maggior diletto si trovi ne la moltitudine, che ne l'unità de la favola.*

(*Prose diverse*, I, 153-154)

For Tasso it is precisely because of its relation to the composite nature of the soul that excessive variety is to be distrusted. But the danger is inherent in all forms of variety, especially that extreme form of tension between variety and unity that Tasso envisages, in which the integrating capacity of the poet's mind is strained to the limit.

It must be remembered that for Tasso the variety of subject matter included in the poem is also the variety of emotions. The early discussion of complex plots, for instance, includes the following:

Composta si dice, ancora che non abbia riconoscimento o mutazione di

---

tion in the mind and impediment in operation, so the imitator of a single plot will operate better than the imitator of many actions.

* Since our human nature is a compound of natures quite different from each other, it is inevitable that it will not always find pleasure in the same thing, but will seek with diversity to satisfy now one, now another, of its parts; since variety is most pleasurable to our nature, they can say that much greater delight is had from a multitude of plots than from unity of plot.

fortuna, quando ella contegna in sé cose di diversa natura, cioè guerre, amori, incanti e venture, avvenimenti or felici ed or infelici, che or portano seco terrore e misericordia, or vaghezza e giocondità: e da questa diversità di nature ella mista ne risulta.*   (*Prose diverse*, I, 47)

The very language here recalls that of the catalogue of subject matter in the statement of the analogy between the poem and the cosmos. Furthermore, the emotional effect of epic poetry, as Tasso conceives it, is a succession of moments of violent and often conflicting emotions; if the readers do not believe in the events, he says in a passage I quoted earlier, "non consentono di leggieri a le cose scritte, per le quali or sono mossi ad ira, ora a pietà, ora a timore, or contristati, or pieni di vana allegrezza, or sospesi, or rapiti." Clearly the imposition of unity on a wide variety of affects—a dialectic moving toward a resolution in admiration—engages the psyche of the poet at its deepest level and brings to the center of attention the nature and degree of tensioned unity among diverse affects in the poet's own subjectivity.[51]

The nature of the problem becomes especially plain in light of the themes of the *Gerusalemme*. The chief obstacle to the taking of the city is the army's tendency toward *distrazione*—dividing into factions or pursuing diverse, self-regarding ends—a tendency that derives from their individual turmoils and multiplicities. The unity of the body politic depends directly upon the inner unity of its members. Both Goffredo and Rinaldo are essential to the taking of the city, and they represent two different kinds of unity: Goffredo's, never endangered, corresponds to the rational faculty; Rinaldo's, won through a difficult process of self-mastery in which the centrifugal tendency for a time wins out, corresponds to the irascible and appetitive faculties.[52] They correspond to conception and operation, and there is thus an important analogy between their relation and the principles of unity and multiplicity in the subjectivity of the poet.

I spoke earlier of a split for Tasso between the processes of invention and disposition, on the one hand, and that of elocution,

---

* It is called compound, even though it does not contain recognition or peripety, when it contains in itself things of diverse nature, that is, wars, loves, enchantments, and adventures, events now happy and now sad, which bring with them now fear and pity, now pleasure and gladness: and from this diversity of natures it becomes mixed.

on the other. To a certain extent, though one must be careful not to oversimplify, the split reflects the two principles of unity and variety. Ideally, the process of elocution ought to combine the principles, but Tasso's conception of the Poet-Narrator and of the rhetoric of the poem endangers the synthesis. The reader is to participate in the achievement of unity in the poem, both affective and poetic unity, and he must therefore be emotionally drawn into the dialectic of the poem. The function of the episode of Tancredi and Clorinda is a good example. The emotions of Tancredi at the death of Clorinda are an indication of the division within him; his inability to conquer this last residue of *motus extra* makes him incapable of the highest heroism, which is reserved for Rinaldo, the only one who can conquer the magic wood. But the reader must share Tancredi's emotions, must feel that he himself would have reacted similarly at the moment of recognition, so that he will have the proper *admiration* of Rinaldo's heroism. In order to reach the thematic synthesis, in other words, the poet must represent as emphatically as possible the local moment, and he must engage the reader in it. As we have already seen, one of his chief means for doing so is the figure of the Poet, which shares the emotions of the characters and is, except in direct thematic statements, immersed in the local moment. The figure of the Poet, then, which comes into being in the process of elocution, tends to represent not so much the fixed principle of the unity of the poetic subjectivity as the principle of operative diversity, of variety.

In order to bring the diversity of the poetic world into being, the poet must himself descend from the contemplation of the idea of the poem to its active fashioning, and there is always the danger that in the process the poet will lose his grasp on the principle of unity. Tasso's recurrent anxieties about the inclusion or exclusion of episodes and the solidity of their connection with the main plot must not be dismissed as mere slavish Aristotelianism and subjection to the *revisori*.[53] What is involved is the difficulty of synthesizing the two phases of creation as he understands them, and that is one reason why he repeatedly cites theoretical grounds for his decisions. In the process of composition and revision he thought of himself as having to overcome threats—internal and external—to the synthesizing operation of his poetic subjectivity. It is striking that his discussion of plot in epic asserts that variety arises from the means and the impediments to the protagonists' progress:

Tutta dunque la varietà nel poema nascerà da' mezzi e da gli impedimenti: i quali possono essere di molte maniere e quasi di molte nature; e non distruggeranno l'unità de la favola, nondimeno, s' uno sarà il principio dal quale i mezzi dependeranno, ed uno il fine a cui sono dirizzati.*54

(*Prose diverse*, I, 164)

Like the plot of the *Gerusalemme*, the process of composition itself is a dialectic between unity and variety; the problem is to allow scope to potentially disruptive tendencies while struggling to overcome the impediments they offer to the operation of the poet's synthesizing power. The result must not be *distrazione*, but rather the *difficulté vaincue* of the true epic poem, parallel to the taking of Jerusalem in the plot, whose allegorical significance is thus relevant to Tasso's deepest poetic concerns.

It is of course a truism to say that the greatness of the *Gerusalemme liberata* depends upon its reflection of Tasso's innermost difficulties. That the unity of his own psyche was endangered in a clinical sense is one of the reasons for the richness of this theme in his work, and of course the *Liberata* is the product of a time when he was still confident of maintaining some degree of unity and willing to be adventurous in giving controlled scope to his own centrifugal tendencies. The pathos of the poem's dedication is, of course, an added proof of the relation in his mind of personal and poetic unity:

> Tu, magnanimo Alfonso, il qual ritogli
> al furor di fortuna e guidi in porto
> me peregrino errante, e fra gli scogli
> e fra l'onde agitato e quasi absorto,
> queste mie carte in lieta fronte accogli,
> che quasi in vóto a te sacrate i' porto.
> Forse un dí fia che la presága penna
> osi scriver di te quel ch' or n'accenna.
>
> E' ben ragion, s' egli avverrá ch' in pace
> il buon popol di Cristo unqua si veda,

* All the variety of the poem will derive from the means and the impediments: which can come about in many ways and be almost of many natures, and nevertheless will not destroy the unity of the fable, if the principle on which the means depend is one and if the end to which they are directed is one.

e con navi e cavalli al fero Trace
cerchi ritôr la grande ingiusta preda,
ch' a te lo scettro in terra, o, se ti piace,
l'alto imperio de' mari a te conceda.
Emulo di Goffredo, i nostri carmi
in tanto ascolta, e t'apparecchia a l'armi.*
                    (I.4-5)

This is the only reference in the poem to the historical identity of the poet, and it identifies the personal travails of the poet with the themes of the poem: Alfonso, the "emulo di Goffredo," has rescued Tasso from his centrifugality and guided him to port, just as Goffredo, as we are told in I.1, united his companions under the holy banner ("sotto a i santi segni ridusse i suoi compagni erranti"). It is not merely a personal outcry, however: in identifying his own experience with that of Goffredo's companions and in calling for a modern crusade (for which the necessary condition is that Christendom be united in peace), Tasso asserts the general validity of both the personal and the political aspects of the poem.[55]

For Tasso, then, the universe fashioned by the poet must include as much variety as possible within a rigorous unity. Because the poet is a finite human being, however, the unity of the poetic universe, like that of his own psyche, is provisional and precarious. Its variety, similarly, falls far short of that of the cosmos, even though the poet risks all in trying to achieve it. Ultimately Tasso turned to the variety-in-unity of the real universe: for not only is there an unlimited variety in the hexaemeral poem, and a unity guaranteed by the transcendent unity of its Maker; but also, if the poet is anchored in God as a transcendent fixed point of unity, the split in himself can be overcome and the infinite variety of creation can be contemplated with affective unity. Furthermore, just as he no longer needs to pretend that an un-

---

* You, magnanimous Alfonso, who withdraw me from the fury of fortune and guide me to port—me a pilgrim wandering and almost drowned among the rocks and the waves—receive with glad brow these pages of mine that I bring as an offering consecrated to you: perhaps the day will come when my prophetic pen will dare to write of you what now it only alludes to. It is right—if it ever comes about that the good people of Jesus live in peace with each other and with ships and horses seek to take back from the fierce Thracian [the Turk] his great unjust prize [the Holy Sepulchre]—that to you be granted the scepter on land or, if you prefer, the high lordship of the seas. Emulator of Goffredo, in the meanwhile listen to my song and prepare yourself for war.

truth is true, so in the process of elocution he need not immerse himself in the dialectical movement of the poem. He is no longer limited by the exigencies of his epic rhetoric to an essential narrowness of reference *within* the poem and its time scheme; he becomes discursive in a pattern that juxtaposes the eldest past, the present, and the furthest future, a pattern that is possible because any given moment of time can be judged from an ultimate viewpoint, transcendent and atemporal.

Spenser

T HE MOST frequently and continuously utilized source of *The Faerie Queene* is the *Orlando furioso*, and Spenser adopts a discursive manner that is clearly based on Ariosto's. Although he may have known Tasso's theoretical writings and may have drawn freely upon both the *Rinaldo* and the *Gerusalemme liberata*, he did not follow either Tasso's demand for unity of action or his adaptation of the Homeric and Virgilian epic Poet. He elected to adapt the intrusive, discursive Poet developed by Boiardo and Ariosto. As we shall see, Spenser imitates and echoes Ariosto's canto openings and endings, interjections, and, less frequently, transitional topoi. The changes he makes are characteristic and important.[1]

1

Spenser's Narrator-Poet refers to himself in several different ways. Many cantos are introduced by moralizing comments on the action of the preceding canto[2] (Ariosto's usual practice) or of the present canto.[3] Many of these exordia adapt exordia of Ariosto's,[4] and those that are verbally independent of him are clearly based on his practice. Interspersed through the narration are comments and exclamations of various kinds: moral reflections, expressions of emotion, occasionally a reference to the poetic process or to the rationale of the poem. Spenser often ends a canto with an adaptation of the formulas used by Boiardo and Ariosto; it should be pointed out, however, that forty-six cantos close without any such formula and instead follow the manner of Virgil or Tasso.[5]

Boiardo adopted a division of his poem into books of irregular length, each opening with an introduction more elaborate than most of the canto exordia. In using the same kind of division, Spenser increased its formal significance by regularizing the number of cantos in each book, and he formalized the proems by sharply distinguishing them from the cantos and by using them consistently both for comment on his purposes and methods and for dedicatory compliments to the queen.[6] We might expect Spenser to be equally consistent in calling attention as well to the formal divisions of his poem at the end of each book, but he does so in only half of the books. The twelfth cantos of Books I, II, and VI have exordia calling attention to the approaching completion of the book; I.12.42 and the 1590 ending of III.12 signalize the end of a unit of construction by the use of a familiar topos, I.12.42 by that of the end of a voyage,[7] III.12 by that of completing the plowing of a furrow. Book VI.12 ends with an envoy to the poet's verses.[8] In addition to conclusions, proems, and interspersed comments, one other type of intrusion of the Poet consists of comments on transitions from one thread of the narrative to another.[9]

Of the verbal parallels between appearances of Spenser's Narrator and Ariosto's, many have been noted by the commentators.[10] One characteristic of these appearances is obvious and perhaps inevitable: they often occur where Spenser is adapting Ariosto's plot material. For example, we find in connection with Britomart adaptations of Ariosto's reflections on Bradamante and Marfisa. Thus in III.2.1-3 and 4.1-3 he adapts Ariosto's two defenses of women, including the idea that it has been the envy of writers that has deprived them of their true share of glory. In Book V, Britomart's mistaken jealousy and excursion to rescue Artegall are based on Bradamante's jealousy of Marfisa (O.F. XXXVI). In V.6.1 Spenser defends Artegall against possible criticism of his surrender to Radegund, just as in O.F. XXXVIII Ariosto defends Ruggiero's decision to return to Agramante (in both cases the events in question contribute to the jealousy of the women). In the story of Florimell the interjections and comments of the Poet are based on Ariosto's comments on the story of Angelica, its source.[11] Book III.8.1, opening the canto that tells of Florimell's narrow escapes from the witch's beast and the fisherman and her imprisonment by Proteus, echoes O.F.

VIII.66-67, in which Ariosto expresses his supposed emotions at the thought of Angelica tied to the rocks. In III.6.27-28, when Florimell is unsuccessfully defending herself against the fisherman, Spenser echoes a different part of the same passage (*O.F.* VIII.68), combining it with an adaptation of the magnificent apostrophe to Angelica's thwarted lovers evoked by her acceptance of Medoro (*O.F.* XIX.31-32). Book IV.11.1 is one of the most elaborate Ariostan comments Spenser makes upon his own conduct of the story. Like the other comments of the Poet in connection with Florimell, it is clearly inspired by *O.F.* VIII.66-67 (and by such transitions as *O.F.* XLI.46). Prince Arthur's protection of Amoret and Aemylia (IV.8.10ff) is similar to Orlando's chaste association with Isabella (*O.F.* XIII), and Spenser's comment (*F.Q.* IV.8.29-33) may have been suggested in part by *O.F.* XIII.1. On occasion Spenser adapts a passage of Ariosto's comments to an Ariostan situation different from the one to which they originally applied. Thus he fits Ariosto's apostrophe of Isabella (*O.F.* XXIX.26-27) to the story of Florimell (*F.Q.* III.8.42-43), and his "O gran bontá de' cavallieri antiqui" (*O.F.* I.22) to a situation derived from the earlier part of *O.F.* I (*F.Q.* III.1.13).

Sometimes Spenser makes Ariosto his model when dealing with material that is similar to Ariosto's but not derived from it. *F.Q.* III.9.1, for instance, which introduces the story of Hellenore, is based on the disclaimer Ariosto prefixed to the canto of Fiammetta (*O.F.* XXVIII.1-3). Like Ariosto, Spenser has two such disclaimers: *F.Q.* III.1.49, which refers to the story of Malecasta, is derived from *O.F.* XX.1-3, which comments on the inclusion of Gabrina. Spenser's apostrophe of Jealousy (III.11.2) owes a debt to Ariosto's full-scale invective (*O.F.* XXXI.1-5). Another good example is II.10.1-4, which introduces the genealogy of the queen: it is based on *O.F.* III.1-4, which introduces the genealogy of the dukes of Este. When Spenser adapted *O.F.* III in *F.Q.* III.3, he inserted another invocation, but as far as its phrasing is concerned it is independent of Ariosto.[12]

As we can see, the great majority of the passages in which Spenser echoes Ariosto's Narrator occur in Book III. The habit of opening a canto with reflective moralizing, however, pervades

The Faerie Queene and is derived from the practice of Ariosto.[13]
Now Ariosto followed several different formal procedures in his
moralizing introductions. The most common starts from a gener-
alized reflection and applies it to the events of the story, as in
this example:

> Quantunque debil freno a mezzo il corso
> Animoso destrier spesso raccolga,
> Raro è però che di ragione il morso
> Libidinosa furia a dietro volga,
> Quando il piacere ha in pronto; a guisa d'Orso,
> Che dal mel non sì tosto si distolga
> Poi che gli n'è venuto odore al naso,
> O qualche stilla ne gustò sul vaso.
>
> Qual ragion fia che 'l buon Ruggier raffrene?*
> (*O.F.* XI.1-2)

Spenser follows much the same pattern in such exordia as II.5.1:

> Who euer doth to temperaunce apply
> His stedfast life, and all his actions frame,
> Trust me, shall find no greater enimy,
> Then stubborne perturbation, to the same;
> To which right well the wise do giue that name,
> For it the goodly peace of stayed mindes
> Does ouerthrow, and troublous warre proclame:
> His owne woes authour, who so bound it findes,
> As did *Pyrochles*, and it wilfully vnbindes.[14]
> (II.5.1)

Like Ariosto and Boiardo, Spenser addresses many exordia
and interspersed comments to specific members or groups of his
audience,[15] notably the queen and the ladies. Apostrophes to
the ladies are numerous, and several are based on specific passages in Ariosto and the rest on his general manner. Like Ariosto,
Spenser turns to the ladies to offer advice in matters of love and
to deprecate misinterpretation of stories of licentious women.
Such passages as *F.Q.* III.5.53-55 and VI.8.1-2, while verbally
independent of Ariosto, are good examples of Spenser's application of Ariosto's formal methods to his own purposes. On one

---

* Although a weak rein often pulls up a spirited horse in full career, it is
nevertheless rare that the bit of reason turns back the fury of lust, when pleasure is available to it; like a bear that will not leave the honey, when once it
has got wind of it or has tasted a drop. What reason then can hold back the
good Ruggiero?

occasion, unlike Ariosto, Spenser includes the male members of
his audience (III.9.1-3—the passage seems to echo Boiardo) and,
on another, singles them out (I.4.1), as Ariosto had never done;
the formal devices are derived from Ariosto, however. The frequent apostrophe and praise of the queen have an obvious
similarity to Ariosto's manner of referring to his patron. One
index of the degree to which Spenser's Narrator follows Ariosto's
rather than Tasso's example is the infrequency of the Virgilian
apostrophe of characters. Characters are sometimes addressed,
but the passages either are directly based on passages in Ariosto
(such as *F.Q.* III.8.42-43) or take his manner as their model
(as in III.1.7-8 and V.10.3).[16]

2

If Spenser owes a large debt to Ariosto for his Narrator, he
changed all that he borrowed to suit his own purposes. The
reader of *The Faerie Queene* notices no abrupt change in the
Poet when he reaches Book III, in spite of the fact that the
direct "imitations" of Ariostan commentary are almost all contained in that book. The reason is that, whether Book III was
written early or late, Spenser in writing his exordia and comments
changed the borrowed material along the lines of the more independent passages. We must now consider the changes and general
differences between Spenser's and Ariosto's Narrators in an effort
to understand Spenser's method.

It might be well to begin by recalling those aspects of Ariosto's
Narrator that Spenser chose not to adopt. One of the most striking
changes is the almost total absence of any reference to the Poet's
personal experience, real or fictitious,[17] and consequently an absence of the recurrent parallelism between the Poet and his
heroes that forms so important a part of Ariosto's method. Furthermore, the value of love is not *en jeu* in Spenser, as it is in
Ariosto; nor is the nature of women or the value of life at court.
The high worth of all is assumed and often proclaimed.

Unlike Ariosto, Spenser never draws explicit parallels between
events of the poem and recent history or current events. Nor
does he ever mention any of his contemporaries, except the
queen,[18] and his praise of her is abstract—he gives no specific
instances of her conduct, as Ariosto does of Ippolito's and Al-

fonso's. Spenser never addresses the rulers or peoples of Europe as Ariosto does (the only passage remotely resembling such an exhortation as *O.F.* XVIII.73-80 is *F.Q.* IV.11.22). There is none of Ariosto's complex play with the reality of events (except in a very different form, when there is a shift in levels of meaning). Spenser never assumes the position of absolute dominion of the world of the poem, which provides so much interest in the *Orlando furioso*.

One of the most striking differences between the two is the lack of humor and irony in Spenser's comments.[19] The tenor of his apostrophes of the ladies, which in Ariosto became the occasion for so much impudence and wit, perhaps best exemplifies this change. At one point Spenser adapts *O.F.* XXII.1-3:

> Faire Ladies, that to loue captiued arre,
>   And chaste desires do nourish in your mind,
>   Let not her fault your sweet affections marre,
>   Ne blot the bounty of all womankind;
>   'Mongst thousands good one wanton Dame to find:
>   Emongst the Roses grow some wicked weeds;
>   For this was not to loue, but lust inclind;
>   For loue does alwayes bring forth bounteous deeds,
> And in each gentle hart desire of honour breeds.
>   (III.1.49)

Spenser has significantly changed the emphasis of such apostrophes as "Donne cortesi e grate al vostro amante." The mention of the ladies as captives of love and their *nourishing* desires, as well as the last lines, suggest that love plays a greater role for them than in the lives of Ariosto's ladies; in Spenser's lines, love has been elevated to a governing principle, and it is, as the word "chaste" reveals, the love that leads to marriage, like that of Britomart and of Amoret, or else to the purely Platonic relationship exemplified by the relationship between Timias and Belphoebe. The context of courtly love to which Ariosto refers has been profoundly changed.

Other characteristic changes can be seen in Spenser's adaptation here. Ariosto stresses, according to his ironic purpose, the rarity of faithful women. In Spenser's stanza, the "sweet affections" and "bounty of all womankind" are assumed; there is but "one wanton Dame" among "thousands good," whereas Ariosto had exploited the contrast between a theory of female goodness and his own empirical findings (*O.F.* XXVII.122ff). Spenser ends the stanza with the sharp distinction between love and lust that is so important in *The Faerie Queene* and so foreign to Ariosto's conception of love. This brings us to another important difference. While Ariosto's Poet is concerned about the ladies' reaction to *himself*, and seeks to retain their favor, Spenser's remarks are directed toward another problem altogether. The ladies' reaction to Malecasta is seen as a specific instance of a general moral problem: the behavior of the good when confronted with examples of the bad. Malecasta is thus identified as an aspect of reality, rather than as the invention or utterance of an author. Much the same change of emphasis occurs in III.9.1-2, further strengthened by the reference to the fallen angel.

When Spenser undertakes to defend the glory of women, it is not their virtue that is in question. He does not have to assert, as Ariosto does, that there have actually been, contrary to appearances, many chaste and faithful women:

> E di fedeli e caste e saggie e forti
> Stato ne son, non pur in Grecia e in Roma,
> Ma in ogni parte ove fra gl' Indi e gli Orti
> De la Esperide il Sol spiega le chioma.*
>   (XXXVII.6)

Spenser defends the ladies' martial prowess and their statesmanship; their virtue is assumed (*F.Q.* III.2.1-2, 4.1-3). In Ariosto's catalogues of glorious women of ancient times, we find examples of valor, statesmanship, chastity, fidelity, and learning.[20] In Spenser's we find Penthesilea, Debora, and Camilla, examples of valor.

Consistent with these changes in emphasis, the terms in which Spenser addresses the ladies are far more exalted than Ariosto's usual "Donne," which becomes an occasional "Donne gentil" or "Cortesi donne."[21]

> Faire ympes of beautie, whose bright shining beames
> Adorne the world with like to heauenly light,

---

* And there have been faithful and chaste and wise and brave ladies, not only in Greece and Rome, but in every place where the sun spreads his locks, between the Indies and the Hesperides.

And to your willes both royalties and Realmes
Subdew, through conquest of your wondrous might.

(III.5.53)

Ye gentle Ladies, in whose soueraine powre
Loue hath the glory of his kingdome left,
And th' hearts of men, as your eternall dowre,
In yron chaines, of liberty bereft,
Deliuered hath into your hands by gift.

(VI.8.1)

It follows from all of this that, just as there is no humor or irony in the commentary of Spenser's Poet, so there is none of the ironic byplot we find in Ariosto. We do find some traces of sequential organization. The direct comments of the Narrator sometimes have a clear relation to the general theme of the book of *The Faerie Queene* in which they appear. The most thoroughly integrated in this respect is Book V, and then VI, II, and I. Book V also manifests the closest approach to sequential organization of the exordia. A panegyric of justice is given prominence in the center of the book (7.1-2), and one can discern a developing complexity in the issues dealt with in the exordia, parallel to the development of the themes in the book, from the necessity of force for the enforcement of justice (4.1) to the relation between justice and mercy (10.1-2). (It is difficult to see, however, the reason for giving V.12.1-2 its prominent position at the beginning of the last canto, except that it is a natural comment on the topical events of the story.) The exordia of Book VI have a direct thematic relevance (except for the problematic VI.10.1-4), but no apparent structure. The exordia of VI.3.1, 5.1-2, and 7.1 form a small logical sequence, similar to a number of others in other books.[22] But the exordia of other books have no discernible rationale of sequence. Those of Book IV are the least integrated of all (as the book is in other respects as well). There is, to be sure, a clear enough connection between the story and the reflections it suggests. This problem of the thematic relevance and structure of the exordia of *The Faerie Queene* is connected to another important change of emphasis. Although structure is noticeable and deliberate among certain kinds of comments in the *Orlando furioso*, Ariosto's remarks in his moral-

izing openings are presented as arising naturally from his reflections on the events of the poem; we do not expect them to
have any formal arrangement, since the structure of the poem is
not expository. The design of *The Faerie Queene*, however, is
avowedly expository. The relation between the reflections and
the events is reversed—the reflections come first and the events
second.

Of the few passages in which Spenser comments on the structure of the poem, the most important emphasize sharply its expository nature. Perhaps the clearest example is VI.12.1-2:

> Like as a ship, that through the Ocean wyde
>> Directs her course vnto one certaine cost,
>> Is met of many a counter winde and tyde,
>> With which her winged speed is let and crost,
>> And she herselfe in stormie surges tost;
>> Yet making many a borde, and many a bay,
>> Still winneth way, ne hath her compasse lost:
>> Right so it fares with me in this long way,
> Whose course is often stayd, yet neuer is astray.

> For all that hetherto hath long delayd
>> This gentle knight, from sewing his first quest,
>> Though out of course, yet hath none bene missayd,
>> To show the courtesie by him profest,
>> Euen vnto the lowest and the least.
>> But now I come into my course againe,
>> To his atchieuement of the *Blatant beast;*
>> Who all this while at will did range and raine,
> Whilst none was him to stop, nor none him to restraine.

The obstacles have been put in Calidore's way by the author
in order to show the knight's courtesy: the book's organization
is expository; the chain that links events is a logical one, not
that of narrative necessity (cf. *Poetics* 1451a-b). In VI.9.1 the
Poet adduces two reasons for including the story of Calidore
and Pastorella: its fruitfulness and the credit it reflects on
Calidore.

> Now turne againe my teme thou iolly swayne,
>> Backe to the furrow which I lately left;
>> I lately left a furrow, one or twayne
>> Vnplough'd, the which my coulter hath not cleft;
>> Yet seem'd the soyle both fayre and frutefull eft,
>> As I it past, that were too great a shame,

> That so rich frute should be from vs bereft;
> Besides the great dishonour and defame,
> Which should befall to *Calidores* immortall name.

If we interpret "so rich frute" as meaning "edification," as it seems most probable Spenser meant it, these two reasons correspond to the fundamental aims of the poem: the "blazoning" of the glory of knights and ladies and the presentation of examples of virtue for imitation. Again, in the proem to Book VI Spenser explicity relates the variety of the poem to its expository nature:

> The waies, through which my weary steps I guyde,
>   In this delightfull land of Faery,
>   Are so exceeding spacious and wyde,
>   And sprinkled with such sweet variety,
>   Of all that pleasant is to eare or eye,
>   That I nigh rauisht with rare thoughts delight,
>   My tedious trauell doe forget thereby;
>   And when I gin to feele decay of might,
> It strength to me supplies, and chears my dulled spright.

> Such secret comfort, and such heauenly pleasures,
>   Ye sacred imps, that on *Parnasso* dwell,
>   And there the keeping haue of learnings threasures,
>   Which doe all worldly riches farre excell,
>   Into the mindes of mortall men doe well,
>   And goodly fury into them infuse;
>   Guyde ye my footing, and conduct me well
>   In these stranges waies, where neuer foote did vse,
> Ne none can find, but who was taught them by the Muse.

> Reuele to me the sacred noursery
>   Of vertue, which with you doth there remaine,
>   Where it in siluer bowre does hidden ly
>   From view of men, and wicked worlds disdaine.
>   Since it at first was by the Gods with paine
>   Planted in earth, being deriu'd at furst
>   From heauenly seedes of bounty soueraine,
>   And by them long with carefull labour nurst,
> Till it to ripenesse grew, and forth to honour burst.

The joy the Poet finds in the ways of Faeryland is an example of the "secret comfort" that the Muses "infuse" into the minds of men. "Guyde ye my footing" is grammatically parallel to its

appositive, "Reuele to me the sacred noursery / Of vertue" (and
there follows another example of the metaphor of virtue as
fruit).

Except for VI.12.1-2, no other comment within the poem so
clearly states Spenser's conception of the expository nature of
its organization as II.12.1:

> Now gins this goodly frame of Temperance
> Fairely to rise, and her adorned hed
> To pricke of highest praise forth to aduance,
> Formerly grounded, and fast setteled
> On firme foundation of true bountihed;
> And this braue knight, that for that vertue fights,
> Now comes to point of that same perilous sted,
> Where Pleasure dwelles in sensuall delights,
> Mongst thousand dangers, and ten thousand magick mights.

The structure ("frame") is "grounded" on the "firme foundation
of true bountihed"; the virtue, temperance, must be so grounded;
a discussion of temperance must be based on certain basic principles; once the virtue has been established in the soul, it can
proceed to its most difficult task (cf. II.6.1), the control of
pleasure; once the discussion has established the nature of this
virtue, it can proceed to analyze the virtue in action in the control of temperance, its formal culmination.

Because of the expository nature of the poem, there is a greater
abstractness in the moralizing comments of *The Faerie Queene*,
in which general principles are related to a clearly understood
and usually explicit hierarchy of values. Whereas Ariosto's moral
reflections have the relaxed and graceful tone, never devoid of
humor (except in the indignant protests against the rape of
Italy), of an experienced spectator and critic of the human scene
who has learned to live calmly with the instability and imperfection of human beings, Spenser's have an obvious programmatic,
hortatory emphasis. For Spenser, knighthood is a living institu-
tion, partly as a metaphor of the Christian warfare of the soul,
partly as a concrete social reality. The moral lessons he wishes
to teach are meant to be applied in a strenuous *vita activa*. They
are the counsel of perfection.

This tonal difference can be seen clearly in passages where

the two poets discuss similar moral issues—for example, the problem of reason's control of the passions. In the passage we have already noted, Ariosto says:

> Quantunque debil freno a mezzo il corso
> Animoso destrier spesso raccolga,
> Raro è però che di ragione il morso
> Libidinosa furia a dietro volga,
> Quando il piacere ha in pronto; a guisa d'Orso,
> Che del mel non sì tosto si distolga
> Poi che gli n'è venuto odore al naso,
> O qualche stilla ne gustò sul vaso.

> Qual ragion fia che 'l buon Ruggier raffrene . . . ?
> (XI.1-2)

Now Ariosto's moral judgment is clearly expressed in the words "libidinosa furia," but the emphasis of the passage is on the contemplation, realistic and clear-sighted, of human action. It is the illumination of Ruggiero's actions as human and comprehensible that is important, and no exhortation to apply the moral lesson is made except in the most indirect way. Here is Spenser on a similar theme:

> A Harder lesson, to learne Continence
> In ioyous pleasure, then in grieuous paine:
> For sweetnesse doth allure the weaker sence
> So strongly, that vneathes it can refraine
> From that, which feeble nature couets faine;
> But griefe and wrath, that be her enemies,
> And foes of life, she better can restraine;
> Yet vertue vauntes in both their victories,
> And *Guyon* in them all shewes goodly maisteries.
> (II.6.1)

The practical urgency of *learning* continence is the dominant note in this passage; it presents an analysis of the problem in abstract, general terms that explain its difficulty in terms of an implied theory of personality. The lesson is stated directly, unadorned by figurative language and humor, and when the point has been made the reader is reminded that Guyon is an example for imitation. Much the same contrast can be seen between Ariosto's excursus on anger (*O.F.* XLII.1-6, where he is of course discussing justified anger) and Spenser's (II.4.1), which again ends by referring to a character as an example—this time of what not to do: "His owne woes authour, who so bound it [stubborn perturbation] finds . . . and it wilfully vnbindes."

If Ariosto sometimes adopts the pose of a courtly Ovidian *praeceptor amoris* (and *repudiator amoris*), Spenser is the Christian-Platonic *praeceptor amoris*. The advice he offers to the ladies is no longer the worldly wisdom of "parcite, Cecropides, iuranti credere Theseo" (*Ars amatoria*, III.457; cf. *O.F.* X.5-7). It is the counsel of perfection, informed with the passionate idealism that is very different from Ariosto's Horatian equanimity:

> Faire ympes of beautie, whose bringht shining beames
>   Adorne the world with like to heauenly light,
>   And to your willes both royalties and Realmes
>   Subdew, through conquest of your wondrous might,
>   With this faire flowre your goodly girlonde dight,
>   Of chastity and vertue virginall,
>   That shall embellish more your beautie bright,
>   And crowne your heades with heauenly coronall,
> Such as the Angels weare before Gods tribunall.
>
> To youre faire selues a faire ensample frame,
>   Of this faire virgin, this *Belphoebe* faire,
>   To whom in perfect loue, and spotlesse fame
>   Of chastitie, none liuing many compaire:
>   Ne poysnous Enuy iustly can empaire
>   The prayse of her fresh flowring Maidenhead;
>   For thy she standeth on the highest staire
>   Of th' honorable stage of womanhead,
> That Ladies all may follow her ensample dead.
>
> (III.5.53-54)

There is nothing of Horace or Ovid in Spenser's Narrator.

Time and time again, then, Spenser emphasizes the fact that his story demonstrates an ethical truth or that his characters are meant to be taken as examples for imitation[23] (or for the reverse):

> So greatest and most glorious thing on ground
>   May often need the helpe of weaker hand;
>   So feeble is mans state, and life vnsound,
>   That in assurance it may neuer stand,
>   Till it dissolued be from earthly band,
>   Proofe be thou Prince, the prowest man aliue,
>   And noblest borne of all in *Britayne* land;

Yet thee fierce Fortune did so nearly driue,
That had not grace thee blest, thou shouldest not suruiue.
(II.11.30)

As I have already said, teaching through example and glorification
was the major purpose of heroic poetry as discussed in the theory
of the age, and we must now consider the ways in which
Spenser's Poet-Narrator, in its contrast to Ariosto's, may reveal
an intent to outdo Ariosto along specifically epic lines, as Spenser
understood them. We may assume that, like Tasso, Spenser found
that Ariosto's poem fell short of the highest *idea* of epic poetry.
Although he rejected the insistence on Aristotelian unity, he was
similar to Tasso in his demand that epic poetry embody the
highest moral seriousness and truth.[24] The differences between
Spenser's and Ariosto's Narrators clearly demonstrate the tendency. Two aspects that remain to be discussed cast further light
on Spenser's use of Ariosto: his habit of elevating the material
of the poem to a position above the Poet (not, as in Ariosto,
below him and at his command) and his statements of the relation of the poem to reality.

3

Spenser avoids Ariosto's attitude of absolute domination of the
poem in favor of a more modest approach. He never, for example,
deliberately violates the reality of the events of the poem, and
exclamations of emotion consistently support the dominant narrative tone. Unlike Boiardo and Ariosto, Spenser uses the mention
of supposed sources of the poem (whether they be the Muses,
records of ancient times, or hearsay) to lend authority, plausibility, or an aura of antiquity to the story—never for humorous
effect. In only one place does Spenser's mention of a source
(not exactly a source, however) imply that his story is an invention:

> Whylome as antique stories tellen vs,
>   Those two were foes the fellonest on ground,
>   And battell make the dreddest daungerous,
>   That euer shrilling trumpets did resound;
>   Though now their acts be nowhere to be found,
>   As that renowned Poet them compyled,

With warlike numbers and Heroicke sound,
Dan *Chaucer*, well of English vndefyled,
On Fames eternall beadroll worthie to be fyled.
But wicked Time that all good thoughts doth waste,
And workes of noblest wits to nought out weare,
That famous moniment hath quite defaste,
And robd the world of threasure endlesse deare,
The which mote haue enriched all vs heare.
O cursed Eld the cankerworme of writs,
How may these rimes, so rude as doth appeare,
Hope to endure, sith workes of heauenly wits
Are quite deuourd, and brought to nought by little bits?

Then pardon, O most sacred happie spirit,
That I thy labours lost may thus reuiue,
And steale from thee the meede of thy due merit,
That none durst euer whilest thou wast aliue,
And being dead in vaine yet many striue:
Ne dare I like, but through infusion sweete
Of thine owne spirit, which doth in me suruiue,
I follow here the footing of thy feete,
That with thy meanings so I may the rather meete.
(IV.2.32-34)

Such a mention of a favorite author is entirely foreign to the Italian poet and reminds one of Chaucer's own discursiveness about his reading. We might recall that Ariosto never mentions Boiardo by name and only once refers to him as the author of the story he is finishing—and then it is to correct him:

Ma non bisogna in ciò ch' io mi diffonda,
Ch' a tutto il mondo è l'istoria palese:
Benche l'autor nel padre si confonda,
Ch' un per un' altro (io non so come) prese.*
(*O.F.* XV.73)

Spenser's attitude is characteristically humble. As above, he usually refers to the poem as "rude," as "my simple rime" (II.10. 50), or to his "Rustic Muse" (III.P.5). The explicit comments on the level of the poem's style relate it to the middle style:

O gently come into my feeble brest,
Come gently, but not with that mighty rage,

* But I need not speak at length about that, for everyone knows the story; although the author is mistaken about the father, for, I know not how, he confused one man with another.

Wherewith the martiall troupes thou doest infest,
And harts of great Heroës doest enrage,
That nought their kindled courage may aswage,
Soone as thy dreadfull trompe begins to sownd;
The God of warre with his fiers equipage
Thou doest awake, sleepe neuer he so sownd,
And scared nations doest with horrour sterne astownd.

Faire Goddesse lay that furious fit aside,
Till I of warres and bloudy *Mars* do sing,
And Briton fields with Sarazin bloud bedyde,
Twixt that great faery Queene and Paynim king,
That with their horrour heauen and earth did ring,
A worke of labour long, and endlesse prayse:
But now a while let downe that haughtie string,
And to my tunes thy second tenor rayse,
That I this man of God his godly armes may blaze.
(I.11.6-7)

The opening of II.10 also implies that the usual stylistic level of the poem is not the *genus grande*. Here Spenser is imitating the beginning of *O.F.* III; he shares with Ariosto (and thus differs from Tasso) the decision to cast his heroic poem predominantly in the middle register, which he occasionally rises above and, unlike Ariosto, seldom if ever falls below.[25]

Not only does Spenser, unlike Ariosto, invoke supernatural aid; he often represents himself as unworthy of the task before him or even as inadequate to it. The very beginning of the poem sounds this note in conjunction with the unmistakable epic reminiscence of Virgil:

Lo I the man, whose Muse whilome did maske,
As time her taught, in lowly Shepheards weeds,
Am now enforst a far vnfitter taske,
For trumpets sterne to change mine Oaten reeds,
And sing of Knights and Ladies gentle deeds;
Whose prayses hauing slept in silence long,
Me, all too meane, the sacred Muse areeds
To blazon broad emongst her learned throng:
Fierce warres and faithful loues shall moralize my song.
(I.P.1)

The difference between this epic beginning, which emphasizes the Poet's humility, and Ariosto's proud and humorous irony is enormous and characteristic. Spenser represents himself as com-

manded by the Muse to write the poem. He is "enforst" to it,
although he is "all too meane" and the Muse's "weaker Nouice,"
his wit weak and his tongue dull.

Later in this proem a reason is suggested for the Poet's un-
worthiness, beyond the ordinary requirements of the heroic
genre: his subject is the queen's "true glorious type"—the pattern
of virtue of which she is a copy (I.P.4). His humility thus becomes that of a mortal before the transcendental (cf. VI.P and
G.L. XX.21). The same reason applies to other occurrences of
the topos, as in the description of the transfigured Una:

> The blazing brightnesse of her beauties beame,
> And glorious light of her sunshyny face
> To tell, were as to striue against the streame.
> My ragged rimes are all too rude and bace,
> Her heauenly lineaments for to enchace.
>   (I.12.23)

In another variety of these expressions of humility, it is the
actual glory and virtue of the queen to whose portrayal the Poet
represents himself as inadequate. Sometimes the reason is that
the queen herself embodies perfectly the virtue under consideration:

> It falls me here to write of Chastity,
>   That fairest vertue, farre aboue the rest;
>   For which what needs me fetch from *Faery*
>   Forreine ensamples, it to haue exprest?
>   Sith it is shrined in my Soueraines brest,
>   And form'd so liuely in each perfect part,
>   That to all Ladies, which haue it profest,
>   Need but behold the pourtraict of her hart,
> If pourtrayd it might be by any liuing art.
>
> But liuing art may not least part expresse,
>   Nor life-resembling pencill it can paint,
>   All were it *Zeuxis* or *Praxiteles:*
>   His daedale hand would faile, and greatly faint,
>   And her perfections with his error taint:
>   Ne Poets wit, that passeth Painter farre
>   In picturing the parts of beautie daint,
>   So hard a workmanship aduenture darre,
> For fear through want of words her excellence to marre.
>
> How then shall I, Apprentice of the skill,
>   That whylome in diuinest wits did raine,

Presume so high to stretch mine humble quill?
Yet now my lucklesse lot doth me constraine
Hereto perforce. But O dred Soueraine
Thus farre forth pardon, sith that choicest wit
Cannot your glorious pourtraict figure plaine
That I in colourd showes may shadow it,
And antique praises vnto present persons fit.

(III.P.1-3)

These more courtly examples echo familiar complimentary addresses from Ariosto and Tasso.[26] They are far more frequent in
Spenser than in the Italian poets, however, and form a fundamental aspect of his Narrator. It is important to keep Spenser's
position of humility in mind when comparing him with Ariosto,
for the special reason that it has a close connection to the problem of the relation of the poem to reality. One of the most significant ways in which Spenser changed Ariosto's Narrator for
epic purposes is to be found in his statements about the truthfulness of his poem.

The relation of *The Faerie Queene* to reality is not hampered
by the insistence on literal historicity that underlies much of
Tasso's thinking about the epic (as it does that of other sixteenth-
century Aristotelian critics); Spenser does not have to ask the
Muse's pardon to interweave ornaments with the truth ("s' intesso
fregi al ver"). On the other hand, he recognizes a responsibility
to historical truth that is foreign to Ariosto. His freedom, based
on a broad conception of the ways in which epic poetry can be
true, bore fruit in a highly complex interplay of shifting levels
of meaning.

The poem is "a continued Allegory or darke conceit," "coloured
with an historicall fiction" (*Letter to Raleigh*), but we usually
find the Poet speaking of the historical fiction as literal historical
fact:

Helpe then, O holy Virgin chiefe of nine,
Thy weaker Nouice to performe thy will,
Lay forth out of thine euerlasting scryne
The antique rolles, which there lye hidden still,
Of Faerie knights and fairest *Tanaquill*,
Whom that most noble Briton Prince so long
Sought through the world, and suffered so much ill,
That I must rue his vndeserued wrong. (I.P.2)

Of warlike puissaunce in ages spent,
  Be thou faire *Britomart*, whose prayse I write,
  But of all wisedome be thou precedent,
  O soueraigne Queene.

(III.2.3)

In a sense it is tautological to say that the Poet speaks of the
fiction as if it were true, since the idea of a fiction presumes just
that pretense. As Spenser points out in the letter to Raleigh, in
making a historical fiction the subject of the poem, he is simply
doing what Homer and Virgil had done before him. Heroic poetry
is supposed to be historical. Ronsard in the *Franciade* or Tasso
in the *Rinaldo* never points out that his story is a fiction.[27]

As Spenser knew, of course, Tasso chose actual history for the
subject of his major epic, identified his Muse with the spirit of
truth as distinguished from the pagan muses, and suggested
that the element of fiction his poem contained was the sugar
coating on the pill of truth (*G.L.* I.2-3); in addition, he published an elaborate allegory of the poem. The way in which
Spenser handles the problem of the truth of his poem is similar
in purpose to Tasso's exordium (the only place in the poem
where Tasso drops the continuous fiction of the Virgilian-Homeric
Narrator). The choice of the discursive Ariostan Narrator made
it possible for Spenser to remind the reader constantly of the
varied semantics of his poem.

Now Ariosto did include some moral allegories in the *Orlando
furioso* and offered interpretative comments about one of them:

> Oh quante sono incantatrici, oh quanti
> Incantator tra noi, che non si sanno!
> Che con lor arti uomini e donne amanti
> Di sé, cangiando i visi lor, fatto hanno.
> Non con spirti constretti tali incanti,
> Né con osservazion di stelle fanno;
> Ma con simulazion, menzogne, e frodi
> Legano i cor d'indissolubil nodi.
>
> Chi l'annello d' Angelica, o più tosto
> Chi avesse quel de la ragion, potria
> Veder a tutti il viso, che nascosto
> Da finzione e d'arte non saria.
> Tal ci par bello e buono, che, deposto

Il liscio, brutto e rio forse parria.
Fu gran ventura quella di Ruggiero,
Ch' ebbe l'annel che gli scoperse il vero.*
(VIII.1-2)

Here we notice that Ariosto translates the allegorical symbol
into literal terms in a manner that explicitly detracts from the
appropriateness of the symbol ("Non con spiriti constretti" does
not say that "constrained spirits signify such and such"). He
preserves the indirection of the story itself by commenting on
the applicability of the allegory of sensuality to the theme of
hypocrisy, and ends with a sly thrust at this story, which again
detracts from the symbol ("Fu gran ventura quella di Ruggiero":
not "the ring Ruggiero was using was his reason," but "how
lucky Ruggiero was to have the ring, since his reason was inadequate").[28]

What Spenser does in a similar situation is quite different:

What warre so cruell, or what siege so sore,
    As that, which strong affections do apply
    Against the fort of reason euermore
    To bring the soule into captiuitie:
    Their force is fiercer through infirmitie
    Of the fraile flesh, relenting to their rage,
    And exercise most bitter tyranny
Vpon the parts, brought into their bondage:
No wretchednesse is like to sinfull vellenage.

But in a body, which doth freely yeeld
    His partes to reasons rule obedient,
    And letteth her that ought the scepter weeld,
    All happy peace and goodly gouernement
    Is setled there in sure establishment;
    There *Alma* like a virgin Queene most bright,
    Doth florish in all beautie excellent;
And to her guestes doth bounteous banket dight,
Attempted goodly well for health and for delight.
(II.11.1-2)

* Oh, how many enchantresses, how many enchanters there are among us,
whom we do not know! who, changing their faces, have with their wiles made
men and women love them. Not by constraining devils, not by observing the
stars, do they perform such enchantments, but with dissimulation, lies, and frauds
they bind hearts with inextricable knots. Whoever had the ring of Angelica, or rather,
whoever had the ring of Reason, would be able to see the real face of each, which
would not be hidden by feigning and art. He who now appears handsome and good,
might, if his makeup were left off, seem ugly and wicked. Ruggiero had a stroke of
good fortune, for he had the ring which showed him the truth.

Here the reverse of what Ariosto did has taken place: although the passage begins as a translation of the allegory into literal terms, at the end of it the literal is suddenly translated back again into the terms of the symbol. Add to that the connection between the rule of reason and the rule of Elizabeth, and a powerful elevation of the symbol has taken place. Thus the distinction between literal and metaphorical discourse, which is so carefully maintained by Ariosto (like that between the "historical" time of the poem and the present), tends to disappear: symbol and referent coalesce, not only in the story itself but in the Narrator's interpretative comments as well.

So also, at certain moments, the distinction between Spenser's characters as fictional personifications and as historical personages disappears. Thus after the trial of Duessa, an allegory whose referent is meant to be understood as primarily the principles of justice and mercy (and only secondarily the trial of Mary of Scotland), Mercilla is suddenly apostrophized, not as a symbol of mercy but in such a way that the reader understands the Poet is addressing the queen herself, not his fictional character:

> Some Clarkes doe doubt in their deuicefull art,
>   Whether this heauenly thing, whereof I treat,
>   To weeten *Mercie*, be of Iustice part,
>   Or drawne forth from her by diuine extreate.
>   This well I wote, that sure she is as great,
>   And meriteth to haue as high a place,
>   Sith in th' Almighties euerlasting seat
>   She first was bred, and borne of heauenly race;
> From thence pour'd down on men, by influence of grace.
>
> For if that Vertue be of so great might,
>   Which from iust verdict will for nothing start,
>   But to preserue inuiolated right,
>   Oft spilles the principall, to saue the part;
>   So much more then is that of powre and art,
>   That seekes to saue the subiect of her skill,
>   Yet neuer doth from doome of right depart:
>   As it is greater prayse to saue, then spill,
>   And better to reforme, then to cut off the ill.
>
> Who then can thee, *Mercilla*, throughly prayse,
>   That herein doest all earthly Princes pas?
>   What heauenly Muse shall thy great honour rayse
>   Vp to the skies, whence first deriu'd it was,

And now on earth it selfe enlarged has,
From th' vtmost brinke of the *Armericke* shore,
Vnto the margent of the *Molucas?*
Those Nations farre thy iustice doe adore:
But thine owne people do thy mercy prayse much more.
(V.10.1-3)

This effect is characteristic of Spenser; it occurs in a slightly different form in the magical episode of Calidore's meeting with Colin Clout, in which the shifting of the planes of reality contributes much of the charm. What happens here is even more complex than in any of the other examples we have discussed. Colin Clout is obviously a symbol of the poet himself; his activity is symbolic of the poet's activities in the writing of his love poetry. When Colin speaks, the distinction slowly evaporates, and the Poet himself finally speaks through him in virtually literal terms:

Another Grace she well deserues to be,
  In whom so many Graces gathered are,
  Excelling much the meane of her degree;
  Diuine resemblaunce, beauty soueraine rare,
  Firme Chastity, that spight ne blemish dare;
  All which she with such courtesie doth grace,
  But quite are dimmed, when she is in place.
She made me often pipe and now to pipe apace.

Sunne of the world, great glory of the sky,
  That all the world doest lighten with thy rayes,
  Great *Gloriana,* greatest Maiesty,
  Pardon thy shepheard, mongst so many layes,
  As he hath sung of thee in all his dayes,
  To make one minime of thy poore handmayd,
  And vnderneath thy feate to place her prayse,
  That when thy glory shall be farre displayd
To future age of her this mention may be made.
(VI.10.27-28)

What makes the effect so subtle is the fact that, at the beginning of the scene, the Poet has apostrophized this symbol of himself:

Pype iolly shepheard, pype thou now apace
Vnto thy loue, that made thee low to lout:

Thy loue is present there with thee in place,
Thy loue is there aduaunst to be another Grace.
(VI.10.16)

This manner of introducing his own amatory experiences into
the poem is very different from Ariosto's references to himself
as lover. In addition to the obvious dissimilarity between Spenser's seriousness and Ariosto's irony, there are other important
differences. Spenser separates and distances from himself as epic
Poet the figure of himself as lover, but Ariosto identifies the two
and represents his poetic activity as determined by his lover's
madness. Spenser refers to himself in terms of pastoral conventions; he does not speak directly, but makes a character who is
a transparent symbol of himself express his attitude. The very
indirection of Spenser's reference helps to create the impression
that the emotions Colin expresses are really Spenser's own and
refer to his actual beloved; the directness of Ariosto's helps us
to identify it as ironic pretense. Furthermore, the effect of Spenser's distancing of his personal emotion is to maintain the humility
of the actual poet and, at the same time, to heighten and make
more impersonal the attitude of the epic Poet.

In Spenser's Narrator, then, we see a shifting of roles that,
though it may have been suggested by Ariosto's Narrator, is
quite different from it. One way of identifying the difference
would be to say that Spenser has adapted Ariosto's chameleonic
method to a view of man that includes the transcendental as a
possible content of representative human experience: Spenser is
able to achieve a continuity and coherence among the potentially
inconsistent roles he plays, whereby they are all reconciled from
above, in terms of a principle that subsumes them. There is of
course an ultimate—and very strong—consistency in Ariosto's
Narrator: the naturalistically conceived *personality* that we infer
or construct and the absolute artistic will that holds the universe
of the poem together. The *Orlando furioso* suggests that man is
ondoyant et divers and that the coherence and consistency of the
personality is at best precarious and difficult; furthermore, the
natural principle of personality that so strongly emerges in the
figure of the Poet becomes the only principle of identity we are
left with in the natural world in which Ariosto represents himself as writing. But Spenser does not represent himself as writing

in a world cut off from the transcendental, and it is therefore possible for him to show how conflicts are reconcilable in terms of a principle higher than that of natural personality, in terms, namely, of the immanent transcendental.

The contrast with Tasso is perhaps even more instructive, since both poets reflect the late-sixteenth-century desire for explicit moral and religious seriousness in poetry. Spenser's choice of the Ariostan Narrator is parallel to his choice of the Ariostan structural pattern (carried even further in the direction of variety). Structurally, *The Faerie Queene* reflects a willingness to let the interrelation of multiple plots remain suspended until a final synthesis is achieved; the figure of the Poet reflects the same willingness to adopt a provisional position, which is later defined in terms of a general principle. Compared with Tasso's attitudes, Spenser's willingness to extend the variety of the poem—and of the self—is staggeringly optimistic. Indeed Spenser probably overestimated his capacity to synthesize the poem, but the important thing here is that there is no indication that he felt endangered by variety; Tasso's whole career, as we have seen, revolved around his sense of the danger. Spenser's undertaking, of course, reflects his sense that the unity of the poem did not depend upon the unity of his own personality, but upon that of the transcendency which spoke through him; Tasso, on the contrary, like other men of his culture, felt less and less confidence in the possibility of divine inspiration. Hence Tasso was also concerned with the central issue of the analogy between the poet and God, an issue that he ultimately resolved by renouncing the effort to create a fictional world and by accepting the mediated transcendency available in ecclesiastical tradition. Spenser was able to transcend this dilemma because he could appeal directly to sanctions that he considered independent of his natural personality as well as directly operative in his poetic activity.

In such a context, then, the humility of Spenser before his material makes far greater claims for the poem than Ariosto's attitude of absolute control does for his. Spenser's different roles complement and mutually support one another. Like Ariosto's differing poses, they dramatize the complexity of mental activity required for an adequate apprehension of reality, but this time the reality includes the transcendental.

Spenser's differences from both Ariosto and Tasso can perhaps be seen with special clarity in the passages about the historicity of the poem. Spenser feels called upon to defend his poem against the charge that it is not historically true:

> Right well I wote most mighty Soueraine,
>   That all this famous antique history,
>   Of some th' aboundance of an idle braine
>   Will iudged be, and painted forgery,
>   Rather then matter of iust memory,
>   Sith none, that breatheth liuing air, does know,
>   Where is that happy land of Faery,
>   Which I so much do vaunt, yet no where show,
> But vouch antiquities, which no body can know.
>
> (II.P.1)

His answer is significant:

> Of Faerie lond yet if he more inquire,
>   By certain signes here set in sundry place
>   He may it find; ne let him then admire,
>   But yield his sence to be too blunt and bace
>   That no 'te without an hound fine footing trace.
>   And thou, O fairest Princesse vnder sky,
>   In this faire mirrhour maist behold thy face,
>   And thine owne realmes in lond of Faery,
> And in this antique Image thy great auncestry.
>
> (II.P.4)

As we have seen, Spenser tells us at the beginning of the poem that his subject is "the true glorious type," the principle or idea, of the various virtues. From this basic position the poem can take on other meanings. The queen's virtues are so exalted that she is herself a "mirrour of grace and maiestie diuine"; if the subject of part of the poem is the idea of justice, the Poet can claim that the proper imitation of justice inevitably involves portraying the queen's justice (V.P.11; cf. III.P.1-3, VI.P.6-7). If that is the case, Faeryland itself is seen as a metaphor for Elizabeth's England (II.P.1-5), and one referent of the fable is history itself. What Spenser repeatedly invokes the Muse to reveal, then, are historical "facts" that he elsewhere shows to be metaphors. And by showing that the "antiquities, which no body can know" are metaphors, he shows that the role of the Poet in asking the Muse to reveal them is also metaphorical. It is a fiction, but a fiction for a real aspect of the poetic process, as becomes clear when that process is described in somewhat more literal terms in the proem to Book VI. Spenser is not juxtaposing the roles in order to dramatize their disparity. Through the shifting reference of the poem to reality and of his comments on it, Spenser is trying to preserve the obligation to historical truth expected of the epic poet, the epic conventions of invoking knowledge, and a genuine sense of transcendent insight, of supernatural inspiration.

These passages reveal an aspect of Spenser's art that is fundamental to the claim of *The Faerie Queene* for consideration as an epic poem: for when the fiction becomes a metaphor revealing the principles that govern history, it becomes more philosophical *and* historical than any such dressing up of the facts as Tasso's.[29] Spenser never draws parallels between the events of his poem and actual history, as Ariosto does, for the simple reason that its meaning includes history as no account purporting to be merely historical can.

Although Ariosto's discursive Narrator was clearly Spenser's model, then, and although many of the passages of his Narrator's commentary are adapted from Ariosto, the changes he made are elaborate and fundamental. All those I have discussed—the omission of irony, the heightening of terms of address, the introduction of expository purpose and structure, the insistent emphasis on glorification and exemplification, the new hortatory tone, the marked attitude of humility before the material, the elaborate distancing of personal references, the recurrent claim to supernatural inspiration, and, perhaps most important, the explanation and dramatization of the poem's shifting allegorical reference to reality—all of these changes reveal a strikingly consistent purpose in Spenser's adaptation of Ariosto's manner. They are clearly the result of his effort to "overgo" Ariosto in the writing of a poem with specifically epic seriousness and dignity. And Spenser, unlike Ariosto or Tasso, does not consider himself restricted to his natural powers. He does not produce the limited reality of the humanly fashioned analogue of the cosmos; he wishes to present that golden nature of which Sidney spoke—nature illumined and transfigured by the light of the transcendental. Spenser looks forward to Milton and ultimately to Wordsworth and Yeats. Ariosto looks forward to Montaigne, Byron, and Joyce. Together they represent two of the most significant literary traditions we have inherited from the Renaissance.

NOTES
INDEX

NOTES

INTRODUCTION

1. *Poetics* 1448a, trans. Ingram Bywater (Oxford, 1909).
2. For a succinct account of the problem of the narrator, see Käte Friedemann, *Die Rolle des Erzählers in der Epik* (Leipzig, 1910), pp. 21-41.
3. See Chapter V below, notes 1, 30, and 59.
4. The "rhetoric" of narrative is thus considerably wider in scope than is allowed for even in Wayne C. Booth's admirable *Rhetoric of Fiction* (Chicago, 1961), to date the most important discussion of the problem in English.
5. The "implied author," in Booth's terminology.
6. Booth's discussion of the "authorial voice" sometimes encourages this obfuscation, as do many of the critics he cites. See, for instance, *Rhetoric of Fiction*, pp. 151-159, 264-266, 271-282.
7. *The Ambassadors*, New York Edition (1909), I, 5.
8. Charles S. Singleton, *Dante Studies I: Elements of Structure* (Cambridge, Mass., 1954), p. 62.
9. See, for instance, René Wellek and Austin Warren, *Theory of Literature* (New York, 1949), pp. 231-232.
10. The common complaint of exponents of the "objective" method, that authorial intrusion destroys the "illusion of reality" (see Wellek and Warren, p. 232; Booth, pp. 40-53, 254-256), betrays a curiously naive notion of fictional illusion and a rigid demand for univocity in fiction, which are curiously parallel to the views of many Counter-Reformation Italian critics (see Chapter VI, note 50).
11. See Bruno Snell, *The Discovery of the Mind*, trans. T. G. Rosenmeyer (Oxford, 1953), ch. 1.
12. Homer represents himself as owing both matter and disposition to the Muse (*Odyssey* I.10). See Walther Krause, "Die Auffassung des Dichterberufs im frühen Griechentum," *Wiener Studien*, 68:67-72 (1955); Steele Commager, *The Odes of Horace* (New Haven, 1962), pp. 1-49; and Leo Spitzer, "Note on the Poetic and the Empirical 'I' in Medieval Authors," *Traditio*, 4:414-422 (1946). The habit of representing stories as received, whether from a natural or a supernatural source, rather than as invented by the writer dominates the narrative art of the Middle Ages. When we find in Ariosto a relentless insistence on the fictitious and invented nature of his story, we have reached a major turning point in the conventions of narrative art. It is important that the protestation of having received the story and that of having invented it are both instances of *ethical persuasion*.
13. There are some significant exceptions among fictitious, participating Narrators, such as Ivan Karamazov and the governess of *The Turn of the Screw*. Their peculiar ambiguity of effect derives from Dostoevsky's having exploited and James's having failed adequately to allow for this basic convention; the fictitious Narrator is not usually supposed to be the inventor of

the story, however crucial his unreliability may be. The factual and moral reliability of Narrators is the central theme of Booth's study.

14.   This has of course been widely recognized (see Booth, pp. 285-309, 422-434), but not always in the full context.

15.   Widely studied, perhaps most perceptively by Booth in *Rhetoric of Fiction*, pp. 221-234, 429-432, and "The Self-Conscious Narrator in Comic Fiction," *PMLA*, 67:163-185 (1952). See also Georges Blin, *Stendhal et les problèmes du roman* (Paris, 1953); Geoffrey Tillotson, *Thackeray the Novelist* (Cambridge, Eng., 1954).

16.   Friedrich Schlegel explicitly relates the irony of Diderot, Sterne, and Jean-Paul Richter to the "divine wit, the fantasy of an Ariosto, a Cervantes, a Shakespeare" (*Kritische Schriften*, ed. W. Rasch, Munich, n.d., p. 10; cf. pp. 19, 270, 274, 306-313, 320). See also A. E. Lussky, *Tieck's Romantic Irony* (Chapel Hill, 1932); M. H. Abrams, *The Mirror and the Lamp* (New York, 1953), pp. 235-244, 272-285; H. Frenzel, *Ariost und die romantische Dichtung* (Studi italiani, 7; Cologne, 1962). On the Hegelian concept of irony in humor, see Chapter V, note 22.

17.   See Chapter II, notes 1-3. On classical literature, see above, note 12, and Brooks Otis, *Virgil: A Study in Civilized Poetry* (Oxford, 1964).

I. TWO ROMAN POETS

1.   *Rhetoric* 1356a, trans. W. Rhys Roberts (Oxford, 1909).

2.   For example, *De inv.* I.15-19; *De orat.* II.178-216.

3.   See I.4.23-5.5, III.6.5-16, and *passim*.

4.   See especially *Institutio* IV.i, VI.i-ii, XI.i. On the whole question, see R. Heinze, "Fides," *Hermes*, 24:148-150 (1929).

5.   *Rhetoric* 1356a; see also 1356b, 1366a-1368a, 1377b-1378a, 1395a, 1403b, 1415a, 1416a-1419b.

6.   Citations of Horace are to *Q. Horatii Flacci Poetae Venusini, Omnia Poemata cum Ratione Carminum* (Venice, Bonello, 1562). In transcription I follow modern conventions of spelling and punctuation.

7.   A. W. Allen, " 'Sincerity' and the Roman Elegist," *Classical Philology*, 45:153-156 (1950); and "Sunt qui Propertium malint," in *Critical Essays on Roman Literature*, ed. J. P. Sullivan (London, 1962), pp. 121, 126-129, 146. See also A. W. Allen, "Elegy and the Classical Attitude toward Love: Propertius I.1," *Yale Classical Studies*, 11:265 (1950); R. Bürger, *De Ovidi carminum amatorium inventione et arte* (Braunschweig, 1901).

8.   See L. P. Wilkinson's excellent discussion of the *Amores* in *Ovid Recalled* (Cambridge, Eng., 1955) pp. 17-82.

9.   See, for instance, Martin Schanz, *Geschichte der römischen Literatur*, 3rd ed. (Munich, 1911) pt. 2, 1st half, pp. 300 ff; and H. J. Rose, *A Handbook of Latin Literature*, 2nd ed. (London, 1949), p. 329.

10.   "Propertius as Praeceptor Amoris," *Classical Philology*, 5:29 (1910).

11.   *Ibid.*, p. 40.

12.   "Ovid himself indicates the character of his work, since he calls his

muse 'iocosa'; he thus wishes his poem to be conceived as playful, as a joke. The playful character springs from the love of *hetairai* being treated as a science and therefore with all the seriousness that, let us say, a treatment of cosmic love would have required. In this contradiction between form and content there is something parodic and gay; the content itself is, however, rightly understood, free from parody" (Schanz, pt. 2, 1st half, p. 304). I disagree with the last clause, as will appear.

13.   Emile Ripert, *Ovide, poète de l'amour, des dieux, et de l'exile* (Paris, 1921). The heroic and "moral" cloaks Ovid throws over the libertinism that is the subject of the *Ars* and the *Amores* are simply further impudencies. See E. K. Rand's delightful discussion in *Ovid and His Influence* (London, 1925).

14.   All citations of Ovid are to *Ovidius De Arte Amandi et De Remedio Amoris cum Comento* (Venice: Ioannes de Triduo, 1494). Again, I follow modern conventions of spelling and punctuation. At *Rem.* 574 and 758 I correct the reading to follow E. J. Kenney's text (Oxford, 1961).

15.   Much of the liveliness of the *Ars* derives from this metaphor, by which we are spectators of a not too serious liaison with all its dramatic little scenes; cf. I.39, 63, 771; II.9-10, 425, 429; III.26, 99-100, 467, 747, 809; *Rem.* 811ff.

16.   An exaggeration of the conceit of *Amores* I.9, which ingeniously explores the similarities between lover and soldier.

17.   Bürger, p. 52, notes the importance of the theme of the triumph in Propertius (III.4) and several verbal parallels with this passage. See also Ovid's *Amores* I.2, 7. Propertius treats the theme more seriously than Ovid, for whom it is already thoroughly discredited.

18.   Cf. II.537-551; III.245-250, 577-590; *Rem.* 499-500.

19.   See Wilkinson, pp. 4-12 and notes, and Bürger, pp. 94-96.

20.   Similar passages are those which attack and defend the present age. In Book II Ovid complains that poetry is unregarded and that this is the true Golden Age because gold buys anything, including honor and love (275ff). But in Book III he hymns modern Rome as the acme of brilliance and refinement, echoing his own language of Book II ("nunc aurea Roma est"), and incidentally poking fun at the skin-clad Homeric heroes and their rustic wives, impudently raising sophisticated vice above the old Roman virtues Augustus was seeking to reinstate—"prisca iuvent alios" (107ff).

II. CHAUCER

1.   The first detailed study is by H. Lüdecke, *Die Funktion des Erzählers in Chaucers epischer Dichtung* (Halle, 1928), which surveys all of Chaucer's narrators and attempts to relate them to those of his contemporaries in England and on the Continent. More recent studies emphasizing the narrators include B. H. Bronson, "Chaucer's Art in Relation to His Audience," *Five Studies in Literature* (Berkeley, 1940), pp. 1-53; J. V. Cunningham, "The Literary Form of the Prologue to the *Canterbury Tales*," *Modern*

Philology, 49:172-181 (1952); Ben Kimpel, "The Narrator of the *Canter-bury Tales,*" *ELH,* 20:77-87 (1953); E. H. Duncan, "Narrator's Points of View in the Portrait-Sketches, Prologue to the *Canterbury Tales,*" *Essays in Honor of Walter Clyde Curry* (Nashville, 1954), pp. 77-101; E. T. Donald-son, "Chaucer the Pilgrim," *PMLA,* 69:928-936 (1954), and *Chaucer's Poetry* (New York, 1958); Dorothy Bethurum, "Chaucer's Point of View in the Love Poems," *PMLA,* 74:511-520 (1959); Charles Muscatine, *Chau-cer and the French Tradition* (Berkeley, 1960); R. O. Payne, *The Key of Remembrance: A Study of Chaucer's Poetics* (New Haven, 1963). For *Troilus and Criseyde,* see note 3 below.

2.   See especially the important study by Wilhelm Kellermann, *Aufbau-stil und Weltbild Chrestiens von Troyes im Percevalroman* (Halle, 1936), and Albert Vàrvaro, *Il "Roman de Tristan" di Béroul* (Turino, 1963).

3.   Recent discussion of the narrator of the *Troilus* includes M. W. Bloom-field, "Distance and Predestination in *Troilus and Criseyde,*" *PMLA,* 72:14-26 (1957); Robert Jordan, "The Narrator of Chaucer's *Troilus,*" *ELH,* 25: 237-257 (1958); S. B. Meech, *Design in Chaucer's Troilus* (Syracuse, 1960); Sister Anne Barbara Gill, *Paradoxical Patterns in Chaucer's Troilus* (Wash-ington, 1960); Bethurum, pp. 516-518; Donaldson, pp. 965-980; Muscatine, pp. 135-137, 161-163; Payne, pp. 216-232; and, most recently, E. T. Donald-son, "The Ending of Chaucer's *Troilus,*" *Early English and Norse Studies,* ed. Arthur Brown and Peter Foote (London, 1963), pp. 26-45.

4.   See Lüdecke, Bloomfield, and Meech (pp. 370-385).

5.   See the valuable discussion in Jordan, pp. 242-246, and the con-venient bibliography in Payne, pp. 333-339. I shall refer only occasionally to Boccaccio's narrator in the *Filostrato;* it seems to me to have been ade-quately described by Meech and others.

6.   Along with the older studies of the problem—Kittredge, Tatlock, Young, Curry—I refer to Jordan (see note 3); A. J. Denomy, "The Two Moralities of Chaucer's *Troilus and Criseyde,*" *Transactions of the Royal Society of Canada,* 44:35-46 (1950); Charles A. Owen, Jr., "The Signifi-cance of Chaucer's Revisions of *Troilus and Criseyde,*" *Modern Philology* 55:1-5 (1957); and the recent essay by S. Nagarajan, "The Conclusion to Chaucer's *Troilus and Criseyde,*" *Essays in Criticism,* 13:1-8 (1963).

7.   This is essentially the view of D. W. Robertson, both in his "Chau-cerian Tragedy," *ELH,* 19:1-37 (1952), and in his recent *A Preface to Chaucer* (Princeton, 1963), pp. 472-502. It will be readily apparent how much this chapter owes to Robertson's work; at the same time, it seems to me that we must find a way of reading Chaucer that enables us to dis-tinguish him from, say, St. Augustine or Innocent III. See R. E. Kaske's re-view article, "Chaucer and Medieval Allegory," *ELH,* 30:175-192 (1963).

8.   See the perceptive comments in Payne, pp. 229-230.

9.   All citations of *Troilus and Criseyde* are to the edition of R. K. Root (Princeton, 1926, 1945; copyright Princeton University Press). Arabic numerals refer to stanzas, not lines.

10.   It seems to me far too simple to see merely a moral decline in Troilus's conduct, as does Robertson (*Preface,* pp. 475-480).

11.   See Payne, p. 230.

12.   I refer in these paragraphs to M. W. Bloomfield's interpretation of this and related passages: "The aspect of temporal distance is the one most

constantly emphasized throughout the poem . . . Chaucer again and again tells us that the events he is recording are historical and past. He lets us know that customs have changed since the time when Pandarus, Troilus, and Criseyde lived. The characters are pagans . . . Their ways of living are different from ours. Their love-making varies from the modern style . . . At times, it is true, Chaucer is very anachronistic, but he still succeeds in giving his readers (or listeners) a feeling for the pastness of his characters and their sad story and *for what we today call cultural relativity*" (p. 16; italics added). This seems to me a patent distortion of the sense of the text and of its rhetorical function.

13. The force of the epilogue, in which all pursuit of earthly happiness is condemned, not merely that engaged in by "olde pagans," depends on, and is prepared by, this identification. See especially V.261: "dampned al *oure* werk that *folweth* so the blynde lust" (italics added); the possessive pronoun does not appear in the stanza from the *Teseida* Chaucer is adapting (quoted in Root's note).

14. As usual, I omit discussion of the function here of formal rhetorical patterns, whose importance in these passages is admirably discussed by Jordan, pp. 242-246.

15. It is the decisive break in the Narrator's participation in the vision of his characters. From the beginning of Book IV on, the movement toward the epilogue is constant and gradual. Jordan's assertion of a radical break at the epilogue seems false to me, as does Donaldson's analysis of the Narrator's "nervous breakdown" (p. 34); both depend on an exaggerated and illegitimate separation of the Narrator from the author. See below, note 19.

16. "The meaning of the poem does not hinge on so fortuitous a fact as Troilus' placing his faith in the wrong woman or in a bad woman" (Muscatine, p. 164).

17. The long debate over the character of Criseyde is usefully summarized in Arthur Mizener, "Character and Action in the Case of Criseyde," *PMLA*, 54:65-68 (1939); in Meech, pp. 395-397; and in Muscatine, pp. 265-267, notes 55 and 61. The idea that Criseyde's actions can be explained as a consistent expression of her character and motivation (thus of her concrete individuality as such) was effectively demolished by Mizener who, however, denies that there is any cause for her betrayal within Criseyde herself (as I read it, Muscatine's theory of Criseyde's "ambiguity" comes to the same thing—see especially pp. 164-165). My own view is that there is indeed a cause within her but that in Augustinian terminology it is a *causa deficiens* rather than a *causa efficiens*, and that her fall is thus an instance of the *habitus ad nihilum* (see Etienne Gilson, *The Christian Philosophy of Saint Augustine*, trans. L. E. M. Lynch, New York, 1960, pp. 143-148).

18. The principle is fundamental in Christian Platonic thought, though it must be made clear that the ontology in question is *essential* and that the question is meaningless in an *existential* ontology. The soul that turns away from the good to the mutable begins an ontological descent: "I do not deny that those who are evil, are evil; but I purely and simply deny that they *are*. . . . A thing *is* when it keeps an order and preserves its nature; what falls away from its nature leaves that being which is situated in its nature. But the evil have power, you say; nor do I deny it, but that power of theirs derives, not from their strength, but from their weakness." (*De consolatione*

philosophiae IV.2; *Corpus scriptorum ecclesiasticorum latinorum* 67; trans. mine). What Boethius says of the cosmos is also true of the soul: "For either there is no one thing to which everything is related and, as it were deprived of their one vertex, all things are fluid without someone to govern them, or, if there is something to which everything hastens, that will be the highest good. . . . This world would never have come together out of so many and so different parts, unless there had been one to yoke together such different things. But the very discordant diversity of their natures would in turn drive apart and uproot these conjoined things, unless there were one who held together what he had joined (*ibid.*, III.11, 12). Cf. Augustine, *Confessions* IV.14ff; XIII.2-18. Troilus' inability to solve the philosophical problem of freedom and foreknowledge and his subjection to external circumstance—that is, the inadequacy of his understanding and the misdirection of his will—are in this view correlatives. Cf. *Confessions* IV.23, IV.26: ("my mutable nature had gone astray of its own accord and . . . to err was now its punishment," trans. Ryan). Fundamental texts here are Romans 1:20-25 and Ephesians 4:14. See Robertson, *Preface*, pp. 473, 494-500.

19. On the question of Chaucer's revisions—especially the addition of Troilus' hymn to love, his ponderings on fate and foreknowledge, and his ascent to the spheres—see Charles A. Owen, Jr., "The Significance of Chaucer's Revisions of *Troilus and Criseyde*," *Modern Philology*, 55:1-5 (1957), which admirably demonstrates the reinforcement of certain important symmetries by the additions.

20. Troilus' vision after death is not, I think, to be taken as an assertion within the story that Troilus went to Heaven, with all the doctrinal problems that would entail. Rather its function is allusive, symbolic, almost operatic. By alluding to the *Somnium Scipionis* here, Chaucer is pointing to an area of doctrine, and the "actual" fate of Troilus is as irrelevant as is the fate of Scipio in the *Somnium*—in both cases the character is a pretext.

21. See my discussion of the allegory of the *Divine Comedy* and *The Faerie Queene* in *Comparative Literature*, 13:172-173 (1961).

III. PETRARCH

1. On the question of dating the composition of individual poems, see Ruth S. Phelps, *The Earlier and Later Forms of Petrarch's Canzoniere* (Chicago, 1925). There is now a consensus that, although there are many noteworthy violations of chronological order, the poems are in general arranged in the order of their composition. The order of composition, however, is quite distinct from the fictional chronology within the work, which is my concern. See also E. H. Wilkins, *The Making of the Canzoniere and Other Petrarchan Studies* (Rome, 1955).

2. Text and translations of the *Canzoniere* are from an edition that I am preparing.

3. See Carlo Calcaterra, *Nella selva del Petrarca* (Bologna, 1952).

4. A moot point in the interpretation of the poem is whether "ove le belle membra pose" refers to Laura's being *in* or *beside* the water.

PETRARCH   247

5. Psalms 148, 149, 150; Daniel 31:1-90.

6. The theme is related to that of Guinizelli's famous canzone "Al cor gentil ripara sempre amore," in which the causal relation between lady and lover is compared to that between God and the angels. See Charles S. Singleton, *An Essay on the "Vita Nuova"* (Cambridge, Mass., 1949), pp. 60-73.

7. The third line, "or ride or piange or teme or s'assecura," is a clear reference to the Stoic theory of the four perturbations of the soul, discussed also in the *Secretum* (Book II), which cites Virgil's famous line, *Aeneid* VI.733-734; the theory underlies much of Petrarch's treatment of the instability of the soul.

8. As is evident, I do not accept the analysis of the structure of the *Canzoniere* on which Ruth Phelps's widely accepted theory of its evolution is based (see note 1 above).

9. The left side is, in medieval thought, the side of the appetitive faculties of the soul. See John Freccero, "Dante's Firm Foot and the Journey Without a Guide," *HThR*, 52:245-281 (1959). Petrarch mentions spiritual limping in several poems, for instance in nos. 88 and 214.

10. A theory of the evolution of the *Canzoniere* needs to take into account the fact that although only one fourth of Part I is later than the Chigi version, two thirds of Part II is later than the Chigi version, and that this two thirds reveals structures not foreseeable in the first third. It is striking that, when Petrarch added the last two thirds of Part II to the Chigi version (if that is the correct theory of the relation of the early and late forms), he did not find it necessary to change the order of any of the poems in Part II, although he changed that of many in Part I. I incline toward the view that Petrarch's conception of the structure of the *Canzoniere* became increasingly clear and controlled toward the end of his life (the vigor of his revisions, insofar as we can date them, is certainly unimpaired); the rearrangement of the last poems in the autograph (renumbered after having been already copied into the codex) supports this view. See below, note 12.

11. Kenelm Foster, O.P., "Beatrice or Medusa: The Penitential Element in Petrarch's 'Canzoniere,'" *Italian Studies Presented to E. R. Vincent* (Cambridge, Eng., 1962), pp. 41-56.

12. The theme of idolatry appears explicitly in 16, 191, 193, and 326, which compare the sight of Laura with the Beatific Vision; in 206, which states a willingness to *adore* her in a dark cell (that of the heart—this is a variant of a well-known interpretation of the myth of Pygmalion); in 264 and 360, both of which include it among the self-accusations. It occurs implicitly in such poems as 78, 123, 173. Medusa is referred to in 309, 51, 179, 197, 213, 366. On the medieval conception of love as idolatry, see D. W. Robertson, *A Preface to Chaucer* (Princeton, 1963), pp. 99-113. It is noteworthy that most of these poems appear only in post-Chigi stages of the *Canzoniere;* Petrarch seems to have decided late in his work on the collection that he wished to intensify the importance in Part I of both themes.

13. The *adúnata* in Petrarch frequently have this sense, as in 57 and 66.

14. See Augustine, *Confessions* XIII.35; *Enarrationes in Psalmos* 92.1; Bernard of Clairvaux, *Sermons on the Song of Songs* 33; Hrabanus Maurus, *De universo* X.iv.

15. A theme Petrarch conceived in a way clearly derived from Augustine's *Confessions;* see XI.14, 26, 29; XIII.2-9.

16. *Senil.* XIII.11.

17. Ernst Zinn, "Fragment über Fragmente," in *Das Unvollendete als künstlerische Form,* ed. J. A. Schmoll Gen. Eisenwerth (Bern, 1959), pp. 161-163, calls attention to Biblical uses of the term *fragment* (notably John 6:12—"Gather up the fragments that remain, lest they perish") and traces some early German instances of the use of the term in an artistic or literary sense, mostly from the eighteenth century. Petrarch's use of it in a literary sense may be one of the earliest instances; however, there was a basis for it in the exegetical tradition—the gathering up of the fragments of John 6:12 was interpreted by Bede and Alcuin as referring to the collation and interpretation by scholars of the obscure portions of Scripture (Migne, *Patrologia latina* 92, 707-708; 100, 823).

18. See Leo Spitzer, "Note on the Poetic and the Empirical 'I' in Medieval Authors," *Traditio,* 4:414-422 (1946).

IV. BOIARDO

1. See the edition by Michele Catalano (Florence, 1940).

2. See II.8.62: "qui sedeti ad agio" (here you sit at your ease). Cf. II.13.2, II.27.2, III.8.1. As Zottoli points out (I, xx), "the cantos of the poem were written down and circulated in manuscript." In I.1.91, the audience are told that they will hear "un bel fatto" if they come back to hear the next canto (cf. I.6.69); in I.19.65, the canto ends with the promise of continuation "questo altro giorno" (cf. II.27.2). Sometimes Boiardo violates the illusion of recitation; the use of "de sopra" in I.6.1 or I.7.1 implies that the audience is reading the poem. In several passages there are explicit references to the poem's being written, as in I.29.35, II.31.50. All citations of Boiardo are to *Tutte le opere,* ed. Angelandrea Zottoli, 2 vols., 2nd ed. (Milan: Arnaldo Mondadori Editore, 1944).

3. See III.1.2, III.9.1-3. But none is mentioned by name, as are so many in the *Orlando furioso.*

4. Cf. Petrarch, no. 71, lines 10-15.

5. Cf. *Orlando furioso* I.3, *Morgante* I.3ff.

6. A similar evocation of an ideally harmonious society occurs in Castiglione's *Cortegiano:* "Thus, all the hours of the day were given over to honorable and pleasant exercises both of the body and of the mind; but because, owing to his infirmity, the Duke always retired to sleep very early after supper, everyone usually repaired to the rooms of the Duchess, Elisabetta Gonzaga at that hour. . . Here, then, gentle discussions and innocent pleasantries were heard, and on everyone's face a jocund gaiety could be seen depicted, so much so that this house could be called the very abode of joyfulness. Nor do I believe that the sweetness that is had from a beloved company was ever savored in any other place as it once was there. For, not to speak of the great honor it was for each of us to serve such a lord as I

have described above, we all felt a supreme happiness whenever we came into the presence of the Duchess. And it seemed that this was a chain that bound us all together in love, in such wise that never was there concord of will or cordial love between brothers greater than that which was there among us all. The same was among the ladies, with whom one had very free and most honorable association, for to each it was permitted to speak, sit, jest, and laugh with whom he pleased" (from *The Book of the Courtier* by Baldassare Castiglione, translated by Charles S. Singleton, pp. 15-16; copyright 1959 by Charles S. Singleton and Edgar De N. Mayhew; all quotations from this translation used by permission of Doubleday & Company, Inc.). There are important parallels in both works to the situation of Cicero's *De oratore* and to the ideal society depicted in the frame of Boccaccio's *Decameron*, both of which were extremely influential.

7.   Boiardo's concern for the decorum of genre may be seen clearly in the elaborate formalism and purism of the *Amores* and the Latin poetry— for example, in the self-conscious effect of the introduction of epic language into the bucolic style of the tenth Latin eclogue.

8.   Cf. II.18.1-3 and I.1.2: it is the supremacy of love that motivates and justifies the mixture of Breton and Carolingian elements.

9.   This remembered situation is clearly similar to Dante's view of Matilda in the Earthly Paradise (*Purg.* XXVIII); cf. also "il tremolar della marina" (*Purg.* I.117), and Poliziano's ballata "I' mi trovai un dí tutto soletto."

10.   The spring as impelling the poet to compose is a dominant theme of the *Natureingang* of troubador poetry, which has been studied in detail by D. Scheludko, "Zur Geschichte der Natureingang bei den Trobadors," *Zeitschrift für französische Sprache und Literatur*, 60:257-334 (1937).

11.   For the traditional ideas of cosmic harmony on which Boiardo is drawing, see Leo Spitzer, *Classical and Christian Ideas of World Harmony: Prolegomena to an Interpretation of the Word "Stimmung"* (Baltimore, 1963).

V. ARIOSTO

1.   Although many critics have commented upon individual passages among those I shall discuss, there is, as far as I know, only one modern attempt systematically to deal with the exordia: Giuseppe G. Ferrero, "Sermone e poesia nell' *Orlando furioso* (gli esordi ai canti)," Università degli Studi di Torino, Facoltà di Magistero, *Scritti vari*, 1:185-202 (1950). This study makes some acute observations on individual passages, but it springs from an inadequate conception of the problem (as its limitation of attention to the exordia may suggest), and it repeats the Crocean commonplaces. It does not relate the exordia to the themes or structure of the poem except in a vague and superficial way.

2.   On the secrecy of Ariosto's relationship with Alessandra Benucci, which was so complete that no sixteenth-century biographers or commenta-

tors refer to it, see Michele Catalano, *Vita di Ludovico Ariosto* (Geneva, 1930), I, 402-403.

3.   I quote the text from the Cornell copy of the 1549 Gioliti (Venice) quarto (Agnelli-Ravegnani, *Annali delle edizioni ariostee*, Bologna, 1933, I, 82), with light modernization of spelling and punctuation. The departures from Debenedetti's 1928 text are exclusively in spelling and punctuation.

4.   For Turpin, see XIII.40, XVIII.175, XXIII.38, XXIII.62, XXIV.44, XXVI.22-23, XXIX.56, XXX.49, XXXI.79, XXXIII.85, XXXIV.86, XXXVIII. 10, XL.84, XLIV.23. Several of these are derived from Boiardo. Sometimes another source is mentioned for information Turpin supposedly does not supply, as in XXIV.44-45. There is no need to discuss in detail the topos of doubt or ignorance: VI.7, VIII.58, XIII.39, XIV.63 (based on Boiardo—*O.I.* I.19.49 and III.1.35), XV.88-89, XIX.22, XVIII.39, XXIV.44, XXIX.6-7, XXIX.47, XXX.71-72, XXXIII.85, XXXVI.58.

5.   Ernst Cassirer, *The Individual and the Cosmos in Renaissance Philosophy*, trans. Mario Domandi (New York, 1963), p. 159. See also M. H. Abrams, *The Mirror and the Lamp* (New York, 1953), pp. 272-277. To avoid misunderstanding, I must clarify the relation between my view and the noted interpretation of the poem by Benedetto Croce (1917). Croce characterizes Ariosto as the poet of harmony, but by harmony Croce means the harmony that *actually*, in his view, resides in things. He was not referring to the conception of cosmic harmony prevalent in the Renaissance, but to his own brand of Hegelianism, as will be clear from his characterization of art in general: "Now, consider that Art in its Idea is no other than the expression or representation of reality, which is opposition and struggle, but opposition and struggle that are perpetually resolved, which is multiplicity and diversity but also unity, which is dialectic and development but also, and because of this motion, cosmos and Harmony" (*Ariosto, Shakespeare e Corneille*, 4th ed., Bari, 1950, p. 23; my trans.). Ariosto is classified with poets who "do not love pure Art, but the *pure and universal content of Art*, not this or that particular struggle and harmony (erotic, political, moral, religious, and so forth), but struggle and Harmony in idea and eternal" (p. 24). This formula empties the poles of the supposed dialectic of any importance; Croce betrays himself in that "and so forth." Now the harmony Ariosto is supposed to have sung in the poem is, according to Croce's aesthetic, a harmony among affects, among sentiments, since "the true material of art . . . is not things but the sentiments of the poet" (p. 31). According to Croce, Ariosto achieves this harmony within himself by destroying the autonomy of his individual sentiments: "All sentiments—the sublime and the playful, the tender and the courageous, the effusions of the heart and the excogitations of the intellect, love speeches and encomiastic catalogues of names, representations of battles and the quips of comedy, all are equally lowered by the irony and elevated in it" (p. 43). Perhaps the clearest statement of Croce's view of Ariosto's irony is this: "One might say that Ariosto's irony is similar to the eye of God, who watches creation moving, all creation, loving it all equally, in good and in evil, in the greatest and in the smallest, in man and in the grain of sand, because he has made it all, and only seizing in it the motion itself, the eternal dialectic, the rhythm and the harmony" (p. 46). This formula is utterly anachronistic when applied to Ariosto; the idea that God loves evil as much as good is a vulgarism

which would have been incomprehensible to him. Brilliant as it is—and it catches something central to the poem—the formula is a *reduction* of the poem to abstractness; Croce has turned away from a reading of the poem to hypostasize the one fundamental sentiment of the poet. The poem is emptied of content, and there is nothing left but "the motion itself."

Such a way of looking at poems makes it difficult to analyze them precisely and also to construct adequate theories about them, but this is not the place further to argue my rejection of Croce's aesthetic. I wish only to make it clear that, whereas Croce was defining what he thought of as the ultimate truth of the poem as it refers to the *real* world, I am analyzing the *primary* sense of the poem as it refers to Ariosto's (not Croce's) idea of the world. I am saying that Ariosto intended the poem to be an analogue of the cosmos both in structure and in content. Croce's perceptive remark about the eye of God was not, by the way, based on any detailed study of the appearance in the poem of the analogy; he does not seem aware that it is intended (his "one might say"). Rafaello Ramat, in *Per la storia dello stile rinascimentale* (Messina, 1953), seems to be the only modern critic who has given this any serious attention, and I have profited from his discussion (see especially pp. 17-21, 65-66).

6. Felix Buffière, *Les mythes d'Homère et la pensée grecque* (Paris, 1956), pp. 155-165 and 472, note 31.

7. See the detailed study by Leo Spitzer, *Classical and Christian Ideas of World Harmony* (Baltimore, 1963). See also John Hollander, *The Untuning of the Sky: Ideas of Music in English Poetry, 1500-1700* (Princeton, 1961); James Hutton, "Some English Poems in Praise of Music," *English Miscellany*, 2:1-63 (1951); Otto von Simson, *The Gothic Cathedral* (New York, 1954); Edgar Wind, *Pagan Mysteries in the Renaissance* (New Haven, 1958), pp. 78-99, 158-175.

8. Augustine, *Epist.* 166.13, quoted in Spitzer, p. 31.

9. Quoted in von Simson, pp. 31-32.

10. *Opera* (Basel, 1576), p. 1455. On the cosmic harmony, see also pp. 1446 and 1737, and *De amore* III.3: "They (sc. musicians) with certain intervals and modulations make high and low tones, natures which differ, more friendly to each other, from which is born the texture and sweetness of harmony. And they so temper to each other slower and faster motions that these become fast friends and exhibit rhythm and proportion" (ed. Raymond Marcel, Paris, 1956, p. 164; my trans.).

11. See Tasso, *Prose diverse*, ed. Cesare Guasti, 2 vols. (Florence, 1875), I, 154-155.

12. On harmony, see Buffière, pp. 467-479; on universality, see p. 73 and *passim*. The topics were available to the late Middle Ages through Quintilian (X.46-53) and Macrobius' *Saturnalia*.

13. Macrobius, *Saturnalia* I.1.18-20, ed. J. Willis (Leipzig, 1963); on Virgil's knowledge of the various arts, see I.24.10-19.

14. Lines 351-367; I translate from *Prose volgari inedite e poesie latine e greche edite e inedite*, ed. Isidoro del Lungo (Florence, 1867), pp. 303-304. See also Poliziano, *Ambra*, lines 21-26 and especially lines 570-574.

15. *Prose diverse*, I, 44-45. The passage goes on to point out that episodic plots are not to be allowed. The epic must be one in the sense of

having one action. Therefore Tasso rejects the precedent of Ariosto's poem with its multiple actions.

16. "And truly he who does not esteem this art strikes me as being quite lacking in reason; for this universal fabric which we behold, with its vast heaven so resplendent with bright stars, with the earth at the center girdled by the seas, varied with mountains, valleys, rivers, adorned with such a variety of trees, pretty flowers, and grasses—can be said to be a great and noble picture painted by nature's hand and God's; and whoever can imitate it deserves great praise, in my opinion: nor is such imitation achieved without the knowledge of many things, as anyone knows who attempts it" (*The Book of the Courtier,* trans. Charles S. Singleton, Garden City, 1959, p. 78). See Cassirer's remarks on Leonardo: "But for Leonardo, art never signifies a mere outpouring of the subjective fantasy; rather it is and remains a genuine and indispensable organ for the understanding of reality itself . . . To traverse the realm of visible forms completely; to grasp each of these forms in its clear and certain contours; and to keep them in their full definiteness before both the internal and the external eye: these are the highest aims recognized by Leonardo's science" (*Individual and Cosmos,* p. 157); "Science is a second creation made with the understanding; painting is a second creation made with the imagination (la scienza è una seconda creazione fatto col discorso; la pittura è una seconda creazione fatta colla fantasia). But the value of both these creations consists not in their departure from nature and from the empirical truth of things, but precisely in their grasp and revelation of this truth" (p. 161).

17. Orazio Ariosto in Bernard Weinberg, ed., *A History of Literary Criticism in the Italian Renaissance* (Chicago, 1961), II, 1002, note 21.

18. See the typical passage in Poliziano's *Ambra,* lines 155-171.

19. Hegel in the *Vorlesungen über die Aesthetik* (Berlin, 1842), in the *Sämtliche Werke,* ed. Hermann Glockner (Stuttgart, 1953), XIII, 220ff; De Sanctis, *Storia della letteratura italiana* (Naples, 4th ed., 1872; ed. B. Croce, Bari, 1949, II, 1-42). Cf. W. Binni, *Storia della critica ariostesca* (Lucca, 1951); Rafaello Ramat, *La Critica ariostesca dal secolo XVI ad oggi* (Florence, 1954); and Giuseppe Fatini, *Bibliografia della critica ariostea, 1510-1956* (Florence, 1958), pp. 213, 259, and *passim.*

20. Notably Ramat (see note 5 above), and Giorgio de Blasi, "L'Ariosto e le passioni (studio sul motivo poetico fondamentale dell' 'Orlando furioso')," *GSLI,* 129 (1952), 318-362; 130 (1953), 178-203. The latter is probably the best essay written on Ariosto since Croce's, than which it is far more sound. The trend was perhaps begun by Attilio Momigliano's *Saggio su l'Orlando furioso* (Bari, 1929). See also the more recent entries in Fatini, and Lanfranco Caretti's introduction to Ariosto (*Opere minori,* pp. vii-xxv, reprinted in his *Filologia e critica,* Milan, 1955).

21. J. W. Bennett, "Genre, Milieu, and the 'Epic-Romance,'" *English Institute Essays, 1951,* ed. A. S. Downer (New York, 1952), pp. 85-125.

22. "Now since humor does not set itself the task of allowing a content *to unfold itself and take shape naturally according to its essential nature,* and to articulate it and round it out artistically in this unfolding, but rather it is the artist himself who steps into the picture; so his principal

activity consists in dissolving and destroying, by the power of his subjective intrusions, flashes of thought, and striking turns of phrase, *everything that wishes to make itself objective and to win a firm appearance of reality,* or that seems to be in the external world. Thereby *every independence of objective content* and the unity of the appearance, given through the thing itself, is destroyed and the representation becomes *a mere playing with the circumstances,* a twisting and distorting of the subject matter" (*Sämtliche Werke*, XIII, 226-227; italics added). The italicized phrases show the characteristic theoretical error of this approach to humor, I believe. The passage depends upon the notion that the content of literature is somehow independent of the words in which it is presented, that the content can have an essential nature, which can be given in the thing itself as opposed to words. Content is even personified in this view; it is something that "wishes to make itself objective and to win a firm appearance (*Gestalt*) of reality." But the fact is that the events of any narrative are not presented in themselves at all, but through and by a narrator. Hegel's conclusion is also erroneous: since all narration presents a narrator, emphasis on his presence does not necessarily reduce the narrative to "a mere playing with the circumstances." The degree of imaginative reality we attribute to the world of a story depends on matters other than our consciousness of the narrator's presence, as the example of *Troilus and Criseyde* may demonstrate. See M. H. Abrams, "Belief and the Problem of Disbelief," in *Literature and Belief. English Institute Essays,* 1957, ed. M. H. Abrams (New York, 1958), pp. 1-30. Hegel further fails to realize that "distorting the subject matter" may be a way of commenting on the degree of reality of the "real" world; in fact, behind his philosophical category lurks the inability of the nineteenth century to deal with the fictional modes of earlier periods.

Hegel's distrust of authorial intrusion looks forward to the modern distrust of authorial commentary, and both are ultimately traceable to the phenomenon we observe so clearly in Ariosto, the rejection of transcendental sanctions of narrative art. The loss of transcendental sanctions for the narrator leads to the sense that he is after all only another man, like ourselves, who possesses no particular claim to be heard as long as he speaks in merely personal identity. But any judgment or statement of value comes to be regarded as the "personal opinion" of the speaker; hence the novelist's need of an "irony," in Lukacs's view, to prevent the reader from rejecting the novel out of hand and to make the values asserted in the novel seem not the *opinions* of the author but the very structure of the world. In other words, the novelist must somehow make up for the decay of publicly accepted values. See L. Goldman, ed., *Etudes pour une sociologie du roman, Revue de l'Institut de Sociologie, Bruxelles,* 2 (1963), which includes a French translation of part of Lukacs's *Theorie des Romans* (1920; reprinted, Neuwied-am-Rhein, 1963).

23.   Abrams, *The Mirror and the Lamp,* p. 276.

24.   Later in the century, Tasso will compare the *favola trovata* but not yet *disposta* to first matter (*Prose diverse,* I, 91); the Platonic analogue is overwhelmingly the dominant one in the sixteenth century.

25.   Cristoforo Landino in his commentary on Dante's *Opere* (Venice, 1484), fol. a (vii)^V, cited by Abrams, p. 273.

26. *Elizabethan Critical Essays,* ed. G. G. Smith (Oxford, 1904), I, 156-157. Cf. Abrams, p. 273.

27. Ariosto thus looks forward to the whole tradition of Romantic irony, and there is a fundamental analogy between his method and such descendants of it as Brecht's *Verfremdungseffekt* (alienation effect), on which see *Brecht on Theatre,* ed. John Willett (New York, 1964), esp. pp. 191-195; and David I. Grossvogel, *Four Playwrights and a Postcript* (Ithaca, 1962), pp. 6-45.

28. See note 16 above.

29. Cassirer, *Individual and Cosmos,* p. 43.

30. Ferrero (see above, note 1), attributes such exordia to "the still burning memory of that 'suffering' of the 'frenzy' which the jealous poet knows well from his own experience" (p. 190), a mixture of naive autobiographical reading and Crocean abstraction, evident also in his attempt to prove the "sincerity" of the exordia, whose rhetorical function beyond that of "resting the poet and the reader from their intense imaginative concentration" does not occur to him.

31. Cf. *The Courtier:* "Then signor Morello said: 'If this Courtier of ours speaks with so much elegance and gravity, I fear there may be those among us who will not understand him.' 'Nay,' replied the Count, 'all will understand him, because words that are easy to understand can still be elegant. Nor would I have him always speak of grave matters, but of amusing things, of games, jests, and jokes, according to the occasion; but sensibly in everything, with readiness and a lucid fullness; nor must he show vanity or a childish folly in any way'" (trans. Singleton, p. 55).

32. Cf. *O.F.* XLIV.1-3 and *O.I.* III.7.1-2; *O.F.* XLV.1-6 and *O.I.* I.16.1.

33. It is important not to mistake Ariosto's attitude, which is similar to Petrarch's, as nationalistic in any modern way. Italy is not a political entity in his mind, but rather an ethnic or geographical one. If he dreams of the unification of the peninsula under one *Principe,* as Machiavelli did, he never tells us.

34. Cf. Horace, *Serm.* I.1.120-121.

35. The term is Ramat's (*Per la storia dello stile rinascimentale,* Messina, 1953, pp. 45ff), who, after accurately noting the presence in the poem of a principle of sharp realism, goes on to maintain that there is a "mutual corrosion of reality and fable." This is a version of the Crocean error, it seems to me. Reality exists outside the poem, and poems do not corrode it. Ramat is right to suggest that Ariosto's view of the real world is that it is in flux (pp. 115-116, for instance); the poem that represents it as such (however indirectly) is by no means corroding it, even within the poem, but rather describing it accurately, if that is its real nature in the eyes of the poet. Ramat's remarks are based on an ultimately positivistic notion of empirical "reality."

36. Cf. Weinberg, *History,* II, 956.

37. See E. R. Curtius, *European Literature and the Latin Middle Ages,* trans. Willard Trask (New York, 1953), pp. 162-165.

38. On the importance of this distinction in Tasso's poems, see Chapter VI.

39. See Catalano's account of Fabrizio Colonna's stay in Ferrara in 1512, *Vita*, I, 343-346.

40. Notably Ravenna (1512) and Rome (1527). But also Urbino (1502), Brescia (1512), Florence (1530), and Pavia (1527).

41. See Catalano, *Vita*, I, 313-325, 339-352.

42. Referred to in III.57; XV.1-2; XXXVI.1-2; XL.1-5; XLVI.97.

43. Referred to in XIV.1-9; III.59; XXXIII.40 (added in 1532).

44. The recapture of Bastia from the Spaniards (1512) is referred to twice (III.54, XLII.1-6). On this occasion Alfonso apparently permitted the slaughter of the entire Spanish garrison as a reprisal for the killing of Vestidello Pagano, Alfonso's deputy, during the capture of the town. In XLII.1-6, Ariosto attributes the slaughter to Alfonso's being unconscious and unable to restrain his men. Apparently this was the official version, but Caretti does not seem to accept it (*Opere minori*, pp. 859, 1109). Once referred to is the battle in which Alfonso defeated the Romagnoli in 1511 (III.55).

45. See Charles Oman, *History of the Art of War in the Sixteenth Century* (Cambridge, Eng., 1957), pp. 130-140.

46. As Oman points out, the French slaughter of the *gens d'armes* at Fornovo (1495) was virtually unprecedented in fifteenth-century Italian warfare (pp. 90-91, 113-114).

47. Cited from *Orlando furioso di Ludovico Ariosto. Secondo le stampe del 1516 e del 1521*, ed. Filippo Ermini, 2 vols. (Rome, 1908).

48. The passage continues for three more stanzas, addressed to the Swiss, the Germans, and Leo X, after which we return to the story with the transition "But from one speech to the other, where have I gone so far from the road I have been following? Yet I do not believe I have so lost it that I cannot find it again" (stanza 80).

49. Ariosto's lengthy condemnation of firearms (XI.22-28) might well have seemed daring, in view of Alfonso d'Este's well-known interest in artillery (see Oman, pp. 43, 130-140; Wind, pp. 95-99; Burckhardt, pp. 111-113). Another important subject of commentary which tends to qualify the tone of courtly adulation is that of the prevalence of hypocrisy and corruption at court, whose importance is reflected in the frequency of exordia on such topics as the impossibility of true friendship among princes (XLIV.1-3), the hypocrisy of courtiers (VII.1-2; XIX.1-2). A particularly interesting example is the following, which was omitted from all editions after the first of 1516 (I translate from Ermini):

"There is a certain something—I do not know whether it should be called wicked or else good and proper, and I am equally in doubt whether it is caused by desire of glory or by fear of infamy—that certain people believe came out of that vase which was the ill gift to the incautious Epimetheus and count it among the plagues and ills that trouble the quiet of mortals.

"This convention, or else duty—for I cannot exactly find its name—often turns one aside from his own wish and pulls him by the hair after that of another. It makes him a slave who would be free, and I do not know how to explain to you how, for in so many cases in so many various ways it binds one with inextricable knots.

"I shall make you, ladies, my first example, you who spoil for yourselves a thousand lovely pleasures, which, if you thought nothing of this, you would have entire. Whether you do well or ill, let some one else say; I can tell you that among the black Indies the ladies who do not pay so much attention to convention do live more happily in their common beds.

"This, which perhaps would be better called opinion than duty or virtue, brings it about that for some slight cause one neglects his own health [or salvation]; blood-ties and close friendship it has violated and held in little esteem; and in the service and pay of tyrants it has done outrage and harm to dear friends.

"I omit ancient examples of soldiers—of Caesar, Pompey, Anthony, and Brutus—who were cruel to their fatherland and to their own blood, helping their leaders in their evil works. How many have you seen, oh glorious offspring of unconquered Hercules, who have been and are friends to you at heart and then, in their actions, like enemies?

"It seems to them by this universal error that being in the service of Venice, or the Shepherd [the Pope], or some other power that is your enemy, obligates them more than their old friendship. It breaks all their hearts to harm you, but still they do it, whenever they are told to by this so-called duty, which beats down all other considerations before it.

"But you, who know the strange style that for good or ill is followed in the world, although the Tuscan cardinal [Giovanni de' Medici, later Leo X] had the place that he of the Alidusi did not use well, nevertheless you did not exclude either him or his brother Giuliano from your friendship, the two branches of the noble Laurel [the two sons of Lorenzo il Magnifico] which, while it was green, made our age an age of gold.

"If the Duke of Urbino [Francesco Maria della Rovere, nephew of Pope Giulio II] was obedient to his uncle in making war on you, it does not mean that his heart is not, like a good relative's, softened with pity by your misfortunes. Nor do you love him less, whence often I hear you raise his green years to the stars, with those highest praises by which one extolls a worthy man.

"I could mention countless others who have been and are friends of yours, although because of this 'duty' they have followed our adversaries in seeking to harm us. I digress in this way to show you that it can be that Ruggiero honors and loves Rinaldo and that still he calls him forth to battle."

One would give a great deal to know whether Ariosto was forced to delete this passage in the later editions of the poem or whether he did so spontaneously. Although it begins in a tone of levity, it soon gets into very deep water indeed, especially if read in conjunction with such passages as (1532) XLIV.1-3, which suggests that so-called duty is merely a cloak for selfish ends. Few passages of political commentary from the early sixteenth century, including those in Machiavelli and Guicciardini, show so clearly the fundamental moral ambiguity, the bewildering complexity, of the public life of these times.

50. Cf. Erasmus' picture of life at court, in *Praise of Folly* trans. H. H. Hudson (Princeton, 1941), pp. 93-96.

51. I paraphrase Horace's famous lines, which passed into the topics of the praise of poetry (*Odes* IV.9.25-28).

52. The full-scale eulogy is in III.10-52.

53. The old man denounces the double standard and proposes that the law condemn to death any woman found in adultery unless she can prove that her husband has also committed it. In any case, he says, incontinence is the worst that can be attributed to adulterous women, whereas not only are no men continent but they are guilty of far worse crimes. Rinaldo renounces the possibility of knowing for certain, by drinking from the magic goblet, whether or not his wife is faithful to him (XLIII.6-8) (the theme recurs in Cervantes' "El Curioso impertinente," in *Don Quixote*).

54. This may be a convenient place to note the many parallels between Ariosto's Poet and the preceptor of Ovid's *Ars amatoria*. In a number of passages, Ariosto's Poet assumes the role of a *praeceptor amoris*, and in XVI.1 he asserts his right to instruct others in the *art*. The question is thus raised of the relation of the two poems, and I believe it is possible to single out some reflections of the peculiar quality of the *Ars*. For instance, the tone and the content of the advice Ariosto offers lovers is often strikingly similar to Ovid's; see *A.A.* III.433-438, 455-460, and *O.F.* X.5-7, where there is a sufficient amount of similar detail to suggest that Ariosto had the Ovidian passage in mind when he wrote. Both Ovid and Ariosto give attention to the advantages of maturity in a lover (*O.F.* X.7-9; *A.A.* II.693-702, III.557-576). Both exclaim at the tortures of jealousy (*O.F.* XXXI.1-8; *A.A.* II.535-599). Both have harsh blame for those who harbor rancor toward women or who harm them (e.g., *O.F.* V.1-4; *Rem.* 655-670). Both, of course, advise both men and women. Like Ovid, Ariosto often refers to supposed experiences of his own, usually ruefully, and urges the reader to profit by his, the praeceptor's, misfortunes (e.g., *O.F.* XVI.1; *A.A.* I.28, II.169-174, III.789-792). Like Ovid, Ariosto gives advice he himself is unable to follow (*O.F.* XXIV.2-3; *A.A.* II.537-554; *Rem.* 311-314). Like Ovid, Ariosto represents himself as betrayed by his emotion into saying what he would otherwise not dream of saying (*O.F.* XXIX.73-74; *A.A.* III.667-672). Both poets claim to have reason in their own personal experience to bewail the avarice of women (*O.F.* XLIII.4-5; *A.A.* II.272, III.547-553), and both compare the present and the "heroic" past, at different times voicing preference for each (*O.F.* XIII.1f, XXII.1, XLIII.4, XXVIII.122-124, XXXVI.1-8; *A.A.* II.275ff, III.633ff—and *O.F.* XX.1-3, XXXVII.1-24, XLVI.1-19; *A.A.* III.107ff). Both Ariosto and Ovid draw humorous parallels between themselves and the heroic figures of legend (the *tertium comparationis* is inverted by Ariosto, however: Ovid compares his control to that of Podalirius and Automedon, for instance, but Ariosto compares his lack of control to that of Orlando).

More important even than this impressive number of similarities in detail is the fact that in both poems the Poet is clearly seen to be adopting different and even conflicting roles, the most important of which are those of attacker and defender of the female sex. For instance, *O.F.* XXVIII.81-83 develops the topos of *A.A.* III.28-32. Although we obviously have to do here with topoi of attack and defense common enough in the huge literature of classical and medieval pro- and antifeminism, I have not been able to discover any poets besides Ovid and Ariosto (and Petrarch, to be sure) who deliberately assume both attitudes *in propria persona*. Perhaps the closest analogue is the "marriage group" of the *Canterbury Tales;* it is not Chaucer himself who adopts the conflicting attitudes, however, but different characters. It might be thought that the *débat* tradition (to which the marriage group bears a certain relation) might afford some examples, but I have not found any: *débats* are usually in dramatic form, with the author using a clearly recognizable spokesman to resolve the dilemma (Ariosto uses this technique also, in Canto XXVIII; on the *débat* see A. Jeanroy, in the *Grande Encyclopédie,* and cf. A. de Montaiglan and J. de Rothschild, eds., *Receuil de poésies des xve et xvie siècles,* Paris, 1875-1880, nos. 97, 127, 161, 177, 193, 194, 200). There is a portion of the *Thousand and One Nights* attacking and defending women (nos. 578-606, in the Payne translation); the host's story of Fiammetta is, of course, an analogue of the frame story of the *Arabian Nights.* Perhaps we have to do here with another instance of the mediation of Andreas Capellanus. In any case it is clear that Ariosto, however closely he may have read Ovid, was also adapting, in characteristically Renaissance fashion, one of the Middle Ages' favorite themes.

55.   Cf. Boiardo, *O.I.* II.12.4 (Rajna, p. 381). See also *A.A.* III.11-17.

56.   Ariosto's offer has a clear affinity with the frequent palinodes of "heretics" against the god of love; the "penance" assigned to Chaucer in the *Legend of Good Women* is the best-known example. Gower's release from the service of Venus at the end of the *Confessio amantis* is a distant parallel, as is the partly Ovidian *Ars amandi* of Andreas Capellanus.

57.   The host says he learned the tale from Gian Francesco Valerio of Venice. Rajna points out (pp. 447-454) that this is a friend of Ariosto's who was an inveterate hater of women but also constantly in love (see XLVI.16). This is another typical Ariostan play with reality, and a further case of the inconsistency the Poet and his characters share. On the belief to be given to fictions and follies, see VII.1-2.

58.   See also XLIII.1-4, and the similar complaint about women's beauty being rarer now than in the olden days, in XIII.1f. See above, note 54.

59.   This stanza was added in 1532; it is usually supposed to refer to Alessandra Benucci, but it could not have been so understood by any but Ariosto's most intimate acquaintances. See above, note 2.

60.   As Rajna points out (p. 547), this catalogue of the varieties of madness is based on Erasmus'. See also the categories of madness as outlined in Horace *Serm.* II.3, on which Erasmus, like Ariosto, draws.

61.   John Arthos has some suggestive remarks on the forest as a symbol in romance, in *On the Poetry of Spenser and the Form of Romances* (London, 1956), on which see below, Chapter VII, note 1. Donald Carne-Ross calls my attention to the frequency in the poem of the phrase *or qua or là* and its variants (some noteworthy examples from only the first few cantos are, in addition to the central one of XXIV.2: I.13, 31, 33, 34; II.30, 53; IV.43-44; V.10; VI.51; VIII.9, 71, 82, 83; IX.4; X.69, 102; XII.9, 10-11, 18, 19, 29, 36, 81; XIII.79; XVI.57, 83), and reminds me of Caretti's note to XXIV.2 pointing out the important parallel with Dante's description of the passion-driven, who are whirled about eternally by a wind: "di qua, di là, di giú, di su li mena; / nulla speranza li conforta mai, / non che di posa, ma di minor pena." Horace is another important source of the phrase as Ariosto uses it. Cf. Petrarch's sestina "Anzi tre dì" (214), and *Decameron* V.3, which Ariosto used repeatedly, especially in the epi-

sode of Orlando's dream (VIII). The extent to which the motif of wandering in a forest was part of the currency of symbolic literature in Ariosto's time may be gauged by its use in that compendium of "mysteries," the *Hypnerotomachia Poliphili*, which draws heavily on Dante, including the phrase in question, for an allegory that is basically Neoplatonic. Cf. also Augustine, *Confessions* X.56; Poliziano, *Stanze*, I, 75. Examples could be multiplied indefinitely.

62. Cf. Chrétien de Troyes, *Yvain*, lines 2781-2826. The madness of lovers as a kind of bestiality appears in Plato's *Symposium* and was discussed by Ficino in terms that fit Orlando: mad lovers "like blind men do not know where they are rushing" (*Commentaire*, ed. Marcel, p. 256).

63. See, for example, Horace, *Satires* II.3, discussed above, and the definition of madness offered at one point by Erasmus' Folly: "by the Stoic definitions, wisdom is no other than to be governed by reason . . . folly is to be moved at the whim of the passions" (trans. Hudson, p. 22), and "All of them (writers) are highly indebted to me, but especially those who blacken paper with sheer triviality" (p. 73).

64. See also *Epistle* I.1.97-101:

> quid? mea cum pugnat sententia secum,
> Quod petiit spernit, repetit quod nuper omisit,
> Aestuat et vitae disconvenit ordine toto,
> Diruit, aedificat, mutat quadrata rotundis?
> Insanire putes sollemnia me neque rides.

(What? when my judgment conflicts with itself, when it spurns what it just sought, seeks again what it just rejected, when it ebbs and flows and has no order in it, when it tears down, builds, changes square buildings for round ones? Then you think I'm doing something important, and you do not laugh at me.)

65. See also Seneca, *Epistle* XXVII.

66. See also Dante, *Purg.* VI.149-151: "Vedrai te somigliante a quella inferma / che non può trovar posa in su le piume, / ma con dar volta suo dolore scherma"; Augustine, *Confessions* VI.16.26. The image is a traditional one. For the first of the two stanzas, cf. Horace, *Epistle* I.11.27: "caelum, non animum mutant qui trans mare currunt"; Seneca *Epistle* XXVIII. The idea is a commonplace of Stoic literature—see *Select Letters of Seneca*, ed. Walter C. Summers (London, 1910, 1932), pp. 194-197.

67. It will not have escaped the reader that Cantos XIX-XXX are the structural and the thematic center of the poem, and that much of what we have been examining occurs within them. It may be convenient to list the appearances in these cantos of passages and stories involving the issue of the evaluation of women: XIX: Angelica falls in love with and herself woos Medoro. XX: Eulogy of women (1-3). The institutionalized lust and female tyranny of the City of the Amazons, and its origin in the mass desertion of the Cretan women by the Argonauts. XXI: Praise of Zerbino's scrupulous keeping of his word (1-2); story of Gabrina's villainous past. XXII: Disclaimer of intent to vilify women, promise to praise a hundred for every one blamed (1-3). XXIII: Gabrina betrays Zerbino; Orlando reunites Zerbino and Isabella; Orlando discovers Angelica's and Medoro's retreat and goes mad. XXIV: Love is all madness; Orlando mad.

XXV: Love that leads to honor is not evil (1-2); novella of Ricciardetto and Fiordespina. XXVI: Few women today love anything but money (1-2). XXVII: Clashes of desire among pagan knights, all of whom quarrel with all the others over some object; Doralice's preference of Mandricardo over her original betrothed, Rodomonte; Rodomonte's desertion of Agramante, Rodomonte's invective. XXVIII: Ladies, skip this canto (1-3); host's novella of Fiammetta (an analogue of the frame story of the *Thousand and One Nights*); Rodomonte falls in love with Isabella. XXIX: How unstable are men's minds! I shall punish Rodomonte (1-3); death of Isabella; Orlando's itinerary; Orlando's one meeting with Angelica; poet's wish that Orlando had done all women in. XXX: Recantation (1-3). XXXI: the pains of jealousy (1-6).

68.   *Selections from Ralph Waldo Emerson,* ed. Stephen E. Whicher (Boston, 1957), p. 153.

69.   See Etienne Gilson, *Introduction à l'étude de St. Augustin,* 2nd ed. (Paris, 1943), p. 186.

70.   Cf. Horace, *Epistle* I.1.90: "quo teneam voltus mutantem Protea nodo?" (By what knot can I hold Proteus as he changes his form?); *Confessions* VI.ix, X.56.

71.   Cf. XXIX.3: "Incontra tutte trasse fuor lo stocco / De l'ira, senza farvi differenzia" (Against them all he drew the blade of anger, without making any distinctions among them), and XXIX.74. The importance of making distinctions is one of Horace's basic themes. The ultimate sense of Ariosto's poem thus seems to me quite different from Croce's notion that he reduces all things to the same level (see above, notes 6 and 27).

72.   *Essais,* ed. Albert Thibaudet (Paris, 1958), p. 371. Essay II.1, "De l'inconstance de nos actions," is a storehouse of the commonplaces on the subject.

73.   Ariosto's readers might have been reminded of the use of the metaphor at the opening of the *Convivio,* among other places. For the topos of the folly of wisdom out of place, see Erasmus, *Praise of Folly,* trans. Hudson, p. 38.

VI. TASSO

1.   Tasso, *Prose diverse,* ed. Cesare Guasti, 2 vols. (Florence, 1875), I, 32-43, 138-154.

2.   All citations of the *Gerusalemme liberata* are to the edition of Luigi Bonfigli (Bari: Gius. Laterza & Figli, 1930).

3.   *The Iliad,* trans. Richmond Lattimore (Chicago, 1951); all translations from the *Iliad* are by Lattimore; copyright 1951 by University of Chicago Press.

4.   *The Odyssey,* trans. George Herbert Palmer (Boston, 1891).

5.   See R. Heinze, *Virgils epische Technik,* 3rd ed. (Leipzig, 1915), pp. 370-373.

6.   See J. Endt, "Der Gebrauch der Apostrophe bei den lateinischen

Epikern," *Wiener Studien*, 28:106-129 (1905), for an exhaustive study of the development of the device into a mannerism in the poetry of the decadence. Although the apostrophe of characters appears more often in the *Aeneid* than in the *G.L.*, it is in the former usually a convenient device for varying narrative method (the conspicuous exceptions are *Aen.* IV.408ff and IX.446ff); except for Dido and Nisus and Euryalus, most of the apostrophized characters are of minor importance, and some of them appear only once, such as Thymber and Larides. In the *G.L.*, however, the apostrophe occurs principally at key moments (e.g., II.35, 37; III.22; IX.86; XI.7; XII.59; XVI.61; XVIII.86; XIX.38). The difference is signalized by the fact that apostrophes are frequent in some books of the *Aeneid* but almost entirely absent in others of equal or greater thematic importance; in Book X the device is used thirteen times; in Book XII, twice.

7.   I quote the Latin from *Opera Virgiliana cum decem commentis* (Lyon: J. Crespin, 1529).

8.   See, for instance, Giuseppe Toffanin, *Il Cinquecento*, 5th ed. (Milan, 1954), p. 616. A variant of the view is that of B. T. Sozzi, for whom Tasso was fundamentally a Platonist whose Aristotelianism was external and given expression in moments not productive of poetry (*Studi sul Tasso*, Pisa, 1954, pp. 270-271).

9.   See the useful survey in Ettorre Mazzali, *Cultura e poesia nell'opera di Torquato Tasso* (Bologna, 1957), and, on the theory and practice of *elocutio*, Fredi Chiappelli's brilliant study *Studi sul linguaggio del Tasso epico* (Florence, 1957). In general, I neglect also the differences between the *Discorsi dell'arte poetica* and the *Discorsi del poema eroico* except as they concern my argument; see Mazzali's comments in his edition of Tasso's *Prose* (Milan, 1959), and Sozzi, pp. 212-215.

10.   See Heinze, pp. 478-493. The *maraviglia* of Tasso's theories must be distinguished from the later concept of the *mirabile* as the *ingegnoso*— the illuminating conjunction of disparates in imagery, which came to dominate the theory of *concettismo*. See Joseph A. Mazzeo, "A Seventeenth-Century Theory of Metaphysical Poetry," *Romanic Review*, 42:245-255 (1951); and "Metaphysical Poetry and the Poetic of Correspondence," *Journal of the History of Ideas*, 14:221-234 (1953). Ulrich Leo's pages on Tasso's concept are suggestive (*Torquato Tasso*, Bern, 1951, pp. 101-118).

11.   Both treatises were written much earlier than their dates of publication: the *Discorsi dell'arte poetica* around 1564, the *Discorsi del poema eroico* largely in 1587 (see Sozzi, pp. 205-210). Although the Aristotelian definition here quoted was added in the later treatise, in conformity with the systemizing of the entire argument, it is implicit in the earlier.

12.   *Prose diverse*, I, 85. It is clear from the earlier statement of the definition, which precedes the discussion of the pleasure proper to epic, that poetry has its moral effect through pleasure.

13.   For instance, René Wellek's and Austin Warren's in *Theory of Literature* (New York, 1949), pp. 151-153, 157, and in Bernard Weinberg's account of Aristotle, in *History of Literary Criticism in the Italian Renaissance* (Chicago, 1961), I, 351. Cf. the definition of the audience in the *Giudizio sovra la sua Gerusalemme, Prose diverse*, I, 511-512.

14.   See *Prose diverse*, I, 18, 271.

15. See *Prose diverse*, I, 51-52, 165-166, and *passim*.
16. See R. Heinze, "Fides," *Hermes*, 64:140-166 (1929).
17. *De oratore* II.189, ed. A. S. Wilkins (Oxford, 1911).
18. *Prose diverse*, I, 52. Cf. Cicero, *Orator* 21.69.
19. *De oratore* II.43-46, II.53; *Orator* 28.97, 17.55.
20. *Prose diverse*, I, 200. Cf. *De oratore* I.16.67-70; *Orator* 20.67-68.
21. *Lettere*, ed. C. Guasti (Florence, 1853-55), I, 119.
22. The text, as in the examples to follow, is that of the *Liberata*. When the passages quoted have been included with no more than minor revisions in the *Conquistata*, the fact will be indicated in the manner used here. In the episode of Clorinda's death, all of the appearances of the Narrator are retained. The pattern is representative, for when Tasso took over portions of the *Liberata*, he tended to include appearances of the Narrator. In sections of the *G.C.* based on the *G.L.*, Tasso omitted only eight appearances (*G.L.* II.54-56, III.21, VII.77, VIII.81, X.25, XIII.57, XVI.35-36, XVIII.89). On the other hand, to those same sections he added twelve appearances, which conform by and large to the manner of the *G.L.* (*G.C.* I.19, I.46, II.11, III.35, VI.119, VII.37, X.50, X.71, X.102, XVII.4 [originally *G.L.* I.36] XVII.133, XXIII.112). In fact, *all* of the important appearances of the Poet's "I" in the *G.L.* are included in the *G.C.*, with the exception of the opening invocation, the dedication to Alfonso, and those in the episode of Sofronia, which was omitted.

As for Tasso's manner in the new parts of the *G.C.*, it is usually that of the *G.L.* in more formal guise (in keeping with the general tendency of the revisions—see Leo, pp. 72-78). Three new tendencies are especially interesting. First, just as Tasso gave in the *G.C.* much greater prominence to the sacrosanct, expanding Goffredo's vision of heaven to fill all of a long canto and having the sun stand still during the final battle, so God is apostrophized either directly or via an attribute, and usually along with the saints, some seven times (*G.C.* I.36, II.11, XIV.9-10, XX.4, XXIII.14, 75) as opposed to three times in the *G.L.* (I.32, XI.7, XIX.38). Second, in keeping with the introduction of long sections of Homeric battle description, as in the defense of the ships at Joppa, Tasso gives prominence to the Homeric rhetorical question (as in *Iliad* V.703-704 or XVI.112-113, where it is addressed to the Muses). He had used the device only twice in the *G.L.* (IV.19, XX.32), but it occurs frequently in the *G.C.* (e.g., XVIII.64-65, XIX.90, XXIV.33); cf. the shifting of *G.L.* I.36 to *G.C.* XVII.4, and the new highly formal *G.C.* I.107. Finally, the increased striving for the monumental is also evident in the inclusion of three new Dantesque boasts of poetic superiority (*G.C.* X.50, XX.41, XXI.102), in the prayer for supremacy in epic in *G.C.* I.3, and in the inclusion as the very last of the overt appearances of the Narrator the long laudatory apostrophe of Charles V. The episodes added to the *Conquistata* serve to increase the degree of variety (cf. *Prose diverse*, I, 520), and to increase the amount of truth (cf. *Prose diverse*, I, 500ff).

23. To Maurizio Cataneo, November [?] 1585 (*Lettere*, II, 452). In his generous reply, Pellegrino agrees that the *Liberata* is rich in "la maraviglia che porta la favola della mutazion della forma [fortuna?] e dal riconoscimento," and, in a fragmentary sentence, seems to agree in singling out the death of Clorinda as a particularly effective example of it: "della

quale maraviglia, tuttochè sia ricca la Gerusalemme di Vostra Signoria sopra ogni altra, in qual poema appar maravigliosa . . . [lacuna] gli animi de' leggitori a confusione della morte di Clorinda" (Angelo Solerti, *Vita di Torquato Tasso*, Turin, 1895, II, 278). Cf. the *Giudizio, Prose diverse*, I, 531-533.

24. So the passage reads in the *Discorsi del poema eroico*. In the *Discorsi dell'arte poetica*, the passage reads (*Prose diverse*, I, 9): "non consentono così facilmente d'essere or mossi ad ira, or a terrore, or a pietà; d'esser or allegrati, or contristati, or sospesi, or rapiti."

25. See Tasso, *Prose*, ed. E. Mazzali (Milan, 1959), p. 524, notes 1, 2, 3; Weinberg, I, 24-26; Baxter Hathaway, *The Age of Criticism* (Ithaca, 1962), pp. 390-396.

26. Cf. the *Giudizio, Prose diverse*, I, 499, and, in addition to the passages already cited, the letters written in 1576 to Silvio Antoniano (*Lettere*, I, 144-146); and to Orazio Capponi (*Lettere*, I, 203-204); cf. *Lettere*, II, 446-449.

27. *Prose diverse*, I, 25. The same principle governs the *Giudizio* (*ibid.*, I, 454, 500).

28. I refer, of course, to the "Allegoria del poema" included in Bonnà's 1581 edition and to the *Apologia in difesa della Gerusalemme liberata* (1585). With characteristic disingenuousness, Tasso represented himself to his censors as having written most of the poem with no thought of the allegory and as deciding to formulate one merely as a defense against the Inquisition (*Lettere*, I, 185, 192-196). What Tasso is really mocking, I think, is the inadequacy of the view that sees justification for the fabulous only in allegory, as well as the essential reductivism of any such résumé of the significance of a poem. See Mario Petrini, "La Vena elegiaco-lirico della *Gerusalemme liberata* e le ambizioni epiche del Tasso," *Belfagor*, 11:415-424 (1956), and, marginally, my "The Bower of Bliss and Armida's Palace," *Comparative Literature*, 6:335-347 (1954). See also the discussion of the allegory in the *Giudizio, Prose diverse*, I, 460-462, 471, and *passim*.

29. It has the effect of arousing expectation and of making the reader attentive (*Prose diverse*, I, 172).

30. *Prose diverse*, I, 187-192. Tasso does point out (p. 192) that the poet also prays for the memory of "cose già sepolte nell' oblivione," but he maintains that before writing the *proposizione* and the invocation the poet has already "ritrovata e disposta la favola" (p. 187). The inconsistency is resolved by the fact that the invocation for knowledge is a pretense.

31. Printed in Angelo Solerti's edition of the *Liberata* (Florence, 1895), II, 3-22.

32. Cf. *Gierusalemme* 3: "Questa, che spiego hor de i gran fatti altrui / antiqua tela, e parte adorno, e fingo" (this ancient tapestry of the great deeds of others, which I now unfold and in part adorn and invent).

33. See above, Introduction, note 12.

34. The objection occurred to a contemporary of Tasso's, the umbrageous Sertorio Quattromani, whose attack on *G.L.* I.1-2 (printed in Solerti, *Vita*, II, 437-441) Solerti considers a rhetorical exercise rather than an actual letter (*Vita*, I, 206n). Although many of Quattromani's objections are willfully pedantic, there is some sense in the following, exces-

sively phrased as they are: "And where did any one hear of a man asking pardon for those errors which he is about to commit? . . . One seeks pardon for things already done, therefore why not restrain yourself and not do them? . . . What do you mean by this weaving of ornaments with the truth? . . . If you mean to say, pardon me if I add false things to the truth, and if I am about to speak lies, you speak like a fool" (*Vita*, II, 440). At one time Tasso considered deleting I.3 (*Lettere*, I, 122), perhaps because it seemed a digression to some of his censors.

35. I cite the Italian text from the edition by Luigi Bonfigli (Bari, 1934). The echoing trumpet referred to is of course the *Orlando furioso*.

36. The phrase echoes Virgil's "sit mihi fas audita loqui," but Virgil's implicit reference is to the Mysteries; the effect is thus quite different.

37. Cf. Weinberg, I, 97, 272, 322-323, 495, 710; Hathaway, pp. 401-436.

38. Cf. P. O. Kristeller, *Il Pensiero filosofico di Marsilio Ficino* (Florence, 1953), pp. 330-339.

39. See above, pp. 123-125. Other instances, both implicit and explicit, in Tasso, are *Prose diverse*, I, 21, 89, 91, 130, 161, 345-355, 440; *Dialoghi*, ed. Ezio Raimondi, 3 vols. (Florence, 1958), II, 901, 909. Cf. Weinberg, pp. 262, 280, 301, 425, 615-616, 721, 733, 735, 740, 1002, 1060, 1062, for other examples of the analogy in the literary criticism of the period.

40. It must be remembered that this is still the method of the *Conquistata*. Cf. the *Giudizio, Prose diverse*, I, 499ff.

41. See the discussion by Giorgio Petrocchi in his edition of *Il Mondo creato* (Florence, 1951), pp. xxxviii-xlv.

42. See Ulrich Leo, *Ritterepos-Gottesepos. Torquato Tassos Weg als Dichter* (Cologne, 1958), pp. 56-60.

43. I thus see the *Liberata,* the *Conquistata,* and the *Mondo creato* as forming a single curve of development in terms of their relation to the central preoccupations of the poet; but I am not trying to defend the literary quality of the two later poems. It must be remembered that even at the very end of his career Tasso still stood by the positions of the *Discorsi del poema eroico;* the *Giudizio* repeatedly cites them.

44. See Weinberg, pp. 957, 969, 973, 975, 982, 991, 994, 1036, 1048.

45. *Prose diverse*, I, 30-32, 141-142.

46. The arguments to be refuted are listed in *Prose diverse*, I, 33-34, 142-143. The *refutatio* itself occupies *Prose diverse*, I, 34-45, 145-157.

47. The last sentence was added in the later version, and paraphrases *Ennead* II.3.16, as Mazzali points out in his note, p. 587.

48. See Weinberg, pp. 1002, 1062.

49. *Prose diverse*, I, 141. The revised passage is cited approvingly in the *Giudizio* (*ibid.*, I, 529).

50. Ariosto's variety—especially in connection with his manner of dropping one thread of the story and taking up another—seemed to many critics of Tasso's age distracting in precisely this sense. See, for instance, the revealing remarks of Filippo Sassetti: "the poet is constrained in this arrangement to interrupt materials that he has begun and now to turn backward, now to pass forward, without paying any attention to the continuity of time. And precisely when he begins to move, as if with the greatest diligence he wished to deprive the reader or the listener of that pleasure, he

quits the narrative that he has begun, jumping into another subject . . . as if it were a pleasurable or a possible thing to feel the soul moved at one and the same time by contrary motions coming from two different objects" (*Discorso contro l'Ariosto,* written ca. 1575, and translated in Weinberg, p. 975). The argument goes back to Denores and Minturno. The former says, "ita omnes partes in eo opere disiunctae: ut lectoris animum, & memoriam confusa narratio uehementer offendat" (Weinberg, p. 957; cf. p. 973).

51.   The unity of the created universe is of course the result of the unity of its Creator; the love that binds together contraries in *concordia discors* is derived from the integrating love of the Creator. For instance, see Ficino, *Opera,* p. 1330, cited in Kristeller, p. 109, and above, Chapter II, note 18.

52.   See the "Allegoria del poema," *Prose diverse,* I, 303-304, and the *Giudizio, Prose diverse,* I, 471, 519, 522-526. Tasso read the *Iliad* in much the same way; cf. *Prose diverse,* I, 522.

53.   See, for instance, *Lettere,* I, 64-65, 75-77, 104, and *passim.*

54.   This passage is part of a section added in the later version. It is noteworthy that in the *Giudizio* Tasso felt called upon to defend the plot as one action of many characters rather than of one character (*Prose diverse,* I, 514-520).

55.   Cf. *Gierusalemme* 2-5, which predicts in fulsome detail the future glories of Alfonso and the reflected glory of his poet. In the long dedication of the *Conquistata* to Cintio Aldobrandini and Clement VIII (I.4-7), there is no longer any mention of *errore,* either of the poet or of his heroes. The emphasis is instead exclusively public; Tasso praises the Cardinal and the Pope for their revivification of the papacy and for their patronage of the arts.

VII. SPENSER

1.   This has also been pointed out in some instances by R. E. N. Dodge, "Spenser's Imitations from Ariosto," *PMLA,* 12:151-204 (1896), and 35:91-92 (1920); and A. H. Gilbert, "Spenser's Imitations from Ariosto—Addenda," *PMLA,* 34:225-232 (1919). Dodge noted, but did not analyze, the differences between *F.Q.* III.1.13 and *O.F.* IX.22, *F.Q.* III.3.1-2 and *O.F.* II.1, and *F.Q.* III.1.1-2 and *O.F.* XXVIII.1-2; and Gilbert remarked the frequency with which Spenser uses Ariosto's method of transition (see below, note 15); neither attempted a comparison of the two Narrators as such.

John Arthos has broached the subject in his *On the Poetry of Spenser and the Form of Romances* (London, 1956), and I have profited from his discussion (see especially pp. 11-12, 22-26, 51-53, 65-73), although I strongly disagree with many of his assertions, such as that Spenser "is as much alone, as much the solitary singer in *The Faerie Queene* as the piper in Arcadia, singing his unrest and his complaint" (p. 26), or that in the proem to Book I Spenser "speaks of himself as a minstrel used to singing warlike deeds to companies of knights and ladies" (p. 12). In general, Arthos disregards the hortatory, practical emphasis of the poem as well as its frequent references to actual history.

2. *F.Q.* I.4.1, 8.1, 9.1, 10.1; II.4.1, 5.1; III.2.1, 4.1, 5.1-2, 11.1-2; IV.2.
1-2, 3.1, 4.1, 8.1; V.2.1, 8.1-2, 9.1-2, 10.1-3; VI.2.1, 3.1-2, 6.1, 8.1-2.

3. *F.Q.* I.5, 7.1; II.5.1, 6.1, 8.1-2, 9.1; III.2.1, 3.1, 4.1, 9.1; IV.5.2, 6.1,
7.1-2, 8.1, 9.1-3; V.4.1, 7.1-2, 11.1; VI.5.1-2, 6.1, 7.1-2.

4. *F.Q.* III.2.1-3, 3.1, 4.1-3, 8.1, 9.1-2, 11.1-2; IV.7.1-2, 11.1; V.6.1;
VI.3.1, 5.1, 7.1, 11.1. Interestingly enough, none appears in Books I and II.

5. The greatest number of these occur in Books I (where such a formula
occurs only once), II (where none occurs), and III (where only two occur).
Here is the list of canto endings in the manner of Boiardo and Ariosto (my
list agrees with Gilbert's, with the addition of IV.7.47); I.6.48; III.8.52,
12.45; IV.2.54, 4.48, 5.46, 6.47, 7.47, 8.64, 9.41, 10.58, 11.53, 12.35; V.3.40,
5.57, 7.45, 8.51, 12.43; VI.2.48, 3.51, 5.41, 7.50, 8.51, 9.46, 10.44. It should
be noted that several cantos end with remarks in a manner derived from
Ariosto, though not from his manner of ending cantos; such are I.12.42 and
III.6.54.

6. Unlike Ariosto, who once allows an exordium to reach the length of
thirty stanzas (XXXVIII.1-30), Spenser limits his canto exordia to one or
two or, at the most, four stanzas. Longer prefatory remarks are relegated to
the proems; that to Book V, for example, has eleven stanzas.

7. Based on *O.F.* XLVI.1ff, as Gilbert pointed out (p. 232).

8. Book II.12 ends without any concluding topos whatever. III.12.45
(1596), IV.12.35, and V.12.43 end with topoi derived from Ariosto's canto
endings; they do not signalize the end of the books as such. As to the openings of these cantos, III.12 has no exordium; IV.12 and V.12 begin with
moral reflections on the events of the poem and make no reference to the
imminent conclusion of the books. The idea that Spenser decided after 1590
to give structural continuity to Books III, IV, and V (rather than make them
sharply distinct like I, II, and III in the 1590 version) is perhaps lent some
support by the fact that in 1596 Spenser changed the concluding passage
of Book III, which in the 1590s had been similar to that of Book I, in favor
of an Ariostan ending which makes no reference to the ending of a larger
structural unit. See Gilbert, pp. 229-230; also J. W. Bennett, *The Evolution
of the Faerie Queene* (Chicago, 1942), pp. 159, 175-177.

9. Gilbert has listed these, with one or two minor inaccuracies and
omissions. Of his "transitions in Ariosto's manner," three are not transitions
from one thread of the story to another: II.2.11, IV.5.2, V.P.13. One of the
transitions he lists is actually made without comment (IV.7.2). Four signalized transitions should be added to his list (VI.2.40, 7.50, 11.24; and
VII.6.37). The revised list, then, reads: II.11.4; III.6.54, 8.43, 11.2; IV.5.28,
11.1; V.9.2, 11.36; VI.2.40, 5.11, 6.17, 7.27, 7.50, 8.31, 9.1, 11.24, 12.14,
12.22; VII.6.37.

10. Dodge lists the following: *F.Q.* I.12.1 and *O.F.* XLVI.1ff; *F.Q.*
II.10.1 and *O.F.* III.1-4; *F.Q.* III.1.13 and *O.F.* I.22; *F.Q.* III.1.49 and
O.F. XXII.1-3; *F.Q.* III.2.1-3 and *O.F.* XX.1-3, XXXVII.1ff; *F.Q.* III.3.1
and *O.F.* II.1 (this seems doubtful); *F.Q.* III.4.1-3 and *O.F.* XX.1-2,
XXXVII.1-3; *F.Q.* VI.12.1 and *O.F.* XLVI.1. Gilbert added: *F.Q.* I.12.42
and *O.F.* XLVI.1ff; *F.Q.* VI.12.1 and *O.F.* XLVI.1. Upton (cited in *The
Works of Edmund Spenser: A Variorum Edition*, ed. Edwin Greenlaw et al.,
Baltimore, 1932-1949) had noted the following, which Dodge overlooked:
F.Q. II.P.3 and *O.F.* VII.1; *F.Q.* III.8.27 and *O.F.* VIII.68; *F.Q.* III.8.42-43

and *O.F.* XXIX.26-27; *F.Q.* IV.1.1 and *O.F.* VIII.66; *F.Q.* IV.6.1 and *O.F.* XXXI.1ff; *F.Q.* IV.6.16 and *O.F.* XLV.80; *F.Q.* VI.P.2 and *O.F.* I.2; *F.Q.* VI.3.1, 5.1 and *O.F.* XXXVI.1; *F.Q.* VI.12.31 and *O.F.* I.53. To these should be added the following, which I believe no one has as yet noted: *F.Q.* III.8.1 and *O.F.* VIII.66-68; *F.Q.* III.11.1-2 and *O.F.* XXXI.4-6; *F.Q.* IV.7.1-2 and *O.F.* II.1; *F.Q.* IV.8.29 and *O.F.* XIII.1; *F.Q.* IV.11.1 and *O.F.* XLI.46; *F.Q.* V.6.1-2 and *O.F.* XXXVIII.1f; *F.Q.* VI.11.1 and *O.F.* XXXI.1. No one seems to have pointed out the following parallels between Spenser's Narrator and Boiardo's; *F.Q.* I.3.6 and *O.I.* I.1.2; *F.Q.* I.11.5-7 and *O.I.* II.22.1-3; *F.Q.* III.9.1-3 and e.g. *O.I.* I.1.1; *F.Q.* IV.3.45 and *O.I.* I.10.6; *F.Q.* IV.7.1 and *O.I.* I.1.2; *F.Q.* IV.9.19 and *O.I.* I.24.14; *F.Q.* V.6.1.8-9 and *O.I.* I.28.1-3.

11.   See Bennett, pp. 138-143, for a discussion of the similarity of the two stories.

12.   One characteristic of several of these adaptations bears mention at this point. We have seen that Spenser used *O.F.* VIII.60-68 in three different places. Dodge pointed out (p. 203) the similarity between *F.Q.* VI.7.1 and *O.F.* XXVI.1ff. The theme and some of the phrasing of the passage also appear in VI.3.1 and 5.1. *F.Q.* I.3.1-2 may have been, like III.8.1, suggested by *O.F.* VIII.66-68.

13.   The differences between the two will be discussed below. Sometimes Spenser opens a canto with a descriptive simile: I.6.1; II.7.1-2; III.7.1; VI.4.1 (the first two and the last are all nautical—cf. *O.F.* XLVI.1ff). Ariosto begins Canto XII with an elaborate simile that gives the effect of a ceremonious exordium and may have suggested Spenser's use of the device.

14.   All citations of *The Faerie Queene* are to the *Poetical Works*, ed. J. C. Smith and E. De Selincourt (Oxford, 1912); used by permission of the Clarendon Press, Oxford.

15.   *F.Q.* I.P.4, 4.1; II.P.10.4; III.P.3-5, 1.49, 2.3, 4.3, 5.53, 6.1, 9.1-3, 11.2, 11.48; IV.11.22; V.P.11. I have not included in this list the occurrences of narrative formulas involving direct address (Gilbert, p. 226, is in error when he states that direct address of the reader occurs only once in *F.Q.*) similar to such formulas as Ariosto's frequent "voi." These are: I.2.11; III.3.8-9, 5.27, 6.53-54 ("thou"), 8.9, 8.52; IV.3.23, 11.2, 12.2; V.1.3, 2.3, 6.31, 9.41; VI.5.2, 5.11, 6.17, 8.46. One might also list, as similar to Ariosto's and Boiardo's "lasciamo" or "torniamo," transition and narrative formulas involving the first-person-plural imperative: II.11.4; III.12.45; V.3.40, 9.1, 11.36; VI.2.39, 7.27, 11.24, 12.22. Members (real or potential) of the audience are referred to in the third person in I.P.1; II.P.1-4; III.6.8, 8.43; IV.P.1-4, 8.29-33, 9.3; V.P.3, 6.1; VI.12.41; VII.7.9. Spenser thus has his audience continuously in mind.

16.   Other examples: *F.Q.* II.7.34, 10.56, 11.30; III.2.3, 5.26, 8.27; IV.6.16-17. There is nothing in Ariosto, of course, even remotely resembling the introduction and apostrophe of Colin Clout (VI.10, esp. 16f, discussed below). Only twice does Spenser echo Virgil in the Narrator (*F.Q.* I.P.1 and *Aen.* I.1a-1e; *F.Q.* II.10.47 and *Aen.* III.56-57). A number of relatively unimportant narrative topoi that Spenser adapted from Boiardo and Ariosto might be mentioned here: those of doubt and ignorance (*F.Q.* I.11.36; II.10.8; III.6.29, 12.26; IV.7.7, 11.40; V.10.1), omission (II.9.47, 10.70; III.1.3, 1.42, 6.30, 6.53, 11.39, 11.44; IV.1.24, 11.17; V.3.3; *O.F.* XXIX.50

seems to have suggested III.6.30, IV.11.17, and V.3.3), and inexpressibility (I.12.23, 12.48; II.3.25, 9.47, 10.2; III.P.2, 8.43; IV.11.9, 11.53, 12.1; VII.7.7). Needless to say, Spenser never uses them for humorous purposes.

17.   There are references in *F.Q.* I.P.1, IV.11.41, and VI.12.41 (perhaps) to other works by Spenser. "My mother *Cambridge*" is mentioned in IV.11.34, "*Mulla* mine" in IV.11.41, and "my old father *Mole*" in VII.6.36. The only significant example is the appearance and apostrophe of Colin Clout in VI.10.

18.   There are two notable exceptions, of course, the transparent reference to Raleigh in III.P and the more veiled reference to Burghley in IV.P. But, characteristically enough, neither man is mentioned by name. There is much topicality in the poem, but it is significantly absent from the appearances of the Narrator.

19.   On Spenser's habit of making serious what in Ariosto is humorous, see Dodge, pp. 168-174, 181-183, 189-190, 195-198. When there does seem to be a note of humor in the Poet's remarks, as in III.1.7-8, the effect is jarring. See Bennett, pp. 18-23, 138-153.

20.   Harpalyce, Thamysis, Camilla, Penthisilea, Dido, Zenobia, Artemisia, Laodamia, Portia, Arria, Ariga, Evadne (XXXVII.6, 18-19); Sappho, Corinna (XX.1).

21.   The same change can be seen in Spenser's manner of addressing the queen as contrasted with Ariosto's "Signor" or "Magnanimo Signor" (*O.F.* XVIII.1) or "Invitto Alfonso" (XLII.1); cf. "generosa Erculea prole,/ ornamento e splendor del secol nostro, Ippolito" (*O.F.* I.3) with "O Goddesse heauenly bright,/Mirrour of grace and Maiestie deuine,/Great Lady of the greatest Isle, whose light/Like *Phoebus* lampe throughout the world doth shine" (*F.Q.* I.P.4).

22.   Other instances: *F.Q.* I.8.1, 10.1; II.5.1, 6.1; II.9.1, 11.1; III.2.1-3, 4.1-3; IV.3.1-3, 5.1-2; VI.1.1, 2.1-2.

23.   Cf. also *F.Q.* I.4.1; II.2.25, 9.1, 10.56, 10.74; III.P.1, P.5, 2.3, 3.3, 8.42-43, 9.1-2, 11.2; IV.1-2, 8.1, 9.1-3; V.P.3, 4.2, 10.5, 11.1, 12.1-2; VI.P.6-7, 8.1-2. Although Ariosto sometimes speaks of Ruggiero's being an "esempio" of virtue (which of course, especially in the early cantos, he is not), and of the Venetians who killed Vestidello Pagano as "esempii" of cruelty, the hortatory accent is usually absent. On only one occasion does he urge his audience to profit by the example set before them (and in so doing echoes Ovid).

24.   Spenser was quite familiar with the common distinction between poetry and the abuse of poetry (*eikastiké* and *phantastiké*) as outlined by Sidney (*Apology* in G. G. Smith, *Elizabethan Critical Essays*, Oxford, 1904, I, 186-187). Tasso bases his poetic theory on the same distinction in the *Discorsi del poema eroico* (*Prose diverse*, I, 97-100), rejecting Mazzoni's position that poetry is *fantastica* rather than *icastica* (cf. Puttenham in G. G. Smith, II, 18-20). On Spenser's analysis of *phantastiké*, see my "The Bower of Bliss and Armida's Palace," *Comparative Literature*, 6:335-347 (1954).

25.   Book VII.6.37 poses a problem: "And, were it not ill fitting for this file,/To sing of hilles and woods, mongst warres and Knights,/I would abate the sternenesse of my stile,/Mongst these sterne stounds to mingle soft delights." And then he goes on and does sing of "hilles and woods." Perhaps the inconsistency reveals an intermediate stage of revision; the appropriate-

ness of the characterization of the style as stern is impossible to judge—perhaps these cantos were to form part of the book concerning the war between the "faery Queene and Paynim king" mentioned in I.11.7.

26. For instance, *O.F.* XVIII.1, *Rinaldo* I.4. The examples of the humility topos are few and far between in Ariosto, and that most of them (such as *O.F.* XIV.108) are humorous.

27. The dedication of the *Rinaldo* does suggest an allegorical historical meaning in language which may have influenced Spenser's in such passages as III.P.3, 5 (*Rinaldo*, ed. Luigi Bonfigli, Bari, 1936, I.4). This is no more than an incidental compliment, however.

28. *O.F.* VII.1 is the closest approach in Ariosto to Spenser's insistence on the metaphorical nature of the *F.Q.* (and from it Spenser took suggestions for the proem to Book II). The differences are quite important. Spenser claims a specifically historical referent for his allegory; Ariosto does not specify (he is of course referring to the story of Alcina, a moral allegory). Spenser claims that his entire poem is allegorical; Ariosto does not (and the reader knows that his allegory is confined to certain sections). Finally, Ariosto's lines include a generous dash of humor.

29. The referent of the allegory can be single or multiple at different times and can shift radically. It is thus possible for Spenser to have the best of both worlds: if the story is for the most part an intermittent metaphor whose referent is true, there are also occasions when it must be understood as literally true in a historical sense (such as much of the chronicles in II.10). On these occasions we may not even have to read "England" for "Faery land" or "Elizabeth" for "Gloriana," as we do when the names have been changed. On a further level of abstraction, Spenser will give a translation of actual events into an allegorical scheme which reveals their inner nature without changing their identity (the story of Burben is a good example). On the most abstract level, the allegorical scheme represents the general principle of which any given historical event is an individual, partial embodiment (thus the trial of Duessa, V.10, is primarily an analysis of the relation between mercy and justice in the abstract; the trial of Mary of Scotland is a secondary referent). Cf. J. W. Bennett, "Genre, Milieu, and the 'Epic-Romance,'" (*English Institute Essays, 1951*, ed. A. S. Downer, New York, 1952), pp. 114-120, which seems to me to overemphasize the abstract principle at the expense of the historical referent. On the whole question, see H. Hotcutt in the *Variorum Spenser*, V, 285-287, and Greenlaw in *ibid.*, I, 485ff.

Index